Magic Island
The Fictions of
L.M. Montgomery

Magic Island
The Fictions of
L.M. Montgomery

Elizabeth Waterston

OXFORD
UNIVERSITY PRESS

OXFORD
UNIVERSITY PRESS

70 Wynford Drive, Don Mills, Ontario M3C 1J9
www.oupcanada.com

Oxford University Press is a department of the University of Oxford.
It furthers the University's objective of excellence in research, scholarship,
and education by publishing worldwide in

Oxford   New York

Auckland   Cape Town   Dar es Salaam   Hong Kong   Karachi
Kuala Lumpur   Madrid   Melbourne   Mexico City   Nairobi
New Delhi   Shanghai   Taipei   Toronto

With offices in

Argentina   Austria   Brazil   Chile   Czech Republic   France   Greece
Guatemala   Hungary   Italy   Japan   Poland   Portugal   Singapore
South Korea   Switzerland   Thailand   Turkey   Ukraine   Vietnam

Oxford is a trade mark of Oxford University Press
in the UK and in certain other countries

Published in Canada by Oxford University Press

Library and Archives Canada Cataloguing in Publication

Waterston, Elizabeth, 1922-
Magic island : the fictions of L.M. Montgomery / Elizabeth Waterston.

Includes bibliographical references and index.
ISBN 978-0-19-543003-5

1. Montgomery, L.M. (Lucy Maud), 1874-1942—Criticism and
interpretation.   I. Title.

PS8526.O55Z94 2008   C813'.52   C2008-902508-3

Cover design: Sherill Chapman

Cover image: Northport Pier, by Anne Gallant, Kensington PE

1 2 3 4 – 11 10 09 08

Oxford University Press Canada is committed to our environment.
This book is printed on Forest Stewardship Council certified paper which
contains 100% post-consumer waste. Printed and bound in Canada.

FSC

Recycled
Supporting responsible use
of forest resources

Cert no. SW-COC-1271
www.fsc.org
© 1996 Forest Stewardship Council

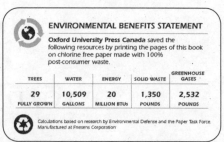

ENVIRONMENTAL BENEFITS STATEMENT

Oxford University Press Canada saved the
following resources by printing the pages of this book
on chlorine free paper made with 100%
post-consumer waste.

TREES	WATER	ENERGY	SOLID WASTE	GREENHOUSE GASES
29	10,509	20	1,350	2,532
FULLY GROWN	GALLONS	MILLION BTUs	POUNDS	POUNDS

Calculations based on research by Environmental Defense and the Paper Task Force.
Manufactured at Friesens Corporation

Contents

List of Illustrations

Introduction

Lucy Maud Montgomery grew up on Prince Edward Island, which lies like the crescent of a new moon in the curve of the mainland coast of eastern Canada. You can reach it by ferry-boat or plane or bridge—a real island of politics and potatoes and tourism.

But there is another island, reflected in Montgomery's fiction: a world of natural beauty and self-awareness, of wit and whimsy and farce, of plot and counterplot and resolution, firelight and starlight and occasional darkening shadow. In twenty-two novels, four hundred-plus short stories, endless poems and autobiographical articles and speeches, Montgomery offered sometimes a wistful glimpse—and sometimes a glowering close-up—of this second, fictional island. She gained access to that world whenever she set aside her "real" life and picked up her pen to write, when, as she put it in her journal, "I am able to escape into my 'dream lives' again and come back refreshed and stimulated."[1] This second island is also easy to access. In her fiction, from *Anne of Green Gables* in 1908 to *Anne of Ingleside* in 1938, Montgomery shared with readers the world of her dream lives.

Each of her novels has the immediacy of description and the subtlety of characterization that made *Anne of Green Gables* so lasting a favourite. From the least known to the most familiar, from the early ones like *Kilmeny of the Orchard* (1910) to the late ones like *Jane of Lantern Hill* (1937), each offers quiet amusement at the self-absorption of children and the self-deception of adults. While the funny parts make you laugh, there are poignant moments that bring tears.

Except for a single short story, all the Montgomery fictions suggest the charm of an island setting. Montgomery herself, however, was not insular. Like all authors, she was open to many pressures. Changes in the reading public, shifts in publishers' demands, universal changes in politics, economics, and technology, reversals in personal experience, emergence of perilous emotions that had to be repressed and sublimated, vicarious sustenance gained from reading—all these complex elements came into play as Montgomery wrote her apparently simple stories.

She left many traces of her development as a writer. She filled scrapbooks with memorabilia: newspaper clippings, scraps of fabric, bits of a cat's fur tied in ribbon, dried flowers from a bouquet. These and a myriad other things pasted into the scrapbooks illuminate memories to be transfigured into fictional motifs. Letters to literary friends listed the markets she worked for and the prices she was getting for her stories. She took excellent photographs depicting her home, and scenes in the woods and by the sea reflecting the sense of symmetry, proportion, and accent that would also shape her written descriptive passages. She carefully preserved the manuscripts of her novels, including notes of all the revisions which adroitly deepen sensual responses and intensify continuity.[2]

Above all, from the time she was fourteen in 1889, until just before her death at the age of 67, in 1942, she kept and saved a diary. She recorded not only her daily doings and thoughts and experiences, but traced also the patterns of her life as a writer. Published almost half a century after her death, selections of the journals of Montgomery now offer an astonishing case history of one writer's flights to her second world.

Daily, monthly, yearly, Montgomery revealed in her journals not only the intimate details of her childhood romancing, her lonely spinsterhood, her marriage, and the birth of three sons, but also her struggles against a closed publishing and critical world, and the embarrassments and tensions of keeping up a professional writing life in the face of marital and social demands. She also reiterated in the journals her joy in the persistent energy of her urge to write. "How I love my work," she noted in her diary, ten years before the publication of *Anne of Green Gables*, when she was still developing her skill as a writer of short stories. "I seem to grow more and more wrapped up in it as the days pass and other hopes and interests fail me. Nearly everything I think or do or say is subordinated to a desire to improve in my work. I study people and events for that, I think and speculate and read for that" (December 31, 1898).

Week after week she wrote into her journal the details of what she called "spade work" as she dug for stories that would catch an audience, and mined her memory of the funny, tangled web of family and community relationships. She recorded, day by day, the push through chapter after chapter, the work on cadences of dialogue, rhythms of scenery, and clash of characters. She groaned over the later gruelling revisions of sentences, chapters, and final manuscript, the work of transcribing the whole story onto a recalcitrant typewriter, and eventually the tussles with editors and publishers and critics over the public presentation of the private dream. Rarely has an author permitted such fascinating backstage glimpses of the way literary creativity fits in with the ordinary rhythms of life.

As the years went by, the everyday pressures noted in the journals were increasingly dark ones. She felt the forces of resentment, terror, and maladjustment and recorded in realistic detail her daily disappointments and physical discomforts. Sometimes re-reading the novels and the journals together brings a strange sense of discontinuity. How could that long series of novels, with their essentially sunny presentation of life, come from the same pen as the darkening diaries? One answer may be that in writing her life-story in the journals, Montgomery deliberately chose to emphasize elements of experience not included in her novels. Each volume of the journals, like each of the novels, seems to be a selective artistic construct, not a full revelation of the woman who created it. The life-record has been tailored to some extent to reveal a mindset different from the buoyancy of the creator of the novels. Re-reading the novels modifies the sense of darkness stirred by the journals.

Conversely, the interest of the novels increases when the full life story of their author is explored. Surprising ambiguities appear in the fictions. Veiled beneath the surface, dark passions add tension to her blithe novels. Montgomery herself scorned those who explored the lives of authors in investigative biographies. The power of her books, however, makes it impossible to resist thinking about the life out of which they rose.[3]

Montgomery was born into a family steeped in the Prince Edward Island tradition of story-telling. Because of the early death of her mother, Clara Macneill, and the departure of her father, Hugh John Montgomery, for the Canadian north-west, young Maud—as she was known to family and friends—was raised in the home of a story-telling grandfather. She was "raised" also by her own urge to capture her world in a web of words

A bookish child, she wanted not only to tell stories but also to publish them. And indeed, at sixteen, at the end of a traumatic year out west with her wandering father (1890–91), she returned to the Island as a thrice-published author. A lyric poem, a documentary article, and a verse narrative about a long-ago shipwreck off the Cavendish shore had all been accepted, each by a different editor. Often using the pseudonym "Maud Cavendish," Maud Montgomery continued to write and publish Island stories during two year-long stays in Halifax, Nova Scotia, first as a college student and later as a newspaper employee.

Back on the Island, she worked from 1890 on through a long and lonely apprenticeship to her craft. She began publishing in a clearly-defined literary convention, as a creator of light short stories, appropriate for the many women's and children's magazines of her youth. She slowly outgrew the formulaic genres of that early work, partly under pressure of changes in publication practices and in the economy, as well as because of changes in the depth of her own experience. Her first full-length novel, *Anne of Green Gables* (1908), became a surprise best-seller, read not only by children but by adult readers, both male and female. Within a year she numbered among her fans such luminaries as Mark Twain. Translation into Swedish in 1909, Dutch in 1910, and Polish in 1912 began the spread of the charm of "Anne's island" to a wider world.[4]

Montgomery left the Island "for good" at the age of thirty-six, in 1911, moving into continental Canada to live as the wife of a Presbyterian minister in Ontario, and to go on with her work as a writer. She would return occasionally to Prince Edward Island, partly to visit family and friends, but

also for renewal of her inspiration. Far away from the sea shore, and far from the people she knew, she kept the beauty of the Island and the foibles of her Island family and friends vividly in her work. They remained as primary literary assets.

Year by year she also filtered into her fictions not only her own experiences, but also all the vicarious life she had accessed through intensive reading. Long after studying Walter Scott's *The Lady of the Lake*, for instance, she could still passionately re-enter its world: "I roamed through its vivid scenery. I talked with its people . . . I was snatched far away . . . and in spirit lived 'one crowded hour of glorious life' oblivious of all my surroundings" (January 30, 1914). She re-entered Scott's world, and also the Barsetshire of Trollope's novels, just before beginning to write *Anne of Avonlea* (1909). Indeed, every time she was readying for a new bout of composition she indulged in a binge of reading or re-reading Trollope, Dickens, the Brontës, Thackeray, Bulwer-Lytton, Mrs. Hemans, and Marie Corelli as well as history books, psychology texts, and current best-sellers.[5] Besides personal sustenance, she no doubt absorbed unconscious lessons in construction, rhetoric, and in stereotypes of characterization from this obsessive reading. In each of her novels, she adopted and exploited narrative techniques and themes absorbed from other writers.

The Montgomery novels also draw from a current world of political, economic, and ethical changes, as the author moved away from the Victorian conventions of her small fishing-farming community in the 1880s and 90s. She absorbed and reflected the lessened assurance of the Edwardian years, the upheavals and losses of World War I (1914–18), the post-war disruptions of family and community, and the new technologies of the 1920s—motor cars, radios, airplanes. She faced the distresses of the great economic depression of the 1930s, and endured the again-darkening years when a second world war was imminent.

Whatever darkness engulfed the world, she continued to create a *joie de vivre* through the vitality of memorable (and memorably named) characters like Anne and Di-ann-a, Rilla Blythe, Emily Starr, Valancy Stirling, and Pat Gardiner. Montgomery outgrew her first audiences and eventually resented being tagged as a writer of books for the young. She knew that her books were being bought by the thousands not by children or by adults buying for children, but by adult readers who had become deeply attached to her style.

In all these increasingly complex novels, sardonic undertones can also be heard. Sub-texts of frustration emerge in the characterization of women like Leslie Moore in *Anne's House of Dreams* (1917), Mary Vance in *Rainbow*

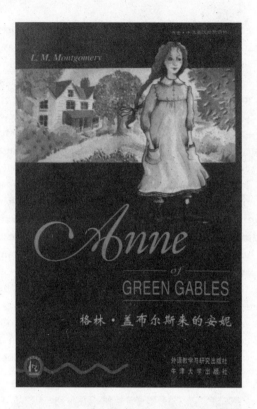

Valley (1919),.Ilse Burnley in the *Emily* trilogy (1923, 1925, 1927), and old Becky Dark, the spider at the heart of *A Tangled Web* (1931). In book after charming book, Montgomery obliquely suggested a private store of anguish, despair, illness, and disillusionment—without disturbing the surface appeal of romance and sentiment and comedy. Notably, Montgomery increasingly used female characters to vent her contrary feelings of mockery and satire— balanced against the effervescent fun of an Anne and the stubborn persist- ence of an Emily. The Montgomery books consequently cast light on historic shifts in gender politics and family patterns.

Montgomery moved with the general tides of her times, adapting to the tastes of her readers and the suggestions of her publishers. She went on to create a whole shelf of full-length fictions—two books every three years, over a thirty year period until 1938, all of them still in print in the twenty- first century.

She drew plots, settings, and characters from the depths of her own experience, including the part of her life she never revealed to the succes- sion of watchers. The home community in Cavendish had never fathomed the frustration of her lonely life. The demanding and generally philistine people in the parishes her husband served had been oblivious of her resentment of their demands on her time. Readers around the globe wrongly assumed she was as happy as her blithe fictional characters. No one knew about the dark passions, obsessively intensified in her later life. They could be vented in her secret diaries. Veiled beneath the surface, they could also give tension to her novels.

Open as the journals are, they do not disclose certain areas in Montgomery's life. There are significant gaps in the journals, where she chose not to recount troubling events or avoided recording embarrassing emotions. Modern research has filled in many of these gaps. New revelations about self-censored events and feelings, though unauthorized by Montgomery and omitted from her journals, illuminate some half-hidden themes in the novels.

Furthermore, full as the journals are, they could not report other facts of which Montgomery herself was unaware. For example, modern research by Mary Rubio has unveiled details about her law cases, her difficulties with literary critics, the nature of her husband's mental problems and the effects of her own pharmaceutical regime. None of these facts were known to her. Yet all facts about her life, both those she herself hid, and those she was unconscious of, help in understanding and evaluating her fiction.

The journals also omit reference to many of the fears and desires hidden in the writer's subconscious. These found their way into her dreams (which she carefully recorded). They also obliquely affected her fiction. She drew, no doubt unconsciously, from emotions repressed, yet sublimated through symbols and metaphors, in colour sequences, and in the suggestive names she gives her characters. Together with other tonal elements and stylistic touches, these deep patterns worked to form a counterpoint to the surface of her stories.

Now, thanks in part to an awareness of iconography and symbol, in part to the surprising revelations in the journals, and in part to scholarly research on her background, it is possible to offer a new and penetrating view not only of Montgomery's fictions but also of the complexity of materials in her creative mind, and of the processes of literary creativity.[6]

So in spite of Montgomery's own emphasis on the limitations of a biographical approach to art, this study sets out to re-examine the novels with every insight offered by contemporary understanding of her life. Each chapter focuses on one of her creations, in the light of new reflections on her experience, her times, her reading, and her professional intentions. The Montgomery fictions, besides their obvious appeal, illustrate the devious paths of the creative mind.

The following chapters explore the whole sequence of novels, from *Anne of Green Gables* in 1908 to *Anne of Ingleside* in 1938. Twenty-two Montgomery books of fiction—twenty novels and two collections of short stories—will be decoded in turn.

Yet no amount of analysis can destroy the ability of these books to come together again. Not all books can live through a comparable dissection, but Montgomery's work survives all interpretations. It will emerge all the stronger after the deconstruction offered in these pages. Readers will return from that dreamed life, as Montgomery herself did, "refreshed and stimulated."[7]

Evidence of her continuing power is that the Montgomery novels are never out of print. They appear in endless formats, large and small, handsome and shoddy, scholarly and child-directed. They propagate material phenomena such as doll versions and look-alike contests, and have been translated into more than seventeen languages already, with new additions to that roster every year or so. They are constantly transmuted into other media, in the theatre, on television and radio, and on the world-wide web.

In spite of this proliferation of approaches to Montgomery, her fictions flourish in their original form. They continue to draw people from all over the world to the island of reading pleasure.

~ Anne of Green Gables ~

(Boston: L.C. Page, 1908)

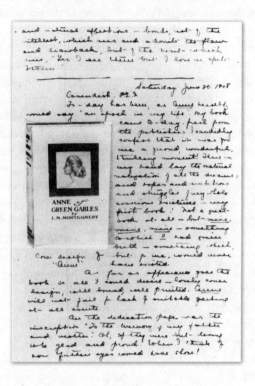

On April 18, 1914, L.M. Montgomery recalled the moment nine years earlier when she began to write *Anne of Green Gables*:

> It was a moist, showery, sweet-scented evening in June. . . . I was sitting *on the end of the table*, in the old kitchen, my feet on the sofa, beside the west window, because I wanted to get the last gleams of daylight on my portfolio. I did not for a moment dream that the book I had just begun was to bring me the fame and success I had long dreamed of. So I wrote, the opening paragraphs quite easily, not feeling obliged to "write up" to any particular reputation or style. Just as I had finished my description of *Mrs. Lynde* and her home *Ewan* walked in. . . . He stayed and chatted most of the evening, so no more of *Green Gables* was written that night.

The two names italicized—"Mrs. Lynde" and "Ewan"—represent the two worlds of Avonlea fiction and Cavendish reality. "Ewan" was Reverend

Ewan Macdonald, the big, handsome, shy minister, recently come to the Cavendish Presbyterian church, and even more recently moved as a boarder into the farm next to Maud Montgomery's home. He had come this evening in 1905 to her farmhouse-cum-post-office home, to pick up his mail and to chat with the thirty-one-year old granddaughter of the postmaster, Alexander Macneill. Conversation with Ewan, a well-educated man "from away," offered welcome relief from the narrowness of the judgmental Cavendish community that for most of her life had been watching her askance.

"Mrs. Lynde" was the imaginary matriarch of the imagined village of "Avonlea," very much like the real Cavendish. She is brilliantly described in the first chapter of *Anne of Green Gables* in terms of her industry and productivity (in bedspreads and children), her control of husband and community, and above all, her curiosity. She is matriarchy personified. But Montgomery adds a touch of surprise to Mrs. Lynde's world. She sits behind her window, but outdoors a little stream tumbles through a flowery, winding course. In one of the many revisions that Montgomery added to her manuscript in the days after that first rush of genesis, the flowers by that stream are given a new specificity.[8] "Jewel-weed" becomes "ladies' eardrops," adding a touch of frivolity and femininity.[9] Soon a bubbly, chattering, free spirit will come into Mrs. Lynde's community.

The second chapter of *Anne of Green Gables* swings the focus from the controlling matriarch to shy, gentle Matthew Cuthbert. Not an alpha male like Maud Montgomery's barb-tongued Grandfather Macneill, or her condescending Uncle Leander, or hostile Uncle John, Matthew has been dispatched to the nearest railway station by his strong-minded spinster sister Marilla. He is to fetch an orphan boy, ordered from the mainland to help with the farm work. "By mistake a girl is sent," as Montgomery wrote in her notebook, in the first jotting about the story. The unexpected little girl will bewitch quiet Matthew with her intensity, her eager flow of questions, and her vivid response to the world around her. She is and will remain articulate and unintentionally amusing—a pitiable but not a pitiful orphan.

Montgomery herself had been a virtual orphan in the home of stern grandparents, her own pretty young mother having died, and her father having left his twenty-month-old daughter behind when he went west to the Canadian prairies. As a child she was well fed and sensibly clothed, but like Anne she knew lonely yearnings for the affectionate encouragement loving parents can give. Like Anne, she was imaginative and independent, but her grandparents and aunts and uncles felt it was their duty to subdue and chasten her pride and spontaneity. Maud Montgomery could never stamp and shout "I hate you," but it must have given her much pleasure to let Anne kick against Mrs. Lynde.

Regardless of this personal connection, the orphaned Anne Shirley has many literary antecedents. Montgomery had read and enjoyed Louisa May Alcott's *Little Women* (1868), Mark Twain's *Huckleberry Finn* (1884), Frances Hodgson Burnett's *Little Lord Fauntleroy* (1886), and Annie Fellows Johnston's *The Little Colonel* (1895), all featuring independent young protagonists. Montgomery as an aspiring young writer had also enjoyed and studied books published closer to the time when she wrote *Anne of Green Gables:* Rudyard Kipling's *Kim* (1901) and Kate Douglas Wiggin's *Rebecca of Sunnybrook Farm* (1903), in which spirited children move alone from a familiar world into a new one. All these books are not fairy tales or animal stories, but realistic accounts of children's needs and potentialities, in the spotlight of a turn-of-the century world. After the publication of *Anne of Green Gables* in 1908, the orphaned, independent child protagonist would recur with new subtlety and charm in best sellers of the next few years: *The Secret Garden* (1911), *Daddy-Long-Legs* (1912), and *Pollyanna* (1913).[10] This widespread use of the orphan motif reflected social facts: high birth-rate and low life expectancy in adults.

Orphanhood also probably matched the self-image of many women writers. In 1905 they could attend college, enter a profession, and travel alone, but could find no support, sympathy, or role models among women of the older generation. Montgomery, like Anne in her inventiveness, pride, and rebellious spirit, had become something of an oddity in Cavendish. In her novel she would make comic use of her life-long sense of being different from the community, like an orphaned outsider, regarded with suspicion.

One thing that separated Montgomery from the neighbours was her addiction to reading. From old-fashioned romances by Walter Scott and Bulwer-Lytton, and from poetry by Tennyson and Longfellow, like Anne she drew a rich vocabulary. Inappropriately applied by Anne, this luscious vocabulary becomes a source of fun. Anne's creator, however, had learned early to manipulate her language more effectively. From the time she was fifteen, in 1889, she had been honing her narrative skill by writing up each day's adventures in a careful diary. As she developed her profession of writing, Montgomery had a unique quarry for stories of childhood and young adulthood in the frank, often naïve, sometimes exaggerated account of growth in spirit and body, up the years from adolescence to maturity. Journal entries on adolescent rivalries, crushes, crises, and triumphs helped her create a believable character in Anne.

There is a marked difference between her careful composition in the journal and the simpler girlish style of her letters to her contemporary Pensie Macneill, as demonstrated in *The Years before Anne*.[11] Those letters came from a time when, at fifteen, Montgomery had left home to take an enlightening trip right across the American continent, to spend a year in Prince

Albert, Saskatchewan, with her beloved father and his unlovable second wife. There she had made new friends, Will and Laura Pritchard. These two fun-loving young people furnished suggestions for the characters of sturdy Gilbert and giggling Diana. Montgomery also had a first suitor during her year out west, in John Mustard (perhaps a model for Mr. Phillips in *Anne of Green Gables*, the awkward teacher smitten by one of his pupils).

When she returned to Prince Edward Island, Montgomery went back to school. Now her class included a red-haired boy, Austin Laird, whom she disliked and teased mercilessly. Compared to the poems she wrote about his redheadedness, the taunt of "Carrots!" would be complimentary! Part of the Austin Laird story was the fact that his father had once wanted to marry Montgomery's mother, according to local gossip. Again art would eventually invert life: here was a hint of Marilla's confession of an early attachment to Gilbert's father.

Since Montgomery's home was also the local post-office, it served as a gathering place for exchange of news, gossip, and local anecdote, all nourishing the love of a good story. Everywhere, local life presented materials she could use as a writer. When she went to Charlottetown to study at Prince of Wales College her journal records of classes and out-of-school fun in her boarding-house could furnish details to make Anne's success at "Queen's College" vivid and convincing.

At this point real life and fiction diverged. Montgomery won no university scholarship. The years of her young womanhood were spent teaching in small Prince Edward Island villages. Nor did she find a soul-mate among the young men of her school and college days. The journal's record of hard and often dreary work is augmented by stories of unhappy relationships with marriage-minded young men, and an unrequited love for an unacceptable suitor.

Her continued life on Prince Edward Island was only broken by two brief interruptions, one in 1895–96 to study at Dalhousie University in Halifax, Nova Scotia, the other a short return to Halifax as a newspaper assistant in 1901–1903. By this time she had given up teaching and was making a thin living as a writer of short stories and poems, sold to a wide-flung number of family and church papers and magazines.[12] Many of the short stories she wrote in the years before *Anne of Green Gables* seem in retrospect like practice exercises. The titles of "The Prize in Elocution" (1897), "The Way of the Winning of Anne" (1899), "What Came of a Dare" (1902), and "The Cake that Prissie Made" (1903) all suggest possible links.

Montgomery's decision to stay home and write was motivated by a situation somewhat like the one Anne finds herself in at the conclusion of the novel. Montgomery's grandfather Macneill had died, and her grandmother could only remain in her old home if someone younger stayed to help her.

Given this situation, however, Maud's mood was not, like Anne's, one of uplift and optimistic acceptance of sacrifice. Resentment of the trammels on her independence pulled her down into a suicidal depression in the years after her grandfather's death.

Then in 1905 the concurrent emergence of Reverend Ewan Macdonald as a suitor[13] and of the inspired conception of Anne's story lifted her spirits. She concentrated her energies in the demanding job of writing her first full-length novel. The years of self-negation and endless work were eventually released and reversed in the creation of Anne's energy and resilience.

Luckily, she had the summer free. For years, her Uncle Leander had brought his family to his old home for two months' summer vacation, expecting his mother and his niece, Maud, to entertain and feed them. In the summer of 1905 Uncle Leander and his wife went elsewhere, leaving Maud free to concentrate on her book. As she worked through that summer, Montgomery created four plots, intertwined in a single long piece of fiction.

First is a plot of developing love between the young Anne and the older woman Marilla Cuthbert. The catalyst is humour. From the outset Marilla is ready to laugh at, as well as to criticize and teach, Anne. The charm of this story lies not in wit or irony, but in a comic sense that makes readers laugh out loud at the clash of generations. This plot develops into the story of Anne's relationships with other older women: Mrs. Lynde, Mrs. Barrie, and Miss Josephine Barry, all converted from revulsion into acceptance of Anne, a volatile alien spirit in Avonlea; and then Mrs. Allen and Miss Stacy, providing models of adult womanhood that can combine propriety with warmth. This first major plot-line connects obliquely with Montgomery's strained and restraining relationship with her grandmother. There is also a reflection here of the relation between herself, a writer in her thirties (feeling old and wise) and the child she once was. That little girl still flitted through her memories, bright, articulate, ecstatic in response to her environment. As Montgomery wrote, she became increasingly certain of what kind of a child she had been. Perhaps she also came to guess how interesting such a child could be to older readers, restoring to them their own capacity for wonder and freshness.

Anne's development within her private world of imagination forms the second plot. She reveals that world at the outset when she asks Marilla to call her "Cordelia," having dropped the earliest dream of being "Geraldine." This shifts into her early facility at "confessions," first to a bedazzled Marilla on the loss of the amethyst brooch, and later to a terrifying Aunt Josephine Barry after a midnight leap into the wrong bed. Later still comes the creation of her Cordelia-Geraldine fantasy for the Story Club. Montgomery lovingly mocks a little girl's ambitious use of pretentious language, remembering her own baffled ambitions as a writer. But

Anne's love of language has given reassurance to many a word-struck child; and many adult writers including Carol Shields and Margaret Laurence have testified that Anne's defence of imagination as well as her love of words boosted their earliest literary aspirations.

The third plot concerns Anne's finding of her "kindred sprits," Matthew and Diana. Diana's light still shines as the novel ends, but gentle Matthew dies, a plot surprise with the power to bring tears—real tears for a loss felt as intensely as if it were not experienced only in fiction. The story of Matthew's response to Anne's needs comes from Montgomery's deep attachments to kind-hearted men: her childhood devotion to her absent father, and her adult appreciation of the faraway correspondents in Scotland and Western Canada who supplied sympathetic, earnest response to a lonely woman's self-revealing letters. As for Diana, Anne's bosom friend, she draws some qualities from Montgomery's cheerful Campbell cousins, and some from pretty Laura Pritchard, Maud's friend in the distant Saskatchewan days. But there is more to her than that. To judge by her name, Diana ought to be associated with the chaste white circle of the moon. Instead, Diana's garden pulses with the sensuous power of flowers, ranging from rosy to scarlet, and carrying erotic suggestions in their names, from "Bleeding Hearts" to "Bouncing Bets" and "Adam-and-Eve." No surprise in Diana's later weakness for raspberry cordial/currant wine, rich fruitcake, and cherry preserves! That vivid sensuality erupts like Montgomery's own ecstatic response to the rich sounds and sights, odours and textures of her environment of woods and sea-shore and farm home. The name "Di-ann-a" hints that she is delicate Anne's hidden second self. She is also of course an essential part of Montgomery herself, sensuous as child and adult.

Finally, the story of Anne and Gilbert is an unusual story of adolescent romance. It begins in a gender-heavy schoolroom, where boy-girl items are "written up" on the door, boys and girls are separated in the seating arrangement, and a boy is punished for impertinence by being made to sit among the girls. The moment when Anne breaks her slate over Gilbert's head remains in readers' memory as the height of humour and surprise. The effect of that chapter is the result not just of a happy inspiration. The manuscript of Chapter 15, "A Tempest in the School Teapot" shows the marvel of craftsmanship. Line after line, Montgomery improved and subtilized her little schoolroom drama. (The full list of revisions to Chapter 15 appear in the Appendix.)

In revising this single chapter Montgomery builds up all four of her plots. Anne chatters to Marilla about her first day in school, and ends with "Can I have some of those pearl beads?" When Anne gets into trouble, Marilla masks her sympathy ("It would never do to say so to her"), and consults Mrs. Lynde about the fracas in school. Other additions develop Anne's romanticism and intensity (so much like Montgomery's own): "I like that lane because you can think out loud there without people calling you crazy" and "Maples are such sociable trees." Her hurt finds extravagant phrasing: "Gilbert Blythe has hurt me *excruciatingly*, Diana," and her love for Diana wings into fabulous dreams of a bride in "snowy garments." Diana's character is also amplified in the revisions: her beauty, her sympathy, and her ordinary joy in group singing, or reading a "Pansy" book. As for Gilbert, he is humanized by the addition of his awareness of Anne's charm ("her little pointed chin and the big eyes") as well as his irritation at her imperviousness to his interest. Still other revisions touch in from sharp memory the details of school life, the boys' cricket races, the hieroglyphics carved on desks, the rivalry over a place to keep milk cold until lunch time.

If the characters in *Anne of Green Gables* and some of the plot-lines come from Montgomery's experiences of other people, the tone of the telling comes from her own nature. The sense of humour and of pathos, the feminist interest in role modelling by the older generation, the reaction against the conventions of boy-girl romance—these were, and remain, the hallmarks of a unique vision. These are the inexplicable qualities that brought Montgomery her devoted and long-lasting readership.

Hardly noticed in a first reading, but deepening the meanings of all these plots, is the author's careful sequencing of images, and the linking of metaphors of colour and shape. Elizabeth Epperly notes that descriptions of sunsets recur eleven times throughout the story, each time enabling a glimpse into changes in Anne's experiences and, often, her hidden feelings.[14] First of these moments comes when, under an arch of snowy apple blossoms, Anne sees glory where "a painted sunset sky shone like a great rose window at the end of a cathedral aisle." This description is the first also of many examples of the way Anne's creator uses metaphors. Double intensity comes when the thought of stained glass—in Chartres or in Montreal or wherever the reader picked up a comparable impression—connects with the thought of a sunset scene. Anne and the reader quickly get a second jolt of the bifocal vision of metaphor when the Lake of Shining Waters comes into view, where "a wild plum leaned out from the bank like a white-clad girl tip-toeing to her own reflection." That description, incidentally, owed nothing to revision: it appears in the first version of the manuscript as it stands now, illustration of the simile-making propensity of Montgomery's mind.

Each such description becomes part of a sequence. The white of the "Way of Delight" for example recurs in the white of Matthew's gift of beads, the white of the snow through which Anne races to help Diana, the misty white of the Snow Queen signifying peace, seen just before Matthew's death, and the white of the "wee scotch roses" that Anne brings to

Matthew's grave. *Anne of Green Gables* can be read as if it were a long lyric poem, with linked images giving depth and unity to the work of art.

At the end of the novel, however, the riot of sensuous colour is replaced by unspecified "flowers of quiet happiness." The sex-laden relationship with Gilbert that began with "angry sparkle" and the "Twhack!" of a slate shifts and pales too, first into intellectual rivalry and then into friendship and mutual admiration. The toning of the expected romance at the end of the book is ambiguous and tenuous.[15] The ambivalence may have its origins in Montgomery's confused feelings about Ewan Macdonald, who had recently come into her life as a potential suitor. Montgomery concludes her work with a gentle diminuendo.

The whole architecture of the book demonstrates a series of similar reductions and adjustments. The key word in the opening movement is "surprise." The coming of Anne into Avonlea results in Mrs. Lynde—and many others—being "properly horrified." But the first ten chapters end with Mrs. Lynde being properly, and amusingly, mollified. After the opening movement, the next eighteen chapters repeat the pattern of Anne erupting, and adult Avonlea learning to enjoy her, to accept some responsibility for her aberrations, and to offer channels for her creative energy. In paired chapters, Anne in a "scrape" is followed by Anne surprisingly victorious. In each pair, Montgomery shows the techniques mastered in her long apprenticeship as a short story writer, creating each time a sudden amusing tension and a surprising resolution. But for a return to propriety after Anne's most dramatic eruption, that crash of a slate over Gilbert's head, the reader is left in suspense until the end of the book.

Montgomery embeds one possible form for the ending, in the chapter on "the Story Club." Here Anne, at the age of thirteen, creates the romance of "Cordelia and Geraldine." The two heroines, named for the two sides of her own earliest dreams, both love "Bertrand"—a twist on "Gilbert." When she imagined Cordelia pushing Geraldine off a bridge into a turbulent stream, to drown in the arms of beloved Bertrand, Anne was using shapes from her subconscious mind: the names, images and actions of this story within the story all prepared her, at a deep level of consciousness, for the ending of the novel.

Before that ending can eventuate, nine chapters present a series of new "surprises." Anne achieves unqualified success, away from Avonlea, on stage at White Sands, and in town at Queen's College. Rivalry with Gilbert is always part of these successes. This hope-filled rising line breaks suddenly in the two last chapters. But Matthew's death and Marilla's impending blindness are balanced by the softening of Mrs. Lynde and the end of the schism between Anne and Gilbert. Anne prepares for a return to Avonlea as an adult and perhaps as a bride. Mrs. Lynde, depositing herself on the stone bench in front of Green Gables, approves Anne's decision to give up dreams of college and stay at home with a mellowed Marilla, accepting Gilbert's offer of a chance to teach in Avonlea. Soon Anne walks with Gilbert up the lane to Green Gables. This moment is shadowed by memory of an earlier scene, when Anne's pride drove Gilbert back onto the pond, leaving her to climb the "steep, ferny little path" alone. Now Gilbert tells her, only half jestingly, "You've thwarted destiny long enough."

The young couple may be moving through an Edenic world, and may believe that "God's in his heaven," but many readers feel a sense of unreality in the reduction of Anne to an orthodox Eve. They may sigh a bit at the loss of Anne's competitive independence: her decision to stay home and help Marilla presents a dubious model for modern girls. For most adolescent readers, however, the ending of *Anne of Green Gables* seems very satisfying. The ending is of course historically realistic in its reflection of rural mores of the period and the pressure of societal assumptions about the nurturing roles proper to women—a value that Montgomery tacitly accepted when she agreed to marry Ewan Macdonald.

In terms of art the final scene effectively completes all the patterns of the book. In the opening scene, Mrs. Lynde looked out of her window at Avonlea, as a rigid, materialistic, self-important regulator of an insular community. Now, thanks partly to Gilbert, Anne looks forward to assuming a comparable but richer responsibility as teacher. Sitting at her window, she looks out not only at Avonlea but also at "her ideal world of dreams." And, again thanks partly to Gilbert, she can see "the bend in the road."[16]

That memorable phrase was a late addition to the novel. Other revisions of the final chapter reveal significant aspects of Montgomery's frame of mind. The "white" motif recurs, muted now as Anne and Marilla sit in a world diminished by the loss of Matthew: "They liked to sit there when the twilight came down and the white moths flew about in the garden and the odour of mint filled the dewy air." Also, coming into focus with another phrase added in revision is Montgomery's obsessive love of trees, especially of trembling poplars: "whose rustle was like low friendly speech." The addition again suggests a mood antithetical to the heightening of passion.

Significantly, and in regard not so much to Anne as to Montgomery herself, one other addition to the final chapter reads: "Don't say anything about this to anyone for a spell yet, anyway. I can't bear that folks should come here to question and sympathize and talk about it." Strangely, in Montgomery's journal, in spite of minute detailing of her daily life, there is no mention either of the writing of this significant novel, or of Ewan Macdonald's increasing visits and ultimate proposal of marriage. She would later tell her correspondents that while she was writing, "I never squeaked a word" to anyone about her ambitious entry into novel-writing. In later years, Montgomery would give exact accounts of her writing progress:

"Began a new book today" . . . "Wrote another chapter" . . . "Finished typing." For later writers, these would be among the most interesting parts of the journals. But her fellow-writers would also be fascinated by the fact of omission in the case of *Anne of Green Gables*. Perhaps because Montgomery told no one about the story that was obsessing her, she could put the full force of her energy and of her life, conscious and unconscious, into the writing of *Anne of Green Gables*.

At any rate, Montgomery had finished her first novel with what is technically a happy ending. The great spurt of energy that had brought *Anne of Green Gables* to existence was over. In Montgomery's own life, Ewan Macdonald had become now a steady visitor. Within a year she would become secretly engaged to him. The coming of Ewan had enabled her to confront and accept and immortalize the Mrs. Lyndes of her world. She concluded her writing, and packed off the manuscript to the first of a series of potential publishers.

Consequently, the book (as Anne would say) began to "weave a spell." Young people dreaming their way into adult life, self-absorbed, feeling little humiliations and embarrassments with excruciating intensity, responding to beauty and honourable ideals with reverence, could identify with Anne. They could laugh with and at her, relive her trial-and-error method of learning, and grow with her. For adults, the novel helped make room for greater appreciation of childhood, and augmented efforts to provide children with more "scope for the imagination." But innumerable adults all over the world also read *Anne of Green Gables* year after year just for pleasure. It offered the joy of re-experiencing, as Montgomery did at the time of writing, the enchantment of growth into a new self, a changing body, a new role, a new relationship.

Thousands of tourists still come each year to the little Canadian Island, just to savour "Anne's country."[17] They come, like Anne, via a "way of delight," into a setting of red roads, emerald fields, dark pines, the sparkling sea and the shining mirroring pond, where a wild plum leans out, "like a white-clad girl tiptoeing to her own reflection."

Home again, they will probably re-read the book that caught the real Island and recreated it as a magic isle of youth and fun and beauty. And then they may well ask for "more about Anne": a sequel.

⊸ *Anne of Avonlea* ⊸

(Boston: L.C. Page, 1909)

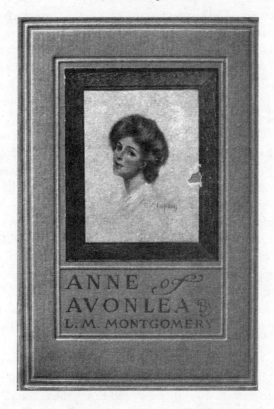

*A*nne of Green Gables was not yet in print when Montgomery began work on a sequel. In April 1907 the first "Anne" book had been accepted for publication. In agreeing to publish it, L.C. Page of Boston had asked for a sequel. Montgomery was delighted rather than surprised by the clause in her contract that obliged her to produce not one book but two. The request accorded with publishing fashion of the time, and she was enough of a professional to recognize that fact.[18] She knew that many of her long-time favourite novels, such as Anthony Hope's *Prisoner of Zenda* (1894), had been followed promptly by sequels.

Among children's books (the genre in which Montgomery hoped at this time to find a secure place), *Rebecca of Sunnybrook Farm* (1903) by her contemporary Kate Douglas Wiggin had now been followed by *New Chronicles of Rebecca* (1907) and Alice Hegan Rice's *Mrs. Wiggs of the Cabbage Patch* (1902) had its sequel in *Lovey Mary* (1904). The habit was catching, and long-lasting. Margaret Sidney's *Five Little Peppers* would eventually run to an eleven-book series.

Montgomery's newly signed-up publisher, L.C. Page, exploited this trend. He had agreed to publish Montgomery's first book in full confidence that she would follow the practice of his other authors, such as Annie Fellows Johnston, whose "*Little Colonel*" series, launched in 1895, had spawned twelve sequels. L.C. Page had also brought Marshall Saunders into his fold, and eventually published nine of her books about animal pets, following the success of *Beautiful Joe* (1894). Marshall Saunders, like Montgomery, was a Canadian Maritime writer. In fact, before the appearance of *Anne of Green Gables*, the Page imprint had recently appeared on several other Canadian Maritime books (with suggestively romantic titles) including Charles G.D. Roberts's *The Heart that Knows* (1906), Theodore Goodridge Roberts's *Brothers of Peril* (1905), and Bliss Carman's *The Kinship of Nature* (1904). Page was also bringing out a series that began with *Our Little Canadian Cousins*, by Elizabeth Roberts MacDonald (1904). All of this marked his recognition of readers' interest in Canadian stories—and his fondness for reaping the profit from publishing sequels and series.

Montgomery was more than ready to write "more about Anne." She was elated by "the joy of creation," especially in light of her feeling that "*Anne* is as real to me as if I had given her birth—as real and as dear" (October 9, 1907). She recorded in her journal the inception of *Anne of Avonlea*:

Yesterday I wrote the first six pages of my new book—the sequel to "Anne." I have been busy all summer collecting material for it, blocking out chapters, devising incidents and fitting them into each other, and "brooding up" the characters. This is the disagreeable part of the work but it is done now and the rest is pure joy. (October 9, 1907)

This time Montgomery started her book with a picture of Anne herself, slim and grey-eyed at "half-past-sixteen." Anne, studying Virgil's poetry, is tempted to let the book slide under the spell of a summer day in Avonlea and a dream of happy days to come as a school teacher.

But just as *Anne of Green Gables* opened with a comic portrait of Mrs. Lynde, representing the community with whom Anne was to come into conflict, so the new novel would swing quickly in those first six pages to a new antagonist. Mr. Harrison, a male opponent this time, berates Anne as a "red-headed snippet" and mocks her for "sitting round reading yellow-covered novels." Montgomery had rummaged among her earlier stories and found a launching-pad in "Miss Marietta's Jersey," published in *Household* in 1899. She lifted the plot of a wandering cow, its furious owner, a misjudged sale of the wrong cow, and the ultimate mollification of the victim. She changed old maid Marietta and her sister Cordely into teen-aged Anne (once almost Cordelia) and Diana. She copied the description of Mr. Morrison (Harrison) word for word: "short and fat and bald, . . . with his round face purple with rage and his prominent blue eyes almost sticking out of his head." But Montgomery now changed the denouement of her story. In her earlier version, Mr. Morrison offered to marry Marietta; Mr. Harrison simply becomes a friend of the "red-headed snippet" Anne. By the end of the third chapter, Anne will have apologized to Mr. Harrison, reminding faithful readers of the parallel moment when a younger red-headed snippet apologized to Mrs. Lynde.

This habit of cannibalizing her own inventions would persist when Montgomery was pushed for time. In this case it results in an appropriate and dramatic opening to the new story.

After the first six pages of *Anne of Avonlea*, however, the writing did not go smoothly. In January 1908 Montgomery reported being subject all through the cold weather to distractions as the neighbours came and went through the post office—which happened to be the kitchen, the only room in the house warm enough for writing. Still, this situation was hardly worse than the earlier times when as a young teacher she had to write early in the morning, in bitterly cold boarding houses, with fingers so chilled they could hardly hold her pen.

Those days were still strong in her memory. The main story-line of her new book would centre on Anne as a teacher. That occupation had been established at the end of *Anne of Green Gables*. Here Montgomery could call on many vivid sources. She herself had gone to school in a one-room wooden schoolhouse, heated by a big square coal stove (stoked by the pupils), with bench seats arranged along two walls, boys on one side, girls on the other. The older children heard the little ones recite lessons while the teacher worked with the middle group, preparing them for semi-annual examinations by trustees and the regional inspector.

Most of the men who taught Maud during her first six grades worked by the rule, "Spare the rod and spoil the child." When she was twelve, she encountered her first female teacher. Miss Hattie Gordon, one of the first women admitted to the provincial teachers' college of Prince Edward Island in 1879, had infiltrated a formerly all-male profession. Miss Gordon brought such enthusiasm into her teaching that almost twenty years later Montgomery dedicated *Anne of Avonlea* to her and allowed Anne to incorporate some of her kindly methods.

Montgomery herself had trained for teaching at Prince of Wales College (the original of Queen's College in *Anne of Green Gables*) in Charlottetown, Prince Edward Island, in 1893–94. Her curriculum there had included

English, history, arithmetic, French, chemistry, music, and agriculture, as well as courses in classroom management, school laws, and teaching. At the age of nineteen she had begun her first teaching job. Memories of one-room schools in the villages of Bideford, Belmont, and Bedeque in the 1890s might be dimming after twenty years, but Montgomery's journals and scrapbooks were crammed with details about students, curriculum, inspectors, and seasonal activities, all useful as a baseline for delineating Anne's professional progress.

Montgomery brought something more than personal experience to bear, however. She had absorbed attitudes to teaching and to education from the culture in which she had been raised. Her Scottish forebears had brought to Canada a belief in John Knox's dictum, "A school in every village, a college in every town." Cavendish treasured its school, nondenominational, free, coeducational, compulsory—and rigidly disciplinarian. As an avid reader of popular American magazines, however, Montgomery had now become familiar with the work of educational innovators like John Dewey of Chicago. *Anne of Avonlea* reflects changes in theory and practice. Anne and Jane and Gilbert argue about the relative merits of the strap, the hardwood pointer, and the power of persuasion as means of discipline. Anne as a teacher substitutes compositions and personal letters for rote recitation. But new ideals will be countered by mean humanity in the person of Anthony Pye, and Anne will mourn her ultimate failure to implement new educational theories.

Here she was adding her own perspective to a kind of story very popular at the time. Eggleston's *A Hoosier Schoolmaster* (1871), Rudyard Kipling's *Stalky & Co.* (1899), and Ralph Connor's *Glengarry Schooldays* (1902) each presented a male view of school life. Montgomery could count on audience interest in working in the same genre, and Anne would add the feminine touch. She lovingly takes one particularly gifted child, named Paul Irving, under her wing and wins his adoration in return.

As in *Anne of Green Gables*, this book will work not just with one plot (the life of a schoolteacher) but with several. In the first chapter, Marilla mentions the six-year-old twins, Davy and Dora, and their doings will constitute one sub-plot. Second, at the outset Anne tells Mrs. Lynde about the idea of a "Village Improvement Society." Third, talking about the new children who will be among Anne's students at Avonlea school, Mrs. Lynde introduces the name of "Lavendar Lewis," a woman left behind by a long-ago lover. Each of these themes as they grow into sub-plots will reveal new elements in Montgomery's life, her reading, and her openness to contemporary concerns.

The twins, Dora and Davy, come less from external facets of the author's own life than from literary conventions. The first of the *Bobbsey*

Twins introduced Flossie and Freddy, Bert and Nan in 1904, followed by sequels—best sellers that would catch a competitor's eye. Their predecessors were Demi and Daisy, Meg's twin children in the sequel to Louisa May Alcott's *Little Women*. The names of Montgomery's twins recall Charles Dickens's *David Copperfield*, where energetic David Copperfield is paired with his pretty, timid child-bride Dora. For Montgomery's "Davy," the mischievous boy twin, there were further literary sources in Mark Twain's *Tom Sawyer* and *Huckleberry Finn*, T.B. Aldrich's *Story of a Bad Boy*, and H.T. Gray's *A Bad Boy's Diry* [sic]. All had been among Montgomery's favourite books.

As in all stories of the double, such as Robert Louis Stevenson's *Dr. Jekyll and Mr. Hyde*, Mark Twain's *The Prince and the Pauper*, or Anthony Hope's *The Prisoner of Zenda*—all also among Montgomery's favourites—the strongly contrasted pair imply a deeper duality of disruption and conformity, both in society and in the individual psyche. The male-female pattern of the twin story in *Anne of Avonlea* connects this conflict with the tense question of gender-based roles. Montgomery had been playing with this motif over and over again in early short-stories. "Ted's Double" in *Men of Tomorrow* (1903), "Millicent's Double" in *East and West* (1905), "When Jack and Jill took a Hand" in *Gunter's* (1905), "Dottie and Tottie" in *Zion's Herald* (1907), and "The Twins and a Wedding" in *Holland's* (1908) are among her more recent stories exploiting the motif of duality.[19]

At the time of writing *Anne of Avonlea*, Montgomery was leading a double life of rebellion and propriety. In correspondence with fellow-writers in the United States, Great Britain, and Canada, she tackled contentious questions, political, religious, and ethical issues, voicing judgments as independent as Davy's. Olive Schreiner's early feminist novel, *The Story of an African Farm*, encouraged thoughts "speculative, analytical, rather pessimistic, iconoclastic, daring—and *very* unconventional. But it is powerful and original and fearless . . . like a tonic, bitter but bracing" (January 14, 1900). Though she related intensely to Schreiner's book, Montgomery could not apply any of these adjectives to her own outward life. Like Dora, she was leading a restrained existence, conforming to her aging grandmother's code of behaviour and to the narrow path laid down for an unmarried woman by a conventional Canadian community.

In Avonlea, Anne manages both Davy and Dora with lavish doses of laughter and sympathy. Maud Montgomery, more seriously torn by the contradictions in her own nature, could manage her own emotions less well. Two months after she began writing *Anne of Avonlea* she experienced a deep depression. "I work and think all day; and when night comes early, dour gloom settles down on my soul. I cannot describe the feeling. It is dreadful—worse than any actual pain. . . . I feel a great and awful *weariness*" (December 17, 1907).

One source of this depression was frustration at her grandmother's refusal to allow any changes in the old home. Working on her new novel, while waiting for the arrival of the published copy of *Anne of Green Gables*, Montgomery fumed, "There are six unused rooms in the house and there is no good reason why I should not have one fitted up and warmed as a library—no reason except the all potent one that grandmother would not hear of such a plan for a moment" (January 12, 1908). Perhaps this frustration gave rise to the idea of a "Village Improvement Society." Anne and her friends hope to see ugly old houses knocked down, or at least painted. They plan to plant gardens at Avonlea crossroads, as Montgomery herself had worked to beautify the Macneill property. Again she found a stimulus for action in her reading. *Elizabeth and Her German Garden* (1898) told the story of another woman's loneliness, sublimated in producing the beauty of roses. "My 'twin soul' must live in *Elizabeth*," Montgomery wrote (May 20, 1905).

The dream of changing and improving the environment was, however, not just a personal dream but also a stylish contemporary concept on rural and village beautification.[20] Frederick Olmsted, the famous designer of naturalistic parks, roadways, and gardens in New York, Boston, Chicago, and Montreal, preached environmental design in the journals that Maud read and wrote for, while Gertrude Jekyll and Edith Wharton showed that women too could become celebrated for fostering beauty in garden and landscape design.

The idea of landscape improvement also had a personal force for Maud Montgomery at this particular time. Reverend Ewan Macdonald had led parishioners in an effort at village improvement when he first served as Presbyterian minister in Cavendish. Groups of villagers followed his lead in tidying, planting, and generally improving the appearance of the graveyard that lay in the centre of the village. Local beautification had an attractive apostle.

Montgomery's situation vis-à-vis Ewan Macdonald underlies another plot-line in *Anne of Avonlea*, a tale of suspended romance. Montgomery had been engaged to this Presbyterian minister for a year now, but he was away, first in Glasgow doing graduate studies (from October 1906 to April 1907), then in the parish of Bloomfield in the western part of Prince Edward Island, far enough from Cavendish to make visits rare and difficult. The end of *Anne of Green Gables* had left Anne in a somewhat similar situation. In order to save Green Gables, Anne must linger in Avonlea as a teacher, while Gilbert Blythe is away, earning enough money to go to college. The fictional couple are young and there is no sense of frustration in their relationship.

Anne reads Virgil rather than romantic novels, and Gilbert is not particularly ardent. Their waiting period will be a happy one, unlike the waiting that their thirty-three-year-old creator was now enduring. So now, working with material closer to her own situation than to Anne's, Montgomery presents in *Anne of Avonlea* an older woman whose lover has been gone for many years. Miss Lavendar Lewis lives "all by herself in that little stone house she calls Echo Lodge."[21] In Miss Lavendar, Montgomery romanticizes her own lonely situation.

Education, beautification, dualities, and suspended romance—Montgomery had a complex of materials to be "brooded up." Any one of these themes could have been worked out in a short story. Indeed, most of them had thus occupied Montgomery in recent years. Titles of some of her recently published short stories suggest these discrete uses of *Anne of Avonlea* materials: "The Schoolma'am's Donation Party" (1903) and "The Spelling-Match at Albury" (1904); "The Little Three-cornered Lot" (1903) and "Dimple's Flowers" (1904); "The Softening of Miss Cynthia'" (1904) and "Lavender's Room" (1905). All were written shortly before Montgomery came to the more complex task of weaving all four themes into a novel.

The writing came hard. "I am pegging away at my new book, but it is rather discouraging work in winter. [T]here is so much coming and going in connection with the post office I am constantly interrupted" (January 12, 1908). Spring came, but in March 1908, after a year of work on the book, she revealed in the journal her dread of a nervous breakdown, and dwelt on her darkest childhood memories. None of this darkness would appear directly in *Anne of Avonlea*, because this was to be a book for young readers, and Montgomery was adept at providing cheerful fare for them. Comic classroom scenes involve children with names familiar from *Anne of Green Gables*: Pye, Sloane, and Bell. Boys are still like the boys in Anne's own schooldays. "Morley Andrews was caught driving a pair of trained crickets in the aisle. Anne stood Morley on the platform for an hour and . . . which Morley felt much more keenly . . . confiscated his crickets." Montgomery had settled to work like a good craftsman.

Then on June 20 came the "wonderful, thrilling moment" when the first copy of *Anne of Green Gables* came into her hands. Within ten days, the book, wonderfully well reviewed, went into a second edition—and her publisher L.C. Page began pushing her again to finish the sequel. "I'm working at it but it will not be as good a *Green Gables*. It doesn't *come* as easily. I have to force it" (June 30, 1908). But the success of *Anne of Green Gables* had reassured her that she was indeed something more than a writer of Sunday School stories for children.

Halfway through the book (probably when she was working on through the summer weather of 1908) she added a new motif. The middle chapters of *Anne of Avonlea* introduce a new female character. Mrs. Morgan, a famous novelist, comes to Avonlea, a free and successful woman. She has the autonomy and power traditionally assigned to males. Montgomery knew, of course, that women writers really could achieve such status: Harriet Beecher Stowe and George Eliot had set standards of independent thought and financial success. But women writers in Montgomery's own time were less revered. Best-sellers, yes; but people like Wiggin, Rice, Saunders, and Gene Stratton Porter were dismissed as pleasant, simple, and sentimental. Mrs. Morgan, in Montgomery's novel, stands for something more. She has kindliness as well as insight, and she deserves her fame and fortune.

At this mid-point in *Anne of Avonlea*, Montgomery recovers her own best voice. She treats the coming of a great woman writer into Avonlea with comic verve. Anne by accident greets the famous author with her nose turned a clown-like red, through a typical Anne misadventure of applying red dye instead of freckle-reducing lotion. This mid-chapter was probably written in July 1908, when glowing reviews of *Anne of Green Gables* were flooding into the little post office. In a comic reductive mood, Montgomery presents the famous author as short and stout. Anne, who has been unsure how to handle Mrs. Morgan's visit is at first comically over-prepared, and then later farcically unready for the famous author's arrival. But the visit turns out happily for all concerned.

Immediately after the encounter with the famous writer, Anne tries her hand at composition. Trapped (in another typical Anne escapade) in an empty hen-house, she creates an imaginary dialogue between the flowers and the birds and the spirit of the garden. Diana admires the finished product: "'*Do* send it to the *Canadian Woman*,'" she pleads; but Anne is dismissive. "'It wouldn't be suitable for publication at all. There is no plot in it. . . . It is just a string of fancies. . . . Editors insist on plots.'" Anne as a would-be writer provides a glimpse of her creator's uncertainties—and perhaps a mockery of her own current composition which seems to have too many plots.

Significantly, Anne composed her scorned "garden idyll" while searching for a patterned platter to replace one broken by ebullient Davy. Anne's concern over her domestic duty reflects the circumstances that Virginia Woolf would later enumerate in *A Room of One's Own*. A girl like Anne is prevented from fully concentrating on her literary work, and consequently writes something more flimsy than a man, fully concentrating on his composition, might produce. This is one of many scenes focused obliquely on the tension between male and female roles.

From this point on, Anne's teaching career recedes into the background. That part of the story had peaked when Anne forced one of the students to throw a package into the school stove, not knowing that the contents were fire crackers. Furthermore, whipping Anthony Pye for insolence when he is accused of placing a mouse in her desk drawer had put a guilty end to her early idealism. In the second half of the book the realistic impudence of a Pye is replaced by the romanticism of young Paul Irving, who dotes on his splendid teacher and offers her sentimental comments like this: "'Do you know what I think about the new moon, teacher? Think it is a little golden boat full of dreams.'" Again Montgomery seems to be mocking her own occasional descents into pretentious poesy.

The theme of teaching dwindles, replaced by that of suspended romance. Not Anne, but Miss Lavendar Lewis emerges as the central figure. The lonely spinster, abandoned by her long-ago lover, turns out to be an interesting happy person, a kindred spirit, in fact. She lives in a pleasant house, surrounded by a beautiful garden, and is looked after by her devoted maid. The principal force for reviving the old love seems to be not the reappearance of the man but the needs of his poetic little son Paul Irving, who has come to love Miss Lavendar almost as much as he loves his dear teacher Anne. This "dream boy" banishes Miss Lavendar's loneliness. When his father Stephen comes back to the Island, a happy ending is obviously on its way.

Readers had been waiting since *Anne of Green Gables* to see what would happen between Anne and Gilbert. Working out a sequel, Montgomery had decided that the answer should be "very little." But she also decided to give her readers a romantic ending—not for young Anne, but for an "old maid" whose prince returns, not too late for happiness.

To balance the romantic story of Miss Lavendar, Montgomery uses Mr. Harrison as a male variant of the "isolate," and gives him a not-so-happy ending. Mr. Harrison is restored to (presumably) married bliss with his daunting long-abandoned wife, a former schoolteacher.

Montgomery pokes fun at traditional romance elsewhere in the book. Diana settles for marrying Fred, the two of them threatening to become a "dreadfully pudgy couple." When young Davy asks, "Why don't *you* get married, Marilla?" Marilla answers amiably that maybe nobody would have her. Davy counters, "But maybe you never asked anybody." Daisy is horrified at this unconventional suggestion, but Davy's question remains as a foray into anti-romance.

The fashion of local beautification also gets comic treatment in the last quarter of the novel. The efforts of Anne and her friends to improve their village with gardens, groves of trees, and general beautification have produced funny and frustrating results. Members of the "Avonlea Village Improvement Society" (AVIS) have discovered the community's reluctance to be improved: they are content with their prosaic agricultural world. Furthermore, a corrupt politician has had to be wooed to help the good cause, and the Community Hall is painted a hideous color with AVIS funds. Finally, near the end of the novel, an old house which has been an eyesore, is levelled: not, however, by human ideals, but rather by a storm.

The storm does more than make a mockery of the society for beautification. It destroys local crops and kills Mr. Harrison's beloved taunting parrot. It also levels the grave of Hester Gray, another abandoned spinster of olden times, like Miss Lavendar. The rebellious part of Montgomery has its correlative in this storm. The enormous success of *Anne of Green Gables* seemed to have released and ratified her unusual creativity. Whipping up an imaginary storm seemed also like a symbolic vent for her own frustration at her grandmother's resistance to change.

Yet the storm subsides. In *Anne of Avonlea*, although the community mocks and opposes the dreams of young people, the conflict ends happily, as most things do in Avonlea (if not in Cavendish).

Similarly, the romantic wedding at Echo Lodge of Miss Lavendar and her prince ends with a double movement, one comic, one conciliatory. The poetic Paul banging on the brass dinner gong makes a noisy, comic coda to Miss Lavendar's pretty, sentimental wedding. Nature, however, softens the brassy noise into the "benediction of sweet sounds" in the valley of echoes. Gilbert and Anne walk together again, as at the end of *Anne of Green Gables*. Once again, however, the ending is ambivalent. "Behind them the little stone house brooded among the shadows. It was lonely, but not forsaken. It had not yet done with dreams and laughter and joy of life." A reader might substitute "she" for "it." Anne had not found the traditional closure of romance.

Neither had Montgomery. She knew that even when Ewan could return from away to claim her as his wife, other prospective problems would loom: how to blend marriage with the stresses of authorship; how to reconcile world-fame as an author with the probable obscurity; and, of course, the responsibility of life as a minister's wife.

Nevertheless, on August 3, 1908, Montgomery finished writing her second book. In spite of "worry and nervous ills" she could say thankfully, "After all I enjoyed writing it" (August 3, 1908). Revising the manuscript, adding linkages and foreshadowings and sharpening descriptions, as she had done in revising the manuscript of her first book, and finally typing up a clean copy occupied her until October 23.

Her success as a writer seemed assured. Since she had received the first printed copies of *Anne of Green Gables* she had been inundated with letters from fans and reviewers. Yet she again slipped into a depression, "prey to indescribable and unconquerable unrest" (October 23, 1908). Nevertheless she reaffirmed her basic intention as an author: "Thank God I can keep the shadows of my life out of my work. I would not wish to darken any other life—I want instead to be a messenger of optimism and sunshine" (October 15, 1908).

As such a messenger she had entered a predictably profitable field, with stories like Louisa May Alcott's *Little Women*. But she had selves to express other than the "Anne" one. After reading Bliss Carman's *Making of a Personality* (Ewan's gift), she felt "better, braver, more hopeful, more encouraged, more determined to make the best of myself and life since I have read it" (February 20, 1909).

Montgomery had given her readers, the Anne fans, a sequel. In it, however, Anne did not just drift toward romance; she accepted responsibility for her community. She still responded to the White Way of Delight, but she also worked to beautify her village. Scenes in the schoolroom recurred—but now from a teacher's point of view. Youthful fun and scrapes appeared, now assigned to Davy and Dora. The wedding at the end is not Anne's wedding, but elderly Miss Lavendar's. Having supplied the requested sequel (even if not quite as expected), Montgomery now stood ready to take her followers to the Island again—without Anne.

Kilmeny of the Orchard

(Boston: L.C. Page, 1910)

In 1909, Montgomery re-read Hans Christian Andersen's *Fairy Tales*, and thought about the "evasive, white-woven enchantment of moonlight" (June 1, June 4, 1909). She was ready to try her hand at something allusive and delicate.

Kilmeny of the Orchard is a fairy tale, but it is told by an adult whose favourite reading also included heavy tomes like Gibbons' *The Rise and Fall of the Roman Empire*. It is a lyric romance of youth, but it is written by a woman in her thirties whose early experiences of love had been awkward and disturbing. It is an easy-to-read story, produced by painstaking craftsmanship. Above all, it is a complex example of the relationship between reality and fiction, between the Island where Montgomery lived and worked and the island of imagination to which she could retreat, taking generations of readers with her.

The basic story of *Kilmeny of the Orchard* had been published first as

"Una of the Garden," a five-part serial, in a "women's magazine" in 1908. It was probably written in the winter of 1906–1907, before *Anne of Green Gables* had been accepted by the L.C. Page Company. Following the success in 1908 and 1909 of the first two *Anne* books, Montgomery began work on *The Story Girl*, but could not write quickly enough to suit her hungry Boston publisher. To pacify him, she agreed to re-work the "Una" serial, and to have finished the revision in time to be published in 1910, as *Kilmeny of the Orchard*.

The serial version of the story is hard to find. Donna Campbell, who has found a rare copy, points out the significance of the many changes Montgomery introduced in revising it to fit a new market—and to accord with the changes that occurred in her life between 1906 and 1909. The two versions of the story also illustrate her extreme care in revision: assigning new and allusive names to her characters; sharpening the sense of appropriate settings; adding tension to the plot.

The shift in the title from "Garden" to "Orchard" suggests a development in Montgomery's vision of love, from a garden's suggestion of the fragile prettiness of flowers, to the orchard's implication of the sturdiness of trees, bearing fruit. Although she claimed at the time that her revisions did not require concentration and that she had "merely to copy and amplify existing thoughts" (January 6, 1910), it seems clear now that subconscious impulses rather than reasoned editing dictated many of them. During the time when she was revising and lengthening the Kilmeny story, Montgomery had become secretly engaged to Ewan Macdonald. Many of the revisions reflect the new perspective he brought into her life.

The name "Una" recalls the Elizabethan poem *The Faerie Queene*, a text Montgomery studied while at Dalhousie University. In Edmund Spenser's epic, Una rides alone and bravely as a female questor, guarded by a lion. When Montgomery changed the name of her heroine to "Kilmeny," she introduced the mysterious note of folklore of the Scottish borders, remembered from a poem by James Hogg, familiar to her from early schooldays when it appeared in Prince Edward Island readers. Kilmeny's surname recognizes a connected debt. In revision, Montgomery changed "Una Marshall" into "Kilmeny Gordon," recalling Hattie Gordon, the teacher who had encouraged schoolgirl Maud in her love of literature. (The surname "Marshall" is reassigned to the hero who will come into Kilmeny's life.)

"Kilmeny" in the old poem is a young woman swept out of a rural glen to "the land of the spirits." Even when she returns to the ordinary world, she still wanders "afar frae the haunts of men." The strange Kilmeny adventure is a metaphor of the out-of-reality experience of creative art. The name shift also changes the focus from a woman of action to a fey wilderness wanderer, suggesting an increase of uncertainty and secrecy in Montgomery, even at a time when her apparent fortunes seemed to be rising.

Both "Una of the Garden" and *Kilmeny of the Orchard* reflect other factors in Montgomery's reading and her life. As a schoolgirl she had memorized long passages from Sir Walter Scott's *The Lady of the Lake*. Stored deep in memory, the pattern of that poem gave her a line to follow. Like Ellen in *The Lady of the Lake*, Montgomery's Kilmeny lives in isolation with her guardians. In Scott's story a king disguised as a huntsman comes to the lady's island and is entranced by the lady's harp-accompanied singing. In *Kilmeny of the Orchard*, Eric Marshall travels to Prince Edward Island to take up the low-level role of school teacher in a north-shore village. There he is entranced by Kilmeny's wordless music, her matchless playing of the violin, as she moves in isolation like Ellen's, "with the moon's beauty and the moon's soft pace."

Eric is not a king in disguise, but at least he is a gifted and high-minded young man and heir to great wealth in Nova Scotia. In "Una of the Garden" the school teacher who comes to the Island from a mainland university, had been named "Eric Murray," recalling perhaps the name of Montgomery's university-educated cousin Murray Macneill. Murray, who had enough funds to complete his college education, had lorded it over Montgomery, who had been denied the same chance. Deleting his name may—always perhaps!—indicate a lingering revengefulness. (Montgomery saves the name "Murray"; many years later it will appear as the name of the prideful New Moon family of "Emily Byrd Starr.")

In "Una of the Garden" Eric simply arrives on Prince Edward Island "from away." In *Kilmeny*, his life is more fully realized in the new first chapters. Eric's friends, his father, and his college days are expanded, perhaps thanks to stories Montgomery was now hearing from Ewan Macdonald, about his life at Dalhousie and at the theological seminary in Halifax. The expanded opening seems to write Ewan Macdonald more clearly into the role of a caring, intelligent man who will break the spell that binds the heroine. For Montgomery, too, hope of escape emerged with the coming of a well-educated stranger.

The new opening of *Kilmeny of the Orchard* emphasizes the pull on Eric Marshall of Prince Edward Island—a pull established in the two "Anne" books as Montgomery's specialty. The young school teacher has also been pulled away from his destined life of wealth and privilege by "a Celtic streak" that fills him with a mysterious dissatisfaction. Montgomery's interest in her Scottish heritage manifests itself throughout *Kilmeny of the Orchard*. In a further echo of Walter Scott's poem, Eric rouses the jealous fury of a darkly handsome youth named Neil Gordon. Fitz-James, the disguised king in *The Lady of the Lake*, has a similar menacing dark rival in Roderick Dhu, who terrifies the Lady. Eric sees this menacing young man when he first arrives on the Island. Neil, the gypsy boy fostered by Kilmeny

Gordon's family, also suggests another powerful literary influence on Montgomery: that of the Brontës. Some memory of the savage gypsy Heathcliff in Emily Brontë's *Wuthering Heights* infuses the dark-browed youth in Montgomery's romantic story. Like Heathcliff, he rouses the reader's sympathy for his doomed possessive love.

Immediately after establishing the dark and mysterious note struck by Neil's appearance, Montgomery swings to another tone as she creates a vivid, folksy community, with Island ways and mannerisms of speech. Here again she is revealing another debt to Scottish literary tradition. The people where Eric Marshall boards resemble folk in the Scottish "Kailyard" novels of J.M. Barrie, Ian MacLaren, and S.R. Crockett. The term "Kailyard" had been applied derisively by critics to a whole group of novels in Britain and the United States that were sentimentally focused on the kindly yet comic lives of poverty-stricken communities, where a front yard cultivation of cabbages ("kail" in Lowland Scots) meant escape from hunger. These stories were enormously popular when Montgomery was a young woman.[22] In 1895, as a student at Dalhousie University, she participated in discussion of the then-popular work of the Kailyard school. Of all the Kailyard writers, Barrie in particular was one of Montgomery's literary gods. His home town of Kirriemuir would be among the places of pilgrimage visited on her honeymoon. In the Barrie manner, Montgomery relishes and effectively recreates the language and manners of rural Prince Edward Island. She catches the rhythm of a woman who explains to the new teacher her son's absence from school: "I had to keep him home to help me put the pertaters in; for his father won't work and doesn't work and can't be made to work." In this style Montgomery resembled another Canadian writer, Ralph Connor, who also imitated the Kailyard mannerisms in his *The Man from Glengarry* (1901) and *Glengarry Schooldays* (1902). Montgomery's unusual achievement was in blending the Kailyard homeliness with that other Highland tradition of haunting mystery.

Other more recent books had absorbed Montgomery during her long lonely years of reading and brooding. Gerald DuMaurier's *Trilby* (1894) was one of these. Trilby is a supremely gifted artist, but her wonderful voice can only be released by the evil hypnotist Svengali. Like Trilby's, Kilmeny's power of expression is inhibited—more tragically, because she has been voiceless since birth. She can be released, not by an evil hypnotist, but by love. In spite of the differences in detail, it is clear that the Trilby story of chained artistry had deep meaning for Montgomery, confident of her own powers, but unable to take full advantage of them.

A bestselling novel by Gene Stratton Porter, one of Montgomery's rivals as a contemporary bestseller, offers puzzling parallels to many other features of Kilmeny's story. Before Montgomery began "brooding up" her *Anne of*

Green Gables, Porter's *Freckles*, published in 1904, had told the story of a red-haired orphan coming into an alien community. There seems to be an even closer affinity between *Kilmeny of the Orchard* (1910) and Porter's *A Girl of the Limberlost* (1909), the sequel to *Freckles*. Both feature a girl who is trammelled by her mother's neurotic response to the past, and who is also a beautiful virtuoso of the violin. The neurosis of the mother in the Porter book, like that of Kilmeny's mother, is rooted in sexual transgression. Elnora's father, like Kilmeny's mother, is accused of adultery by judgmental family members. In both cases, a sensitive man saves the girl who has been made to suffer grievous social consequences for the sins of the elders. Both stories are connected with frightening concepts of sin and doom.

In both cases, furthermore, the suffering has also involved restrictions on self-expression through a musical gift. Both Montgomery and Gene Stratton Porter can be presumed to be releasing deep-seated resentments against a patriarchal society still reluctant to recognize outstanding artistic talent in women. The publication dates pose a puzzle about possible indebtedness. The American author may have read "Una of the Garden" (1908) in serial form in a mid-western magazine; or the Canadian author may have read the best-selling *Girl of the Limberlost* while her revised *Kilmeny* was going through the press in 1909; or both authors may have responded independently to the same literary influences of Brontë and DuMaurier and have independently meditated on the repression of talent in young women.

Although in a later journal Montgomery would write, "Kilmeny reflects very little out of my own experience" (January 27, 1911), there are in fact many parallels. Like Kilmeny, Maud Montgomery had been raised by older relatives because of the death of her mother, and the sense of loss was very strong in the author's mind at the time she was creating the story of Una/Kilmeny. The first entry in the journal of 1905 is a cry of grief over the death long ago of her mother. "It is a dreadful thing to lose one's mother in childhood!" (January 2, 1905). Like Kilmeny, Montgomery lived a lonely life. She too escaped to a natural world of beauty and to books. She too found solace in practising her art. Increasingly she too felt locked into her own life, unable to communicate fully, in spite of her amazing success as a writer of little essays, stories, sketches, and poems. Yet a new sense of repression accompanied her hope. Courting under her grandmother's eye must have seemed like Kilmeny's inhibited voiceless state, the sense of being under a spell.

When Montgomery turned the "Una" story into *Kilmeny of the Orchard* she kept unchanged the first description of the beautiful, mysterious, solitary girl:

> On a stone bench under the big branching white lilac tree a girl was sitting, playing on an old brown violin; her eyes were on the faraway

horizon and she did not see Eric. . . .

Her face was oval and delicately tinted, marked in every line and feature with the expression of absolute purity found in the angels and Madonnas of old paintings, a purity that had in it no faintest stain of earthliness. Her head was bare and her thick, jet-black hair was parted over her brow, "one moonbeam from the forehead to the crown."[23]

Like the other Kilmeny, she lives "far frae the haunts of men."

The nature of the spell that binds her is much darker and more complex than anything Montgomery had handled in the "Anne" stories. In a distorted version of Scottish Presbyterian theology, Kilmeny appears fated to suffer for the sins of her forebears. She is trapped, like all humans, according to rigid Calvinist doctrine, in a fate not of her own making, sealed by her mother's sin of bearing a child out of wedlock, her grandfather's sin of prideful rejection of his daughter and her baby, and her mother's sinful refusal to speak in response to the old man's wrath in the months before Kilmeny's birth. Behind this story lurks the theological notion of a stern, retributive God, so aware of human sin that He doles out a fate undeserved by the individual, whose faith and good works might be supposed to earn salvation. Kept away from the world by the dark secrets of her family, innocent Kilmeny lives in isolation, deprived of speech, unable to communicate except through her magically articulate violin.

The concept of Kilmeny as a person fated by sins not her own reflects a largely outdated version of the Presbyterian theology of predestination. Yet that theology in all its harshness was still adhered to by many of Montgomery's contemporaries, including—sadly—the man she had promised to marry. Ewan Macdonald had been brought up in a rural Gaelic-speaking community at the east end of Prince Edward Island. He apparently harboured a suppressed feeling that he was not himself one of the "elect," the people chosen for salvation by God's predestining will. His sense that he was doomed to damnation was dormant at this time; it would emerge later in their married life with terrible consequences.

Perhaps as part of an ongoing discussion with Ewan, the graduate of theology, Montgomery raised the old dogma of predestination in her novel only to reject it. She had been reading books of psychology, such as *The Law of Psychic Phenomena*, and discussing the possibility of psychosomatic healing with her correspondents (February 3, 1906).[24] Eric, as a scholar coming fresh from university, brings new ideas about human destiny. He calls in a college friend, a physician, to examine the impaired Kilmeny, searching for a cure of her inability to speak. On December 23, 1909, Montgomery wrote of *Kilmeny*, "It is a love story with a psychological interest—very different from my other books and so a rather doubtful experiment with a public who expects a certain style from an author and rather resents having anything else offered it" (December 23, 1909). The "psychological interest" comes from the doctor's theory of psychosomatic impairment caused by "trauma" and his hope that Kilmeny may be shocked into a cure. This plot development seems to articulate a probably unspoken difference in theological/psychological assumptions between Montgomery and the man she was preparing to accept as a future husband.

Besides being held in silence by the force of ancient sin and by the physiology of trauma, Kilmeny is trapped by her lack of positive self-image. No mirrors have been permitted in Kilmeny's world; she has no inkling of her own beauty. Eric, presenting her with a mirror, convinces her that she is lovely. Like Kilmeny, Montgomery sadly needed support and reassurance about her value—as an attractive woman, not just as a successful professional author.

The stranger discovering Kilmeny in her strange isolation cannot however free her by mere love and admiration. She must free herself, and she does so when Eric is threatened by the foster child in her family, Neil, the dark gypsy. In Jungian terms, if Kilmeny externalizes Montgomery's *anima*, and Eric her *animus*, Neil Gordon is the *shadow* in her psyche. Like Montgomery herself, Neil is motherless, abandoned by his father, and brought up in an adoptive family. Kilmeny's fate hangs on the menace of dark depressive Neil. She is wakened to full life by recognizing and facing the danger he poses to the man she has come to love, with whom she has "conversed" only by writing. Terrified when Neil threatens Eric's life, she magically regains her voice in a desperate warning. She is freed, not only into speech, but into love.

The original story had come from a time when Montgomery was reaching the end of a very troubled period. She knew that she was perceived in her home community not so much as an artist, but as a spinster, a woman unable to find a proper husband. Certainly there were few men in the rather isolated community of Cavendish who could match her in intellectual vigour or sensitivity. She could look back on her earlier life, however, as a time of wrenching romantic involvements. She had suffered from an inappropriate engagement to Edwin Simpson, an intensely intellectual and self-absorbed young Baptist minister. She had heard with sorrow of the death of Will Pritchard, a happy-go-lucky boy who had loved her in her time out west. She had found herself passionately attracted to Herman Leard, a young farmer, a natural, vital man with "no trace of intellect, culture or education." Montgomery's journal affirms that she could never imagine herself marrying him. Modern research discovers that as a matter of fact he was not eligible, being engaged to someone else at the time; but whatever the case, her connection with Herman was a source of suffering. It had ended traumatically when her grandmother casually read from the local paper in 1899 the news that Herman Leard had died, suddenly, reportedly of influenza. She had dismissed Edwin Simpson, though he lingered at the threshold of her consciousness. Licking her romantic wounds, she had continued to write and publish up-beat stories of courtships—some gently romantic, some wildly farcical.

In 1905 she recorded mood swings as she faced the insecurities of her life and her writing:

> It is well I am used to dullness or the unutterable dreariness of these past two days would have mildewed my very soul. As it was, I kept myself sane by working; a story was finished, a lot of typewriting done, a fancy collar made, and a book re-read that took me away from my snowy prison into a wonderful world. (January 27, 1905)

She fed her melancholy by reading and re-reading the journal accounts and the letters that had survived from happier days when dreams of love and passion were strong. In April 1906 she heard that Nate Lockhart, her earliest school boyfriend, was not only "*married*," but also "*very gray*" (April 5, 1906). She was already "brooding up" *Anne of Green Gables*, drawing from memories of Nate and others. Worries were "moth-eating" her soul. "There is no one in Cavendish to whom I can turn for advice or assistance. I cannot bear to expose the seamy side of my life to the gaze of any outsider. To all here I preserve the same unbroken front of smile and jest and composure" (March 6, 1906). This is the personal plight from which Una's initial situation was drawn.

But within a few days of this entry came the "sweet-scented evening" when Ewan Macdonald first came to call, and Montgomery wrote the opening lines of *Anne of Green Gables*. Her mood had lifted. In 1903, Ewan Macdonald had taken on the position of Presbyterian minister in Cavendish. Even before he declared himself as a suitor, his very presence had been stimulating. Montgomery began serving as church organist and attended a wedding where he officiated. There is only a single reference to him by name in these years, yet in October 1906 he proposed and she accepted his proposal of marriage. So, besides literary influences, there is another source of the "salvation part" of the Una story: Montgomery's own life, transmuted no doubt unconsciously into a fairy tale.

Beside the fairy tale quality, this story, in the enlarged ending of *Kilmeny of the Orchard*, held other charms. Eric's "amazement and joy" is matched by Kilmeny's more realistic preparation to join the local society now that she is free and preparing to be married. She will go to church and to the Missionary Society meetings. For Neil, too, the dark other, good Kailyard realism is invoked in his banishment. He goes west on a harvest excursion train—a fit disposal of a villain from a farm community. Then the highly charged story ends in an apotheosis that is at once pastoral, sexy, and regal. Kilmeny sits under a lilac tree, in a blue dress "simply and quaintly made, as all her gowns were, revealing the perfect lines of her lithe, slender figure." She is presented to Eric's kingly father, "like a young princess, crowned with a ruddy splash of sunlight that fell through the old trees."

The story of Kilmeny the marvellous violinist thus ends not with Kilmeny's artistry but with her happy preparation for marriage to Eric the teacher, or as he is always called, the Master. Here the likeness between the book and the author's life ends. For Montgomery, too, hope of escape had emerged with the coming of a well-educated stranger, in her case Reverend Ewan Macdonald, but she would move into an unexpected debacle in marriage, with a man unable to master his own moods and delusions. Even from the outset a new sense of repression had accompanied her hope. The separation that followed her acceptance of Ewan's offer of marriage sent her back into depression. Kilmeny's creator was still in thrall to her own nervous illnesses and black moods. Within days of sending off the manuscript of *Kilmeny* she suffered "a month of nervous prostration—an utter breakdown of body, soul, and spirit" (February 7, 1910).

Montgomery prepared to outface the depression by continued flight into the world of her imagination. Montgomery's real hope in 1910 was of escape through art. Aware of her own powers, she might well dream of moving into a wider world, not through musical performance like Kilmeny's, but by masterful performance in words. With the phenomenal success of the two "Anne" books to bolster her dream, she could envision a steady climb up the "Alpine Path"—the road to fame as an artist. *Kilmeny of the Orchard* was one of just three books written by Montgomery in which adult characters dominate. "Una of the Garden," like many of Montgomery's early stories, had been written for a magazine directed at an adult audience. In its later form as a novel it received favourable reviews, noting the move into "adult fiction."

In 1910, however, *Anne of Green Gables* had established such a strong reputation for appealing to younger readers that her publisher pushed her to return to *The Story Girl*. The word "Girl" in the title signalled a return to the very lucrative "young adult" audience. Practicality—or predestination?—shifted Montgomery back in that direction.

(Boston: L.C. Page, 1911)

The he title of *The Story Girl* is a story in itself. It tells of a moment in Montgomery's development when she was ready to try something new and ambitious, something different from the books that had established her as a best-selling writer, but that had also seemed to fix her work into a predictable pattern. Her previous titles—*Anne of Green Gables, Anne of Avonlea, Kilmeny of the Orchard*—had promised a focus on one person in one place. This book would not limit itself in that way. It would play games with the idea of *storying* and would dramatize a notable example of *girlhood*.

As "story" it would present, first, a narrative about young people enjoying summer life on an ordinary farm in Prince Edward Island. This framing story would be enriched by a wild variety of other stories (legends, comic anecdotes, ghostly tales, romances) that would carry readers away from the Island to ancient Greece, Scandinavia, pioneer Canada, and out to the Milky Way. A "girl"—an unusually gifted girl—would be the teller of these absorbing embedded tales. Montgomery was ready to celebrate the gift of narrative that she recognized in herself, and to show the kind of impact that a female story-teller could have on an admiring group of listeners, both male and female. But a man named Bev King, who once came with his brother Felix to the happy isle, will purportedly tell this story of the summer spell of joy woven by the Story Girl.

Many years earlier, Montgomery had used a male narrator to tell a rollicking adventure story titled "Our Charivari,"[25] based on memories of the two Nelson boys who had come from Toronto to spend a summer at the Macneill farm. Perhaps, in using a male narrator again in her new book, Montgomery merely hoped to reach out to a readership beyond the female audience established by the two *Anne* books. She had recently sold several short stories to "boys' own" magazines such as *Boys' World* and *Men of Tomorrow*.[26] Perhaps, however, she now intended to mollify literary critics, who generally assumed that a male point of view was more significant than a female one. In *Una of the Garden/Kilmeny of the Orchard,* Montgomery had presented a longer and more complex story through the focus of Eric Marshall from a male point of view. Perhaps she was ready to mock those same critics, by making Bev King's story so much less colourful than those the Story Girl tells.

At any rate she begins her new book when thirteen-year-old Bev King tells of coming with his younger brother Felix (like Wellington and Dave Nelson) from distant Ontario, to join a family circle on an Island farm.[27] The first chapter of *The Story Girl* enlarges on the sense of homecoming that Bev and Felix feel as they are welcomed to the King homestead and its orchard—the feeling many readers, male and female, would now have as they re-entered Montgomery's Island.

Near the entrance of the blossoming orchard stands Sara Stanley, the Story Girl, "gay and graceful." She offers to tell the newcomers stories, including some "witch stories" that "will freeze the blood in your veins." Sara Stanley is presented, not as a child like the funny eleven-year-old Anne who first amused readers with her incredible fantasies, and not as a young woman like Anne in the sequel about a teacher who has drifted beyond dramatic story-telling; certainly not as a full-grown adult like romantic Kilmeny. Sara at fourteen is exactly the age Montgomery was when she wrote in her journal "Life is beginning to get interesting for me" and added, soon, "I like writing compositions" (April 2, 1889) and "I . . . got honorable mention" (February 19, 1890) for a story submitted to the *Montreal Witness* school competition.

The long apprenticeship which had probably drawn some mockery and jealousy as well as some admiration from her home community now seemed thoroughly justified. Montgomery could insert into her scrapbook adulatory reviews of the *Anne* books from the Boston *Spectator*, the London *Observer*, the Toronto *Globe* among many others. She gloried in imputing her own story-telling power to her new heroine, and retracing the early development of that power.

Fourteen-year-old Sara Stanley (named for Montgomery's own birthplace of Stanley Bridge) is an idealized self-portrait of the author as a young girl. The Story Girl lives on the farm adjoining the old King homestead, with a bachelor uncle and aunt, since her beloved father is far away (like Hugh John Montgomery). She is not beautiful (neither was Maud Montgomery), but she is able, like Montgomery, to beguile listeners with her dramatic flair for story-telling.

The circle of listeners includes Felicity, Cecily, and Dan King (aged thirteen, twelve, and eleven), with Sara Ray as a virtual sister and Peter Craig as a young farm helper who shares the family's leisure time. It is perhaps coincidental that this constellation closely parallels that of the March family in *Little Women*, where Jo is the story-teller to Meg, Beth, and Amy while nearby Teddy Lawrence adds a male listener to her circle. "Big family" stories like Alcott's perennial favourite were still in style when Montgomery began writing *The Story Girl*: the *Five Little Peppers* series was just one of a host of books satisfying young readers' fascination with the genre.

Montgomery, however, had a personal memory of big-family life, in spite of being an only child. Felicity, Cecily, and Dan King match the real-life circle of her cousins—Clara, Stella, and George Campbell, with whom she had spent long happy visits as a child and young girl, playing her part as a nearby cousin who joined them to tell fabulous tales.[28] Personal memories joined awareness of a popular genre in creating the framing narrative. But the star of the novel shines with Montgomery's current pleasure in her own success.

Montgomery had grown up in a family of noted story-tellers, and in a Scottish-Canadian community where shared legends, tales, and anecdotes about ancestors and neighbours held the clans together. In *The Story Girl*, Montgomery would fit traditional stories like those her elders once told, adding flash and variety and sensationalism to the framing picture of "real life" on the family farm. Near the outset of the story, in a miniature version of her own experience, she will show the Story Girl winning the ultimate accolade in the eyes of a Scottish community, when her facility at telling an old story squeezes a five dollar donation out of an old curmudgeon. (Montgomery had earlier sold a version of this winsome story, drawn from Macneill family tradition, as "A Pioneer Wooing" to *Farm and Fireside*, in 1903).[29] To a good simple story, Montgomery now adds Sara's voice and gestures to provide drama. The listeners, unwillingly seduced by her art, add comedy. Similarly, throughout the early chapters of the novel, each spellbinding moment of story-telling is set in a framing drama, always starring the Story Girl.

The prime obvious source for the framing drama is Montgomery's journal. Just as Bev the narrator claims he is writing about the Story Girl and the summer on the Island with his old "Dream Books" close at hand, so Montgomery could access her own adolescent feelings by rereading her treasured diary. Revisiting her spring time there, she creates a legend of youth, setting the story in an orchard of plentiful blossoms and a few forbidden fruit. For the author, the sense of the charm of the Island was intensified by a feeling of uncertainty. How long would she be staying in her old haunts, now that she was engaged to marry a man who would probably accept a call to a parish far away from Prince Edward Island?[30]

Yet Montgomery was enjoying a mood upswing that summer of 1909 as she wrote the first chapters of her new novel. Her journal records elated walks in Lover's Lane, relishing her current success and brooding up a series of scenes in which Sara would exercise narrative power over a responding audience. She records reading Keats and Tennyson and dismisses Keats as too "luscious" and Tennyson as too "well-ordered." She admits to a hope that she could capture something of the "indefinable, elusive, 'bouquet'" of her Island home—a quality neither luscious like Keats nor well-ordered like Tennyson. She recalled her grandfather's stories of sea voyages and the verve with which he told them.

Then she walked again in Lover's Lane, this time with a powerfully attractive cousin. At the same time she re-read her earliest journal, with its emphasis on boys and girls playing at romantic attachments, exchanging notes, talking, and "walking around together"—and she touched into her new story about fourteen-year-olds a hint of what Evelyn Waugh in *Brideshead Revisited* would call "the thin bat squeak of sexuality." One of the first stories in the new book would be about a young girl "with red lips and black, black eyes and hair" who kisses a sleeping poet. The Story Girl reports that the young people like to act out this story, especially effective when Felicity plays the girl and Peter the poet is kissed. Late in the book the theme will be lifted into mythic proportions when Sara tells the story of "how kissing was discovered," in response to Felicity's fury when Peter tries to kiss her, not as an enactment. Montgomery, admitting her arousal by her cousin Oliver Macneill, and at the same time keeping secret her engagement to Ewan Macdonald, was venturing into a tone different from the way she had presented her Anne as shuddering away from romance.

Through the summer of 1909 and on into the fall, she worked well, without the depression that had floored her in the previous year. Montgomery's joy in writing the opening chapters was short-lived, however. In November 1909 she suspended work on *The Story Girl*. She was induced to write a different, more quickly publishable novel for L.C. Page, so that a 1910 offering could exploit the current popularity of her name. She dutifully set her new story aside in order to refurbish "Una of the Garden" as *Kilmeny of the Orchard* (a book very different in tone, structure, and focus). Not until *Kilmeny* had been sent to Page in January 1910 could she return, wearily, to *The Story Girl*.

The pressure to work through a hurried revision had destroyed her creative mood. By the time she finished *Kilmeny* she was hovering on the brink of nervous prostration. It was March 1910 before she could face any return to writing on her *Story Girl* manuscript. Then a bracing Easter visit from her favourite cousin, Frederica Campbell, strengthened her morale. (*The Story Girl* would eventually be dedicated to Frederica.) In revived spirits Montgomery returned to work in May. She could now write happy passages like the opening of the sixteenth chapter, where Cecily and Sara Ray "'talk secrets'" while Paddy the cat purrs his satisfaction, Felicity bakes a gorgeous new kind of cake, all the children pick raspberries, and the Story Girl tells a story of being whisked straightaway to fairyland.

Unfortunately a long summer visit in 1910 from her Uncle Leander's family, "home for the holidays," again suspended all hope of any writing. "I have accomplished almost nothing these past six weeks," she wrote (April 26, 1910). After "the Leanders" left at the end of August, she turned again to *The Story Girl*, "The best piece of work I have yet done" (November 29, 1910). Part of its excellence lay in the way it reflected the swings of mood that had beset her.

She was in an elated mood as she wrote her way toward the end of the novel that September, because of an honour paid to her by the Governor-General of Canada. Lord Grey had particularly asked to meet her during an official 1910 visit to Prince Edward Island. Returning home to Cavendish, she rushed to finish the book, because now she had been invited to Boston in October to meet her publisher and to discuss future publications.

Again, the joy of these exotic visits was followed by irritation. Returning home to her grandmother's "petty tyranny" she exploded, "I certainly ought to keep a servant. To do the housework I do in connection with my increasing literary work is too much for me" (September 10, 1910). This explosion against the duties of housekeeping manifests itself in the Story Girl's domestic ineptitude—and in Bev's reassurance that her gifts are more significant than Felicity's perfect cupcakes. *The Story Girl* was finished and typed by the end of October 1910.

Montgomery's journal in its published form enriches a reader's understanding of the working-out of *The Story Girl*. In return, reading *The Story Girl* adds an understanding of the author not available through the journal. *The Story Girl* may have begun as an amalgam of memories, literary influences, and awareness of marketing possibilities. Fictional characters, however, as most fiction writers will admit, have a tendency to develop a life of their own. Richer characterization results from the release of repressed or forgotten fears or delights. For the two outsiders who enlarge the family circle, neighbour Sara Ray and hired boy Peter Craig, Montgomery would draw not on memories of her childhood, or on records in the journal, but on suppressed dramas of her more mature days.

Melancholy Sara Ray represents the pathetic downside of Sara Stanley's euphoric zest. This "other Sara" personifies the depressive self that Maud Montgomery was aware of in herself, the gloom into which she had slipped several times since adolescence. Weepy Sara Ray creeps like a sad shadow through the Story Girl's world, like the affective mood disorder that increasingly afflicted Montgomery herself. A conflicting duality is manifested also in Felix and Felicity. In spite of their twinning names (they are called after loving twins of a past generation), pretty, proud Felicity and fat, self-doubting Felix are at odds throughout the story.[31] Felicity is also often in some conflict with Sara the Story Girl. Felicity's prettiness, her dimpled domesticity, arouses Sara's jealousy. Creativity and femininity live uneasily together in the novelist as well as in the novel.

Peter Craig suggests another psychological tension in his creator. Peter works as a hired boy at the farm where the Story Girl lives. He is is a type that recurs in other books by Montgomery, as Neil Gordon who stalks Kilmeny and as Perry Miller, the hired boy who admires Emily at New Moon. Good-looking and curly-headed, Peter in his appearance recalls the description of Herman Leard, the central figure in Montgomery's first real romance. In her journal, Montgomery had claimed she rejected Herman because she considered him her inferior. Research suggests, however, that he was in fact engaged to a pretty Bedeque girl at the very moment that Montgomery fell prey to his charms.[32] The situation was too humiliating to be mentioned in the journal. Montgomery, however, can twist facts into a more satisfactory fiction. Peter Craig is devoted not to gifted Sara Stanley but to pretty Felicity; but Felicity scorns him because he is lower in caste than the King family. In an ultimate revenge, Montgomery ordains that Felicity's charms are outshone by the Story Girl's: "Her face was like a rose of youth. But when the Story Girl spoke, we forgot to look at Felicity." Sara, like her creator, has perception, humour, and a mystic sense of the double beauty of the world and of words—better attributes than prettiness and good housekeeping, whatever Peter (or Herman) may believe.

Perhaps unconsciously, Montgomery in later parts of the book introduces women characters exemplifying other contradictory aspects of her complex self-image. Peg Bowen, the menacing eccentric considered a witch by the young folk, shows what a lonely, intense woman can become. Aunt Olivia, twenty-eight years old, though charming and kind, is dismissed by the young people as un-marriageable. More cheerfully, homely Rachel Ward is remembered as a woman who, after losing her lover Will, locked her treasures in a blue chest and left for the Canadian mainland. All these characters suggest an ambiguity in Montgomery's own conception of the feminine.

Yet in spite of this uncertainty, and in spite of the start-and-stop pace of composition, the main story in the new novel is unified by a tone of gentle irony. Adolescent agonies and ecstasies are reduced by the narrator's amusement. Fear of death, obsession with sin, puzzles over theology, nibblings at romance, and indulgence in youthful rivalries—all themes to be treated with melodrama in Sara's embedded stories, are all reduced in the enfolding narrative of summer on the Island, and hence controlled. The framing story—its characters and its incidents—reflects in a cool way the major concerns of the author at the time of composition. In Sara's stories, the same concerns flame into intensity.

While working on this novel, for instance, Montgomery was obsessed by the thought of death. She lived in the shadow of the anticipated death of her frail grandmother, whom she both revered and resented. That imminent death would mean that Montgomery's uncle would at last inherit the home place, and consequently that she would no longer have a home in Cavendish. Simultaneously she was working through her memories of other deaths (her hated stepmother in April 1909, her well-loved Aunt Mary McIntyre in January 1909, and more distantly, her mother, her father, Herman Leard, and Will Pritchard). In spite of this obsession, the frame story reduces the danger of death to a case of measles or the bewitchment of a cat. But Sara's legends lift to a higher, terrifying key, starting with the tale of the proud princess, who spurned love and found death.

Romantic love also concerned Montgomery intensely at this time. She worried in her journal over her inability to feel for Ewan the kind of passion aroused once by Herman and more recently by her cousin Oliver. Yet Montgomery does not feature falling in love or being married in the framing story. Attraction between the sexes appears in mild and amusing form as the young people inch toward romance in the covert and comic courtship between Peter and Felicity and the "crushes" involving Cecily, Sara Ray, and the boys at school. Only the older generation seem involved in the distant marriage of a cousin away from the Island. It is left for Sara to introduce more heated notions of love, in the Indian myth of the lovers of Shubenacadie, and the Greek myth of Aglaia and Glaucon, whose love moves beyond the discovery of kissing to a trembling moment clasped in each other's arms.

Theological issues offer another example of the way Montgomery reduces difficult issues in the framing story but lets Sara tackle them head-on. As "sinners," the King children transgress in petty ways. Sara Ray defies her mother and goes to a church meeting, and Dan eats green apples (twice).

The children cheat in order to experience a stellar dream life, pray against each other's dominance, change the clock to fool an adult. A hint of the deeper sin of heresy tinges the three most dramatic scenes in the novel: when Peter preaches about Hell; when the children obtain a terrifying picture showing God as "the stern, angrily-frowning old man with the tossing hair and beard," a creature like the terrifying "Urizen" imagined by the mystic poet William Blake; and when the young circle wait in trembling for the "Judgment Day" as announced in a newspaper. In each case, the reaction of the remembering narrator to theological terrors is affectionate amusement, augmented by the scornful mockery of the adults in the story. This treatment of sin is light, compared to Sara's story about the sin of the archangels whose forbidden love changed the constellations, or the sin of a blasphemous man, clawed by Satan in punishment of the sin of pride. Perhaps Montgomery's obsessive emphasis on the theme of sin simply reflects her community's insistence on self-examination for traces of sin. More likely she is releasing a residual fear that her growing scepticism and agnosticism is sinful. In *The Story Girl* she confronts the idea of sin in two ways: with laughter, and with horror.

As for sectarianism, the outward form of theological dissension, Peter's dithering between Presbyterianism and Methodism reveals a view (surely inappropriate in Montgomery) that such divisions within the church are really a comic and childish matter. Notably, many of Sara's reductive stories concern ministers—for instance, the tale about the minister too fat to get into the pulpit. Sara proffers an inordinate number of stories mocking Presbyterians (confused with "perspiration" in one story), mission meetings (where a drunken man makes a fool of himself), and ministers (one who hides in a cupboard, another who admonishes his wife from the pulpit, and yet another who recapitulates an entire sermon for the benefit of late-comers). Maybe this preponderance reflects the community's focus on its church officials, just as Sara's "cannibal story" reflects how exciting a missionary's lecture would be to people in the bucolic village of Cavendish. The number of these embedded "minister stories" seems peculiar, however, considering the imminence of Montgomery's marriage to a Presbyterian minister.

The main plot of summer on the Island certainly lacks the high drama of Sara's embedded stories. Sometimes in exalted style, sometimes with the flip of a funny phrase, Sara works with a panache and a wide imaginative range:

> from the afrites and jinns of Eastern myth, through the piping days
> of chivalry, down to the homely anecdotes of Carlisle workaday folks.
> She was in turn an oriental princess behind a silken veil, the rider who
> followed her bridegroom to the wars of Palestine disguised as a page,
> the gallant lady who ransomed her diamond necklace by dancing a

coranto with a highwayman on a moonlit heath, and a "Buskirk's girl" who joined the Sons and Daughters of Temperance "just to see what was into it" (162).

Montgomery wove thirty-two of Sara's stories into *The Story Girl*, as if to demonstrate all the kinds of work she could turn her hand to. She had once kept a notebook of ideas which had already proved to be a valuable storehouse. Others of Sara's stories came from old school readers: "The Prisoner of Chillon," an excerpt from the *Iliad* about Helen of Troy, and the legend of King Cophetua and the Beggar Maid as retold by Tennyson. From favourite American authors, Hawthorne and Poe, came weird stories, like the tale of the proud princess whose bridegroom was Death. Other ghost stories represent the stock in currency among children everywhere: the tale of the skeleton of a long-lost baby, or the one about the ghost with eyeballs but no eyes. While concocting *The Story Girl*, Montgomery wrote in her journal, "To this very day I like nothing better than a well-told ghost story, warranted to send a cold chill down your spine" (June 1, 1909). Local gossip was another fruitful source for another group of Sara's stories, comic anecdotes such as the one about the man who lost half his whiskers in a fire and refused his wife's urging that he shave off the other half. No doubt a family story-teller (Grandfather Macneill, or Great-Aunt Mary Lawson) was the originator of the romantic stories about the Miss Dunbar whose lover left for the gold rush and died far away, or about the poet who was kissed.

Montgomery's scrapbooks, like "Aunt Olivia's scrapbook" which the Story Girl acknowledges as her source, contained the more elevated legends: the myth of Shubenacadie; the story of ancient Thebes, where kissing was discovered; the legend of a bridge of stars, the Milky Way; or the Norse legend of a hero who follows his god Odin, undergoes sacrificial death in a bitter and perilous flood, but reaches immortality.[33] Montgomery had pasted copies of her own early publications in that scrapbook.[34] For *The Story Girl*, she chose only two for re-telling by Sara: the story of Betty Sherman's "pioneer wooing," and the story of Rachel Ward and the Blue Chest, first published as "The Old Chest at Wyther Grange" in *Waverley Magazine* in 1903.

In the final scene of the novel, Sara's stories and the reality of family life fuse. Rachel Ward's sorrow has been the subject of a sentimental tale proffered early in the summer by Sara. At the end, the chest is opened in "real life," and its contents revealed. Remnants of Rachel's material goods are divided among the children—handkerchiefs for the boys, ornamented vases for Felicity and Cecily, dress goods for the adult aunts, and for the Story Girl, a candlestick. Those gifts clarify the differences between Sara and her cousins, the difference between imagination and materialism. Earlier the same differentiation was clear. When the Story Girl says, "I'd like a dress of moonshine with stars for buttons," Felicity retorts, "It wouldn't do. You could see through it."

With a practicality like Felicity's, the romantic mystery ends. Rachel Ward's letters, picture, wedding dress, and bridal veil are to be burned. But nature, as if in protest, has flung a "filmy veil of lace over the dark evergreens, and the hard frozen ground." The first snow fall marks the death of summer, in a "fairy beauty that lasted all day." This ending recalls the ambiguous response to the tradition of a "happy ending" in both *Anne of Green Gables* and *Anne of Avonlea*.[35]

Was Montgomery aware of the thematic disjunction between the framing narrative and the embedded stories? She was a very clever writer, showing off through Sara's stories the breadth of the range of her interests, while keeping her unsophisticated readers happy with what looks like another visit to the magic island of the *Anne* books. She was also a woman still living in a small community that was watching her work closely for indications of eccentricity. Sara acts as a mask for the disruptive strain in her imagination.

In this complex, ambiguous novel, Montgomery had opened her own version of the blue chest. She celebrated not only her own memories, passions, and experiences, but also her own ambition and her own accomplishments, her books and life documents. When she wrote this book, Montgomery had achieved any artist's double dream—world-wide fame plus monetary success. Almost in awe, she could reconstruct a portrait of the artist as a young girl.

Montgomery recreates Sara's world with the extra intensity of someone destined to leave it very soon. There are many elegiac touches in the loving descriptions of the King orchard, especially in the final autumnal scene, "crisp and mellow with warm sunshine and a tang of frost in the air, mingled with the woodsy odours of the withering grasses." In a world of "royal magnificence of colouring, under the vivid blue autumn sky" where "the big willow by the gate was a splendid golden dome, and the maples that were scattered through the spruce grove waved blood-red banners over the sombre cone-bearers," Sara stands with her head garlanded with the crimson leaves of fall.

Montgomery repeated the note of leave-taking when she wrote on November 29, 1910, about the ending of her work on *The Story Girl*, "I was sorry to finish it. Never, not even when I finished with Anne, had I laid down my pen and taken leave of my characters with more regret."

Closing the book on the Island of her imagination, she knew she would also soon be taking leave of the real Island that had provided stimulus for her stories ever since she began writing.

Chronicles of Avonlea

(Boston: L.C. Page, 1912)

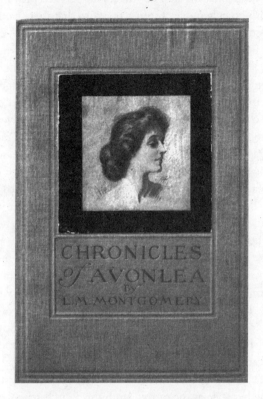

In 1911, Maud Montgomery looked over her pile of published short stories. At least 375 of them had appeared in American and Canadian magazines since 1895, and she had already pillaged some of them for re-use in *The Story Girl*. Now she was trying to choose a few that could be up-dated and presented as a new book. Her publisher reported an undiminished demand for "more about Anne" and urged her to produce still more of the kind of writing that had made *Anne of Green Gables* a phenomenal success in 1908, *Anne of Avonlea* a worthy successor in 1909.

In November 1910 she had made a trip to Boston to meet that demanding publisher in person. There L.C. Page had shown her the delightful side of literary fame (as against the "secret mortifications" of being a celebrity in a narrow-minded village). He had arranged social events and newspaper interviews for her. But he had wheedled her into signing a new contract for the just-completed *The Story Girl*, including a binding clause, guaranteeing that she would give him the right to publish her new works for the next five years. She was disturbed: he offered the same minimal royalties as those she had accepted in advance (and gratefully) for *Anne of Green Gables*. Nevertheless she signed the new contract, and also accepted his urging that she get to work quickly on yet another book, so that there would be a "new L.M. Montgomery" to keep up the yearly series.

Early in 1911, however, Montgomery was in no state of mind to create a new novel. She was growing older, more worried about the deteriorating health of her grandmother, and more frustrated by her long-drawn-out engagement to Ewan Macdonald, who had now accepted a call to the Presbyterian church in the Ontario village of Leaskdale, over a thousand miles away from Cavendish. But, as she wrote in the journal on January 17, 1911, "Mr. Page wants to bring out a volume of short stories sometime and I am rewriting such of them as are worth including" (January 17, 1911). In order to capitalize on her publisher's demand, she had turned to the scrapbooks and folders in which she had kept copies of her earlier work.

Her routine in the days between 1899 and 1910, when she wrote those stories, had been taxing: an hour's work at writing in the morning and another in the evening, sandwiching a day-long rehearsing in her mind of scenes and dialogues and description as she moved through her house work and the routines of church and post office (where she was now assistant postmistress). Her journals continued to be the receptacles of a secret outpouring of moods and a painfully honest recording of destructive family tensions. Yet the short stories written in that period were generally neat little studies of amusing entanglements, easily resolved in happy endings.

In these early stories, Montgomery had learned to satisfy a wide readership, adapting her style as she moved from the church-school papers, which bought her first efforts, to general family magazines, some simple and some sophisticated. Her stories for children had centred on youthful pranks and domestic mishaps; her stories for adult magazines had featured courtships, death scenes, and family tensions. Now, from this big pile, Montgomery chose stories of adult relationships in which children either were absent or played a minor role. This kind of choice suggests that Montgomery or her publisher realized that her books were now being purchased less by or for children and more by adults who had developed a taste for her way of writing. The stories in *Chronicles of Avonlea* would hold much less appeal for young readers than was the case with *Anne of Green Gables* or *The Story Girl*.

The new book republishes six stories written and published before *Anne of Green Gables* was conceived, and six others, probably written and certainly published after that bestseller. Individually, the stories record Montgomery's initial response to the demands of contemporary magazine publishers, and her later sense of the new market for which she selected these particular samples of her work. Several of the stories introduce names or plot situations that Montgomery would re-use in later novels. Read in their original sequence, they offer an interesting flashback to Montgomery's development as woman and writer in earlier years.

Fortunately, the stories in *Chronicles of Avonlea* can indeed be reconsidered in their original order and form, thanks partly to Montgomery's own care in preserving records—her scrapbooks, her business ledgers, her correspondence with fellow-writers, and her journals—and thanks also to two researchers, Rea Wilmshurst and Donna Campbell.

From her early published stories, Montgomery chose two dealing with love concealed. In "Old Lady Lloyd," Sylvia Gray, a young musician, receives secret help from a terribly poor old woman who once loved Sylvia's father. The old lady sends flowers, sells a heritage jug, and begs for help from a hated cousin. Happy recognition follows after the old lady takes a dangerous long walk in the rain and falls ill. In the story's conclusion, the young artist, like Montgomery around 1898, delays her flight to the world outside in order to be a companion to the old lady. A source of the story may have been the revelation by her friend and cousin, Tillie Mackenzie Houston (to whom *Chronicles of Avonlea* is dedicated) that she had once loved Maud's father. Certainly the theme of love concealed was close to Montgomery's own experiences: she had carefully hidden since 1898 her passion for Herman Leard. The focus on Old Lady Lloyd's near-death existence at the outset of the story may reflect Montgomery's almost suicidal depression near the turn of the century. This story (placed second in the final volume) is the only one not yet dated or traced to its first publication. It was probably published in the New York *Family Story Paper* in the late 1890s, since the copy pasted in Montgomery's scrapbook is in the same font and on the same kind of paper as the many short stories she sold to that cheap all-fiction magazine. This early story contains many elements that foreshadow later uses: the name "Sylvia" will be allotted years later to another secret friend, in *Magic for Marigold*; a treasured heirloom jug will be re-used in *A Tangled Web*; and Old Lady Lloyd's walk in the rain and subsequent deathly illness will reappear many years later, when Jane experiences a rain-walk and illness, in *Jane of Lantern Hill*.

"Little Joscelyn" (allotted fourth place in the *Chronicles*) was published September 1, 1904, in the Boston *Christian Endeavor World*, a respectable evangelical magazine. It is another story of ties between an older woman and a younger artist. After Aunty Nan's tearful deathbed scene (appropriate for a religious publication), young Joscelyn sings a "grand old hymn" about mercy—then hands out judgment to the relatives who have made the older woman's life a misery. In "Joscelyn" Montgomery portrays a confident artist who can dismiss an impercipient world: "Thank you, . . . but I cannot possibly stay longer." Proud words written by an author whose stories had brought her respect as well as money: $500 over the year 1903–1904.

First of the courtship stories, and placed first in *Chronicles of Avonlea* is "The Hurrying of Ludovic," published May 1905 in the Toronto *Canadian*, a general readership magazine, which unfortunately paid only $8 for the story. Slow Ludovic Speed holds Theodora Dix in thrall for fifteen years while she waits for him to propose. Montgomery had used this theme of dragged-out courtship obsessively for several years: witness the titles of "The Setness of Theodosia" (1901), "A Long-delayed Wedding" (1902), "The Romance of Aunt Beatrice" (1902), "Miss Madeline's Proposal" (1904), and "Miss Juliana's Wedding Dress" (1905). She was converting her own position as a thirty-year-old single woman from a social embarrassment into an amusing plot situation.

A second example, chosen now for republication, was "Aunt Olivia's Beau" (placed seventh in the new book). *The Designer* of New York, June 1905, a handsome magazine catering to women interested in patterns and styles, paid $20 for the story. In this tale, prim Aunt Olivia's life is disrupted by a vigorous suitor who tracks mud into her house. Murray Macpherson's manners—and his grammar—do not match her ideals. Her propriety almost costs her the chance of a renewal of romance, but in the fiction she is offered a second chance, and she runs to catch her man before his train leaves. Montgomery (who claimed she had rejected Herman Leard on the same grounds and lost him permanently) had assigned the name "Olivia" to the pretty aunt in *The Story Girl* who marries at the age of twenty-nine in *The Golden Road*.

A different kind of love—between father and daughter—appears in "Old Man Shaw's Girl" (placed sixth in the series) from the Springfield, Ohio, *Farm and Fireside* (June 15, 1905), a regional agricultural semimonthly that paid $14 for a 3000-word story. The blissful life of father and daughter Sara, reunited and keeping house together, recalls George Eliot's *Silas Marner*, one of Montgomery's favourite novels. The story breaks open the scar over Montgomery's childhood trauma at separation from her adored father. Lyrical descriptions present an orchard by the sea; a similar orchard will bloom in "The Old South Orchard," *Outing Magazine* (1908), *Kilmeny of the Orchard* (1910), and *The Golden Road* (1913), in which another Sara is reunited with a beloved father.

Montgomery returned to the theme of delayed engagement in "The Winning of Lucinda" (fifth in the new order of stories) titled "A Case of Atavism" when it appeared in *The Reader* of Indianapolis (November 15, 1905). For this sophisticated and relatively new monthly, Montgomery wrote in a less sentimental style than when writing for farm papers, but showed the same delicate precision in describing silver harvest fields and frosted birches. She also gave Lucinda the mix of beauty and sexiness that recalls the description of Kilmeny: "The ruddy light of the autumn afternoon gave a sheen to the waves of her hair and brought out the exceeding purity of her Greek outlines." Elegant Lucinda Penhallow slips into a "swear word" which even the stylish *Reader* did not dare spell out in full—and ends a fifteen-years' silence between herself and Romney. She gets a comic dowsing, but salvages her pride. The end of the story slyly suggests that jaunty Lucinda Penhallow's fate will be different from that of submissive Olivia and Theodora. The Penhallows will reappear in a similar family assembly, twenty-six years later, in *A Tangled Web*.

"Pa Sloane's Purchase" (placed as number nine in the *Chronicles*) had appeared as "Pa Rudge's Purchase" on February 22, 1906, in *Christian Endeavor World*, one of Montgomery's most consistent markets, appealing to a more commonplace readership. Written while Montgomery was also working up materials for *Anne of Green Gables*, this story pictures a kindly old man and a rigid old woman who adopt an orphan almost by accident. The people talk like Matthew and Marilla, and like the real farm folk of Cavendish. Brief, taut, anecdotal, with a good touch of dialect and a real feeling for rural eccentricities, this story in its brisk confident tone reflects the pleasure of the artist in complete control of her materials. The comic tone reflects Montgomery's re-reading of Dickens's *Pickwick Papers*, as reported in this period to her correspondents.

The new brilliance of tone reappears in "The Quarantine at Alexander Abraham's" (eighth in the new volume). *Everybody's*, reputedly the leading American magazine in contents, circulation, and advertising, published it in April 1907. "To appear in [*Everybody's*] is a sign that you are getting somewhere," Montgomery wrote in her diary (December 2, 1906). She was tickled to tell her western correspondent Ephraim Weber that this story, for which *Everybody's* paid $100, had been rejected twice, "once by a magazine that pays $30 per story, and once by a magazine that pays ten!"[36] "The Quarantine" is comedy with a bite, a spoof of the patriarchal assumption that women are meek beings needing care and direction, and that old maids are to be pitied. Reversing the stereotype, Montgomery shows the old bachelor as pitiable, for all his fierce ways and his ferocious dog. The old maid, Peter Angelina MacNicol, with her salty tongue, her strong mind, and her six cats, shoulders "woman's work" in his house, cleans, cooks, and acts as a nurse. Then she mellows and accepts him as a suitor—but on her own terms. Montgomery could now make sparkling fun out of this old maid's capitulation. In October 1906, she had accepted a proposal from an amiable man, not at all like the rampant fictional "hero" Alexander Abraham. She wrote to her Scottish correspondent George Macmillan, "If two people have a mutual affection for each other, don't bore each other, and are reasonably well mated in point of age and social position, I think their prospects of happiness together would be excellent, even if some of the higher upflashings of the 'flame divine' were missing."[37] Peter Angelina and Alexander Abraham approach marriage in a similar wry mood. In April 1907, the same month as "The Quarantine" was published, Montgomery signed the contract for *Anne of Green Gables*.

A month later she saw the double publication of another story: "The End of a Quarrel" (placed in the final position in the *Chronicles*) was published simultaneously in the New York *American Agriculturist* and the New England *Homestead* (July 20, 1907). Montgomery was doing a professional job of mining possible markets. Here is yet another story about a middle-aged courtship. A successful career woman, aged thirty-eight, has quarrelled long ago with her admirer over his ungrammatical language. She slips into his pitifully disordered house, to tidy and beautify it. Her reward is ungrammatical: "Them strawberries look good!" followed by the diminishing phrase, "Nancy, my girl!" as the man declares proprietary rights over a mature, intelligent woman.

"The Courting of Prissy Strong" (placed near the end as number ten) appeared in July 1909, in the Greenfield, Massachusetts *Housewife*, a respectable domestic journal. Here a timid, clinging girl outwits her domineering sister and marries her long-denied lover. As the successful and widely recognized author of *Anne of Green Gables*, published a year earlier, Montgomery might now identify with the competent, effective Emmeline. At home, however, Montgomery was still locked into a claustrophobic situation; she could therefore identify also with the weak and lonely sister Prissy. Like her author, Prissy is not allowed to choose her own friends, or to read whatever novels she chooses. With the help of her neighbours, she is finally rescued. The language of this strong story is folksy: a late-blooming romance is dubbed "cold soup warmed over." This is the only story in the *Chronicles* that ends with a wedding. The final moment, however, is anti-romantic: the older sister whirls into the house and slams the door. Many years later Montgomery would re-use the "two sisters" story in *Rainbow Valley*. There the gentle dominated sister marries a lonely, unworldly minister.

"The Miracle at Carmody" (second-to-last in placement) had been originally named "The Miracle at Mayfield" in *Christian Endeavor World* (October 28, 1909). This is another story of two sisters locked into a shared life. Withdrawn from the community and the church, they have adopted a little boy. Like *Kilmeny of the Orchard* (revised in this same year), this story concerns psychosomatic impairment. The younger sister, Salome, is a pious woman, held from worship by her domineering sister, Judith. (The theme will recur, modified, in *Rainbow Valley*.) Salome becomes "crippled" by agonizing over the effect of social isolation on the boy. A miracle occurs when, in the need to protect the child, Salome drops her crutch and runs. As in *Kilmeny of the Orchard*, Montgomery inserts an old doctor's explanation that emotion has overcome the inertia of long-disused muscles. The names of characters add another subtext. Salome is named for the dancer who wheedled Herod into beheading John the Baptist, Judith for the biblical queen who did her own beheading of Holofernes. Between them the women tame little Lionel, sleeking down his golden leonine curls, feminizing him in velvet and lace when they finally take him to church, thus reducing the virile force of the little heathen. This complex story shows the maturing and deepening of Montgomery's philosophy and technique. She had been re-reading Gibbon's agnostic work, *The Rise and Fall of the Roman Empire*, and wrestling with her own unorthodoxy as she prepared to marry a minister. The portrait of Judith, who has ceased to believe in God's justice and stubbornly distances herself from old beliefs, is balanced by pious (and crippled) Salome. Yet Salome performs the strongest act in the story when she defiantly sets off for church. Montgomery gives her orthodox audience the ending it wants, the miraculous conversion of Judith from doubt to belief.

Mr. Leonard, another Lion, appears in "Each in His Own Tongue" (third of the *Chronicles*) published first in *The Delineator* (October 1910), a long-established family magazine with a huge circulation. This minister believes that art is frivolous and dangerous. He must learn to accept the boy Felix's artistic gift, which, like Kilmeny's, is a wonderful facility on the violin. The story is enriched by old Abel, the drunkard, outcast from the village (like another Abel, who will appear much later in *The Blue Castle*), and by three women: Naomi, bearing the scarlet badge of sin; Janet, the peaceable housekeeper; and Maggie, a retarded girl. The gothic tone, the heightened style, and the setting in village, forest, and outcast's hut, all recall Hawthorne's *Scarlet Letter*, another long-time favourite of Montgomery's. The real sin in this intense story however is not the sexual one but a sin of denial. The minister is blind to his own sin in repressing the gifted Felix. Naomi tells him this truth, in her own tongue. In the climactic scene, the minister's prayer, in the stylized rhetoric of Christian theology, is replaced by the violin's song, "glad," "wild," "sweet," "soft," and "innocent." Felix has earlier been forced to promise to give up his art—just as, years later, Montgomery's new heroine, Emily, will be made to promise her aunt not to continue writing. Montgomery's own early pain at family rejection, disinterest, and mockery of her art had perhaps been revived by the opposition, tacit rather than open, of the orthodox clergyman who was now her fiancé. In her fiction, the minister is converted from dangerous negation to acceptance of the freedom of art.

This dream of acceptance was no doubt furthered by Montgomery's growing income from her writing. The numbers reflect her climb: The

Detroit *Pilgrim*, in March 1906 paid $10 for "The Box of Violets"; *Gunters*, a short-lived New York magazine, paid $35 in April for "The Education of Sally"; *The National Magazine* of Boston paid $10 in August for "The Girl at the Gate"; *Holland's Magazine* of Texas paid $3 in November for "The Story of a Love"; and the Minneapolis *Housekeeper* in March 1907 paid $25 for "Paul, Shy Man." Montgomery re-sold "Pa Rudge's Purchase" to *Everybody's* for $100.

These then were the twelve stories chosen for revision. Before she could tackle the job of revising them, however, Montgomery's life changed radically. Her grandmother died in March 1911. She could now make arrangements for her marriage to take place in July. She must now leave Cavendish, "the old trees that encircled home, the graveyard on the hill with its new red mound, . . . Lover's Lane—the sea-shore, the pond, the houses of friends" (January 28, 1912). What with a summer honeymoon abroad and then the distraction of settling into marriage, a new house, and a new community, it was January 1912 before she could resume literary work, "re-writing and revising several of my magazine stories" (January 28, 1912).

Her publisher had requested that the revisions should locate the chosen stories in or near "Avonlea." Accordingly, Montgomery changed place names: "Avonlea" is substituted for "Deepdale" in "Little Joscelyn;" "Carmody" replaces "Mayfield" in "The Miracle;" "Delandville" in "The Speeding of Ludovic;" "Duxbury" in "Pa Rudge's Purchase;" "White Sands" replaces "Oriental Road" in "The Quarantine of Alexander Abraham;" and "Cranford" in "Pa Rudge's Purchase." As she worked in the Leaskdale manse, Montgomery revisited her imaginary island for the first of many times.

That last substitution suggests why Montgomery accepted freely the idea of linking all these stories to one small rural neighbourhood. Ewan Macdonald had given her *Cranford*, the local-colour classic by Mrs. Gaskell, as part of a Christmas gift. Mrs. Gaskell's deft touch is echoed in the Avonlea allusions in the *Chronicles*. People are also renamed to conform with the Green Gables story. The Sloane name makes several appearances: Pa Rudge becomes Pa Sloane, and Jordan Lowe in "Little Joscelyn" becomes Jordan Sloane. Several people are renamed "Pye" in "Prissy Strong" and other stories, as mean as Anne's enemy Josie Pye or the younger Pyes that bedevilled the teacher in *Anne of Avonlea*. Other characters are renamed "Gillis" and "Blair" to link with the clans that filled Anne's world. Poor Moody Spurgeon Macpherson gives his name to Peter Angelina (once MacNicol) and to "Aunt Olivia's Beau," changed from Norman Nicholson to Murray Macpherson. To recall the menacing alternative to Marilla in *Anne of Green Gables*, "Mrs. Peter Blewett" is the revised name of "Martha Walters" in "Old Man Shaw" (originally "Old Man Reeves"). Reverend Aaron Crickett in "Quarantine" becomes our old friend Reverend Mr. Allan.

Finally, the stories are now woven together by interlocking references. Mr. Leonard, Naomi Clark, and Abel Bird now appear in more than one story, substituting for people with different names in the originals. Nancy Copeland in "The End of a Quarrel" becomes Nancy Rogerson, and appears incidentally in two other stories as a Sunday School teacher. Other minor changes include some grammatical tidying up: "ain't" is changed to "aren't" to maintain Avonlea propriety (though the hired boys still say "ain't"). Montgomery tucks in some new "fine writing" of the kind Anne fancied: "A thick grove of birches" in "The Hurrying of Ludovic" becomes "a green meadow bestarred with the white and gold of daisies. A wind, odor-freighted, blew daintily across it." Such changes are minimal, mostly occurring in "Ludovic."

These are acceptable changes. References to Anne herself are less deftly introduced. The original "speeder" of Ludovic was Juliet Sherman, romantically named. Substituting "Anne" means losing the suggestion of young romance in Juliet's name, and creating the unlikely situation where a stranger resolves Ludovic's problems. Rosanna, the narrator of "The Courting of Prissy Strong," effectively ordered her fat husband to clamber up a silo to run up signals for Prissy's lover. The addition of Anne in the revised version (glad as we are to see her up to her old courageous tricks when she climbs a ladder in the service of romance) destroys an ironic point, when bossy Rosanna congratulates Stephen on his acquisition of an obedient wife. Comparable loss of point occurs when in "The Quarantine of Alexander Abraham," salty Peter Angelina, who in the original story comically preferred to teach boys as a way of gaining the upper hand over males, is given in the revised version an added unconvincing motive—she doesn't feel capable of teaching a girls' class because of Anne Shirley's presence there. In "Little Joscelyn," Aunty Nan uses Anne's charm, unnecessarily, to explain the sway of "Little Joscelyn." Nancy Rogerson drags a quotation from Anne into "The End of a Quarrel" with inartistic results. Anne has no business in these stories. No wonder the author felt a great relief when she finished the thankless task of tinkering with her chronicles.

Reassembled in a new order as a book, the stories undergo a deeper change. When she regrouped them, Montgomery devised a new order. Placed at the centre of the book stands the rhapsody of father-daughter reunion in an old orchard. Near the beginning of *Chronicles of Avonlea* cluster the three stories of young artists abetted by loving older people, with the story of triumphant Joscelyn placed at the end of the group. Near the end of the book appear the two pictures of children with adoptive parents, the comic Sloanes and little Leo, ward of Salome and Judith. In both cases foster children bring renewal into their guardians' lives. Framing all, and interspersed throughout, are the six stories of spinsters moving slowly toward marriage. The opening tale presents a woman who cannot change her fate, the final one tells of a career woman who gaily chooses her own way of life. The irony of the first modulates into the gaiety of the last. The book consequently offers the reader an experience quite different from the single impact of the individual stories.

In spite of the darkness of Montgomery's own experience during the period when she was writing these short stories, *Chronicles of Avonlea* as a whole offers to readers an ultimately affirmative vision. Slow time, dragging and repetitive, does eventually shift, in each story and in the book as a whole, into a liberating change.

Chronicles of Avonlea was published in June 1912. Page had chosen the title ("somewhat delusive" Montgomery suggested). *Chronicles I* and *II* in the Biblical Old Testament recount the fall of dynasties and the rise of prophets. The title had its own ironic appropriateness. Montgomery had domesticated the Biblical archetypes and sentimentalized them. Significantly, she had also converted them to a female perspective. In these stories, written much earlier in her life, battles for power were waged not by kings but by spinster sisters; faith in life was revived not by David the boy harpist but by the young woman Sylvia, singing hymns in the splendour of moonlight.

The Golden Road

(Boston: L.C. Page, 1913)

The Golden Road, Montgomery's fifth novel and sixth published book, was the first she composed as a married woman. A sequel to *The Story Girl*, it shows some of the tensions imposed when she tried to satisfy the demands of her publishers and the pleas of her fans at the very time she was making a difficult transition, switching from a quiet private life on the north shore of Prince Edward Island into a new role in Leaskdale, an inland village sixty miles east of Toronto, Ontario. *The Golden Road* also reveals the deep impact of marriage on the woman who had been forging a successful career as a writer but was now expected to subordinate her own work to the demands of her husband and his parish. She faced a complicated change in status as the bride of an old-fashioned Presbyterian minister.

Her wedding, a simple, old-fashioned ceremony, had taken place in the farmhouse parlour at Park Corner in July 1911. Her feelings on that wedding day, as recorded in her journal, climaxed in a strange mood. "When it was all over and I found myself sitting by my husband's side—my husband! I felt a sudden horribly inrush of rebellion and despair. . . . Something in me—something wild and free and untamed—something that Ewan had not tamed—could never tame—something that did not acknowledge him as master—rose up in one frantic protest against the fetters which bound me. . . . I was as unhappy as I had ever been in my life" (January 28, 1912).

If life denied her the kind of marriage she wanted, writing fiction offered a chance to compensate. In *Anne of Avonlea* and *Chronicles of Avonlea*, she had resisted the fans' call for the traditional happy ending for "Anne;" but in *The Golden Road*, a "non-Anne" book, she gave full play to romantic notions about weddings—though she added dark undertones. The first of the Story Girl's tales in this new book is about a long-ago elopement. Masterful old Hugh Townley, who, like Montgomery's domineering great-grandfather, boasted that he knew "every man, woman, and child" in the Island, forbids his daughter to marry the man she loves. She puts on her best gown (green silk, like the one Maud's mother wore when she married Hugh Montgomery) and escapes from the Island, bound for Buenos Aires.

Later in the story, however, a less romantic elopement story is described by Peter Craig, the hired boy, as his contribution to the magazine launched by the circle of children. Peter carries the story of Jemima Parr beyond "happy ever after" to recount the ultimate death of the groom as a very old man. "He felt quite well when he went to sleep and when he woke up he was dead." Peter's poor narrative style undercuts the seriousness of the "happy-ever-after" debate.

A wedding-day climax, not in the interpolated stories but in the main narrative, comes when the "Story Girl," Sara Stanley, acts as bridesmaid for Aunt Olivia King. Romantic Olivia is married at five o'clock under the late apple tree—which has "most obligingly kept its store of blossom until after all the other trees had faded and then burst lavishly into bloom." Aunt Olivia's groom, unfortunately, turns out to be forty, bald, short, and stout. He also turns out to be a "jolly good fellow." Readers may have missed noticing the odd metaphor that describes Aunt Olivia, beautiful "amid the frost of her bridal veil."

A second bride in the main plot-line of *The Golden Road* is "Beautiful Alice," the young woman who has come to the King home to teach music (the role Maud Montgomery once played at Park Corner, after her return from the West). Alice, "like other girls . . . had her dreams of a possible Prince Charming, young and handsome and debonair." She finds a mate, instead, in the shy, dreamy Awkward Man.

Alice's wedding is upstaged in the story, however, by the sudden appearance of the Story Girl's long-absent father, brown-bearded Uncle Blair (whose description seems like a photograph of Montgomery's beloved father Hugh John). After the ecstasy of that reunion, on the morning of Alice's wedding-day, the Story Girl's father hides at the gate, "calling out gay mirthful jests" while the young people scatter flowers on the path of Alice and the Awkward Man. Asked what he thought of the bride, Uncle Blair replies, "When she dies white violets will grow out of her dust." Prosaic Felicity comments that Uncle Blair "says even queerer things than the Story Girl." He does indeed! Yet Blair King seems to have been conceived as a delightful antidote to the two unromantic bridegrooms. He is poetic in response to the beauty of nature, childlike in gaiety, yet deep in feelings. He has come to take fifteen-year-old Sara away from the Island, not, as when Maud's own father whisked her off when she was fifteen to a prairie town and an unlovable stepmother, but to Paris and a bohemian life of art and laughter. This truly happy ending of *The Golden Road* is one not achieved in a marriage—perhaps an admission of the growing sense of uncertainty in Montgomery's own marriage.

The equation of happy endings with marriage in adult books was very binding in the first decade of the twentieth century as a holdover from Victorian conventions. But the true happiness in this book is perhaps more meaningful to younger readers. Total acceptance by a loving and interesting parent would surely make any young heart sing.

Again, Peter Craig provides a sardonic version of the Story Girl's father-centred romance. The dream-like motif of a father's return has been previewed earlier in *The Golden Road* in Peter's story. Peter has worked as the Kings' hired boy because his drunken father had abandoned him. This father returns, subdued—and converted to Methodism (a fate only slightly less dire than conversion to Roman Catholicism for this little community). Poor Peter feels forced to confess to his long-lost father that he has become a Presbyterian! Peter's father's answer is plain and effective: "The main thing is that you must be good and do right."

This downright answer is a very welcome alternative to Uncle Blair's twitterings about ethereal beauty, such as "the flicker of a pixy-litten fire." Montgomery was developing the trick of assigning an idiosyncratic style of speech to each of her characters. Here she distinguishes Uncle Blair's poetic mannerisms (which sound like a parody of young Anne, in *Anne of Green Gables*) from the down-to-earth sayings of a character who, like Marilla, is anti-romantic.

The Golden Road, in other words, offers a subtle play of text and counter-text, a juxtaposition of romance and mockery of romance. It is, in fact, a more complex book than *The Story Girl*, and a proof of Montgomery's development in vision beyond the level of the *Anne* books and *Kilmeny*. Perhaps marriage had given her a new perspective on romance.

Readers of *The Story Girl* would expect to find in this sequel an abundance of little fictions, told in Sara Stanley's inimitable way. The Dedication

"To the memory of Aunt Mary Lawson" seems to promise as much. It memorializes the great-aunt who had told Montgomery "many of the tales repeated by the Story Girl." Sara Stanley is indeed back, but not so firmly in the centre, and not armed with anything like as many stories. In spite of the promise in the Dedication, the idea of a "story girl" in full control of wide-ranging creative powers has now been side-tracked. Perhaps Montgomery had fully milked her old store of short fiction in concocting *Chronicles of Avonlea*. Perhaps she was too absorbed in her new life in Leaskdale to put her full energies into composing a new collection. Certainly there are now fewer of the folk stories and myths with which Sara Stanley had regaled the listeners in *The Story Girl*. They are good stories, but they are not the central driving force of the new book. Montgomery was still to some extent memorializing her own role as "a story girl" but the main interest is now on the framing story about the life of young people on the Island.

In the stories that Sara Stanley does tell, family anecdotes dominate. The wedding motif recurs in her first full-length story, featuring a long-ago belle who ran away from home with a handsome brown-bearded man. Other family romances are dealt with more summarily: Great-Aunt Georgina, whose husband came to his wedding on the wrong day, and Alice's Aunt Una, who died on the eve of her wedding, leaving a groom to life-long mourning.

Most of the Story Girl's non-family tales are told very briefly, almost casually: the story of the Christmas Harp that sounded at the Nativity when a clumsy shepherd made unexpected music; the story of the sighing reed, set free by suffering; the legend of the trembling poplar, involved in the Crucifixion (an alternative Greek myth about the poplar is tucked in). At other times Sara merely hints at a story, as in the suggestion of a First Nations' legend about mayflowers. Indeed, so diminished is the notion of the Story Girl as marvellous elocutionist that the book offers a comic moment when she suffers humiliation at the hands of the other Sara, silly Sara Ray.

Only near the end of the book does Sara Stanley offer strong full-length narratives. She tells the tale of the "Yankee Storm," with its postscript, about the fated sailing-ship Franklin Dexter; and the story of the Awkward Man's secret room, a romantic alternative to the Bluebeard legend. This story is purported to be written out by the Story Girl forty years later—a blurring of the narrative edge as the book shifts into the future tense.

In this sequel to *The Story Girl*, in other words, Montgomery swings her focus away from the sporadic tales of a gifted young narrator, and develops instead a more fully worked-out cover story. The plot involves the whole group of children who gather at the Kings' farm. Montgomery is moving back from a collection of "chronicles" towards the organic novel form which she had used for the first time in *Anne of Green Gables*, and which would remain her forte for the major part of her creative life.

Several sub-plots twine throughout the book. The children's adventures with Peg Bowen, the local "witch," climax in the scene at church where Peg stars as commentator, with wicked little stories about each parishioner entering the church. The children's devotion to Paddy Grayfur, the cat, ends sadly with his death and burial.

Cecily, rather than the Story Girl, emerges as central character in yet other plots. She tackles scary Mr. Campbell in the name of missionary work; she suffers agonies when she curls her hair with mucilage; she copes with an unwanted admirer, whose devotion leads to her humiliation in school. These Cecily stories are clearly aimed at a young audience. It seems as though Montgomery is writing so hastily to meet her deadlines that she slips back from the subtlety of *Anne of Green Gables* into the kind of stories she had written for children's magazines in earlier days. She is inadvertently paving the way for critics who assign all her books to the children's shelves in bookstores and libraries.

Again, it is not the Story Girl but Bev, the boy cousin from "away" who tells these stories about the King children and their circle.[38] Their production of a magazine to which all contribute clarifies the differences between the children and also suggests the movement of time as one issue succeeds another. Montgomery pulled off a *tour de force* here. Each of the contributions bears unmistakable marks of its originator, both in style and content. Like *The Diry of a Bad Boy*, Montgomery's own childhood favourite, "Our Magazine" plays with funny spelling and grammar. In this it is probably like her own first literary effort, a would-be comic work she titled "Dere Diry," in imitation of her favourite. "Our Magazine," the children's literary effort, also includes wonderful spoofs of the stories in the family magazines to which Montgomery had contributed hundreds of formulaic narratives.

The title of *The Golden Road* reflects the mind set of the time. Childhood was seen as a time of "clouds of glory." Many writers had offered the same gentle mockery of the self-absorbed children who live in their own little world, unconscious of the prison-house of adulthood awaiting them, as William Wordsworth had suggested long ago in his "Ode: Intimations of Immortality from Recollections of Early Childhood." Montgomery admired Kenneth Grahame's *The Golden Age* (1895). Other literary models were available in the world of children's books: older ones like the *Elsie Dinsmore* books by Martha Finley (published from 1867 on), the *Katy* stories by Susan Coolidge (1872 and on), the *Five Little Peppers* series by Margaret Sidney (beginning in 1881), not to mention the more recent *Patty* series by Jean Webster (1911 and on). The notion of a series of sequels was still thoroughly understood as part of the literary marketplace in this "golden age" of print publication.

Specifically, *The Golden Road* seems to reinforce the idea that Louisa May Alcott's *Little Women* and its sequel *Good Wives* were at the back of

Montgomery's mind when she moved from *The Story Girl* to *The Golden Road*. Again there is a cast consisting of one girl who is a domestic adept (Meg in Alcott, Felicity in Montgomery), another who is a gifted, independent story-teller (Jo in Alcott, Sara Stanley in Montgomery); a third sweet girl, doomed to an early death (Beth in Alcott, Cecily in Montgomery); a nearby curly-headed boy (Teddy Lawrence in Alcott, Peter Craig in Montgomery). Alcott's pretty, selfish Amy contributes something to Felicity.

For her inspiration, however, Montgomery had a real as well as a literary circle of children to draw from. Dan King is probably modelled on George Campbell, sole boy in a family of girls, Clara, Stella, and Frederica. The real-life Nelson boys from faraway Toronto had suggested adopting the point of view of fictional Beverly King and his brother Felix. Wellington and Dave Nelson had made Montgomery's childhood lively and satisfying. They had been two cheery conduits to carry her away from the rather gloomy and repressive family of grandparents and aunts and uncles.

The plethora of uncles and aunts in the background of *The Golden Road* is also like Montgomery's extended family: Aunt Annie and Uncle John at Park Corner, Aunt Emily and another Uncle John at Malpeque, Aunt Mary McIntyre in Charlottetown, Uncle Leander and his family coming each year to the old farm from New Brunswick, Uncle John F. and Aunt Anna Maria next door. As in *The Golden Road*, this was a crowded adult world against whose values the children played out their own lives. The sense of family history, the lingering memories of members of the family who have died, this too is like Montgomery's kind of childhood. There is nothing quite like it in other children's books, though the "Olympians" in Grahame's *The Golden Age* are an interesting English variant.

Montgomery's book reveals another specialty that had set her apart from Grahame, Alcott, and all the others. She was again recreating the unique qualities of Prince Edward Island, carrying her readers to a remembered world through her extraordinary power of evocation of orchard and seashore, farmhouse, and firelight.

But Montgomery as an ordinary person had entered her own "sequel." She had left the idyllic isle and moved to the Upper Canada village life of Leaskdale. Her dreams of marriage as an escape had been realized in July 1911. She recognized, of course, that she and Ewan Macdonald were an older couple, like Aunt Olivia and her Nova Scotia doctor, and an ill-matched couple like Alice and her Awkward Man. Nevertheless she arrived in Leaskdale, Ontario, as the minister's bride in October 1911. When Ewan Macdonald had announced his imminent marriage to the Ontario church he had been called to, he had been asked whether his bride was "the author L.M. Montgomery." In an ominous revelation of his attitude, he had answered, "Yes, I believe the lady does write books."[39] Ewan would never respond to the "Story Girl" he had married, as her audience all over the world was doing already. He would never serve her, as the young King cousins did, as enthralled fan or eager requester for more.

Writing up her journal notes on January 28, 1912, she recalled her bitter heartbreak and homesickness on first arriving. Her home was not a house of dreams. It was owned by the church, as she had known it would be, and its decoration and facilities were subject to the decisions of the church session. In *The Golden Road*, many of the comic stories are concerned with the church, including Peg Bowen's running commentary on the parishioners and the minister, and the children's delighted recounting of the oddities of Reverend Mr. Davidson. "Stories are always funnier if they are about a minister," says Peter. Just as well Ewan Macdonald did not read the book!

How would these mocking comments in *The Golden Road* square with Montgomery's role as the minister's wife? Did Leaskdale take it amiss that she looked askance at the righteous? Perhaps it was consoling to believe these were all Island stories, not Leaskdale ones. Of her new neighbours in Leaskdale, she was soon writing in her journal, "There isn't one interesting or really intelligent person in it" (January 28, 1912).

"Home life and work" compensated. Of course the most compensating work was when she left Ontario behind in her imagination and moved back to the Island world to begin work on "a second Story Girl." She set up her desk in the room that was designated "the minister's study" and went back to her writing. "To shut the door of my soul on the curiosity and ignorance displaced by so many and retreat into a citadel of dear thoughts and beautiful imaginings—this it affords me peculiar satisfaction to do" (April 4, 1912).

In April 1912, her spirits were rising, for the best of reasons. "If I can get the skeleton of it [*The Golden Road*] blocked out before my confinement I shall be content," she added. She was now "making *tiny little dresses*" (April 4, 1912) having learned with delight that she was expecting a baby. Chester Cameron Macdonald was born on July 7, 1912.

She enjoyed an "annus mirabilis," a happy time, with baby Chester, a long visit by Frederica Campbell, and a good maid in the manse, Lily Reid. The book had been part of the year. "I have not enjoyed writing it," she admitted; "too hurried and stinted for time. But it may be as good as those written with less hurry." She did not finish *The Golden Road* until May 21, 1913. It ended with a sentence that might well have worried her fans: "The Story Girl was gone." But no one needed to worry about Maud Montgomery Macdonald's literary avocation. The book came from the publisher on September 1, 1913. On that same day she began writing *Anne of the Island*, a novel about the time that "Anne" first leaves Prince Edward Island and finds new friends and new interests.

~ Anne of the Island ~

(Boston: L.C. Page, 1915)

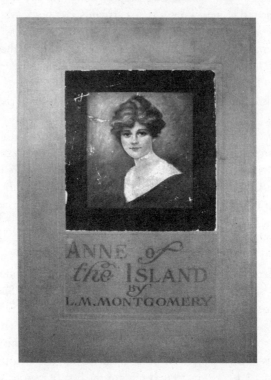

In *Anne of the Island*, Anne finally moves (as her creator had done) *off* the Island. She prepares to take her rightful place—"the first Avonlea girl who has ever gone to college," as Gilbert says—at a university on the mainland.

Montgomery was setting out to write a *bildungsroman*, an important and maybe unique story of a young woman's intellectual aspirations, in a time of critical changes in the status of women.[40] She planned to call her new book "Anne of Redmond" emphasizing the shift to a brilliantly coloured world on the mainland (a "red-*monde*"), where Anne can enjoy "the widening of horizons and interests." Such a widening would be different from the Story Girl's ambition to perfect her art through studies in Paris, or Montgomery's own desire to "climb the Alpine Path" as a creative writer.

The previous two "Anne" books had prepared the way for a book about college life. Matthew and Marilla had from the beginning meant Anne to "go as far as she wanted to go," and Marilla made her going possible by inviting Mrs. Lynde to move into Green Gables to help with the twins and the farm management. But when Anne sets off, she trails awareness of what the Island thinks of college for girls. In *Anne of Green Gables*, Mrs. Lynde had pronounced, "I don't believe in girls going to college with the men and cramming their heads full of Latin and Greek and all that nonsense." In *Anne of Avonlea*, Mr. Harrison had added his scorn of "B.A.'s so chock full of book learning and vanity that there ain't room for anything else." *Anne of the Island* sounds the sceptical theme again at the outset. Older women cite the danger to a girl's health, the cost, the folly, the probability that she will face snobbery as a country girl among the Kingsport stylish co-eds. When Mrs. Lynde summarizes, "I don't believe . . . that the students in such colleges ever do much else than flirt," Marilla can only respond dubiously: "They must study a little."

Such attitudes were not surprising in Anne's time. The trickle of women into academic life was still new and still tiny. In 1874, the year that Montgomery was born, only a very few, very daring girls would have dreamt of applying for admission to university. Some women's colleges had been founded (Vassar in the States in 1861, Girton at Cambridge in England in 1873), and some formerly all-male universities had admitted women undergraduates into degree courses (Cornell in 1870, some of the western state colleges a few years earlier). In 1875 the first Canadian woman to get a degree graduated from Mount Allison University in New Brunswick; ten years later Dalhousie University in Nova Scotia, the model for "Redmond College," awarded its first BA to a woman. Ten years later again, Montgomery enrolled at Dalhousie in 1895.

She faced difficulties greater than those she assigned to Anne. Her grandparents were not keen on furthering her ambitions (although the grandmother, who eventually facilitated Maud's leaving the Island, was more sympathetic than Montgomery admits in her retrospective journal). Her Uncle Leander, whose son Murray had preceded her to Dalhousie College in a cloud of family pride, made no effort to help his niece. No women in the Macneill or Montgomery families had been college students. Like most people in the late nineteenth century, Cavendish folk worried that college studies might lead women into agnosticism, threatening the religious basis of home life, and that educated women either would not marry, or would be distracted from giving primacy to raising children. A widely accepted medical theory held that higher education would cause a woman's uterus to atrophy, preventing child-bearing.[41]

In spite of such worries, Montgomery enrolled at Dalhousie College in Halifax, one of a handful of girls among the 300 students in Arts Science, Engineering, Law, and Medicine. Even with her grandmother's help she only had enough money for a single year, but her journal records that it was a busy, productive time. She took a double number of English courses, played a part in the "Philomathic" discussion society and in the fun of midnight feasts and torchlight processions. She lived in residence at the Halifax Ladies' College, under the austere eye of Miss Kerr, the Principal, a Girton college graduate, "no doubt very clever" but with "no charm or imagination"—not an attractive role model.[42] Her reaction to the male professors was not much more kindly. She summarized the Dalhousie faculty: Professor Murray of Classics, "a bit stodgy at first" but charming; Professor MacMechan, "nice" but "rather a weak man."[43] She enjoyed concerts and theatrical productions and the busy life of a city many times the size of Charlottetown, let alone Cavendish.

In the spring term, at the request of the editor of the Halifax *Herald*, she submitted a jaunty article published as "A Girl's Place at Dalhousie College." It set forth firmly a belief in the academic ambitions and accomplishments of such a "girl" and added a quotation from Tennyson.[44] It began with an epigram from Tennyson's "The Princess" which voices the dream of intellectual entitlement:

> Girls:
>> Knowledge is now no more a fountain sealed;
>> Drink deep until the habits of the slave,
>> The sins of emptiness, gossip and spite,
>> And slander, die.

Seventeen years later, in 1913, Montgomery seemed to herself to have returned to a world of "emptiness and gossip." She was living in Leaskdale Ontario, a long way from her Island, and a long time after her own days at university. Her "pastoral duties" as the minister's wife in a small rural community meant endless visits to parishioners, as well as attendance at equally endless church and Sunday School meetings, Missionary societies, Women's Auxiliary, Young People's Union, and on and on. Her marriage had led her into a life dominated by the demands of her husband's profession. She dreamt of saying to Ewan's parishioners, "Begone! I refuse to waste my precious time catering to your petty vanity. . . . I have other and more important work to do. You have no right to expect me to sacrifice that work to your trivial round and common thought" (June 29, 1913).

The "more important work" was the writing of *Anne of the Island*. One stimulus for getting at it was that the previous year's bestseller had been *Daddy-Long-Legs*, a story with a college setting, by the American novelist Jean Webster. Nine years earlier Webster had published *When Patty Went to College* as a sequel in her popular "Just Patty" series. But Webster's books dealt with a residential women's college, where girls did not face the distractions of fitting studies into coeducational social life. *Anne of the Island* would be pioneer in presenting four years at a city college, where women students live off-campus and study and flirt and form friendships in the shadow of a long male tradition of collegial life.

Her Dalhousie journal would be a prime source. Other help would come from her cousin and friend Frederica Campbell, an intelligent and ambitious young woman who had gone to Macdonald College of McGill University near Montreal, thanks to Montgomery's support, moral and financial. In 1913, when Montgomery was gathering her resources for moving on with Anne's story, Frederica came as a very welcome guest to Leaskdale, fresh from a year on the staff of Macdonald College.

Montgomery confessed to reluctance at the thought of opening her memories of her own college days. "I did not want to do it—I have fought against it. But Page gave me no peace and every week brought a letter from some reader pleading for 'another Anne book.' So I have yielded for peace sake. It's like marrying a man to get rid of him!" (September 27, 1913).

It was lucky her sense of humour was still strong (as *Anne of the Island* would demonstrate), for finding time and energy to write was very hard indeed in that fall of 1913. Beyond the "pastoral duties," she was looking after her son Chester, now just over a year old, who offered constant distraction. She began the book in September; by November she discovered that she was again pregnant, and suffering debilitating nausea. All the more reason to settle into a revised version of her college experience, assigned to Anne. But her mood was acerbic and the tang of irony shows itself in the way she handles the required romantic scenes in the new novel.

Therein lay a problem. As a sequel, the book would find an established audience. Montgomery prefixed *Anne of the Island* with a dedication to "all the girls all over the world who have wanted 'more about Anne.'" As she began writing the novel she grumbled, "I must at least engage Anne" (September 27, 1913). She must have presumed that "all the girls" would be more interested in flirting and friendships than in classes, essays and examinations. So to please her public, *Anne of the Island* emerges, apparently closer to love story than to *bildungsroman*, in spite of the fact that the plot takes Anne into the halls of academe. She began the book with an epigram from Tennyson, very different from the stirring intellectual vision of "The Princess." This time she quoted from the sentimental love story of Sleeping Beauty waiting to be awakened by the coming of a prince:

Love in sequel works with Fate,
And draws the veil from hidden worth.[45]

Love, not intellectual aspirations, will dominate in Anne's new life. Anne may feel the charm of social and intellectual life, but she will answer the sensual and future-minded call of the mating time. Montgomery's own experience of romance and marriage, however, was too complex to allow her immersion in a simple bath of sentiment. Although the new novel draws on Montgomery's memories of creative days at college, it is also deeply tinged by the troubles of her subsequent life. She subtly adds a strain of mockery and fear to the cheerful story of the "fair seed-time" of the soul of a post-adolescent girl. The result is both romance and anti-romance.

The story begins when Anne and Gilbert, looking forward to a "splendid four years at Redmond," saunter beyond the Haunted Wood and discover apples, "delicious. Under the tawny skin was a white, white flesh, faintly veined with red; and besides their own proper apple taste, they had a certain wild, delightful tang." The suggestions are erotic. Four years later, at the end of the book they walk home, over "haunted meadows" beyond the marsh, in the dusk, "king and queen in the bridal realm of love." Formality and dignity have replaced the rhapsodic quality of the first scene. Montgomery's manuscripts show how carefully she inserted these linked yet opposed descriptions. Every element teases the contemporary reader into ironic reading of the apparent closure of a happy marriage.

Between the opening and the closing, the story swings through a series of proposals of marriage, normally moments of romantic exhilaration. Anne's response to most of these proposals is strangely near hysteria.

The first, a comic proxy offering of Billy Andrews by his sister Jane, leaves Anne unsure whether to "writhe or laugh" at this "grotesque" proposal.[46] It is a funny story, but it comes on a night with rather frightening associations: "wild white bluster and blow . . . when the storm-wind hurtles over the frozen meadow and black hollows." This imagery links with the previous chapter, where metaphors for the change of seasons suggest an uncomfortable idea of marriage: "The far-away slopes and hills were dim and wraithlike through their gauzy scarfing, as if pale autumn had flung a misty bridal veil over her hair and was waiting for her wintry bridegroom."

Billy's proxy proposal is followed in the next chapter by Charlie Sloane's proposition, which sends Anne into "tears of humiliation and rage." Understandable enough—but Anne soon also finds Gilbert's first quiet proposal "grotesque or—horrible." In fact, his proposal is stiff and pallid, rather like an imitation of the language in Anne's story "Averil's Atonement." It is hard to understand Anne's horrified response.

Next summer, when Anne is back on the Island on a summer teaching job, she gasps and responds "haughtily" to Sam Tolliver's genuinely grotesque offer of marriage. Less predictably, she reacts "wildly," "desperately," and "miserably" to Royal Gardner's more elegant approach.

Although these desperate reactions remain mysterious and without adequate explanation in the novel, an early description of the Halifax harbour, written as a sort of set piece by young Maud in her first term in the city, suggests something in Montgomery's own nature as their source. At the end of her first term at Dalhousie, she wrote of a walk to "to look over the harbor," and described a deeply suggestive scene, to be re-worked at three central moments in the novel:

> On my left lay the city, its roofs and spires dim in their shroud of violet smoke that drifted across the harbor and stained the fair blue of the sky darkly, as if some fell angel had spread his murky pinion across the calm beauty of heaven. George's Island loomed out of the mist and the water lay before me satin smooth in sheen and silver gray, while the gentlest of wavelets lapped against the granite crags. Far to my right stretched the harbor, taking on tints of rose and coppery gold as it reached out into the sunset until it lost itself in dull, fire-fringed clouds. . . . [O]n George's Island the lighthouse beacon flared through the smoke like a baleful star and was answered by another on the far horizon. And far above all, in a concave of stainless blue, where no soil of earth could reach, shone a silver-white half moon with a maiden veil of pearly vapor drawn chastely over her pure face. (December 23, 1895)

The perception of opposed sexual forces in this scene—the "looming" island with a masculine name, George's Island, and the "baleful" flaring of its lighthouse, set against the maidenly chastity of the moon—suggests fears and inhibitions which she perhaps unconsciously imputed to Anne.

Significantly, Montgomery uses part of this description (very carefully rephrased) in Chapter 6 of *Anne of the Island*, when Gilbert and Anne join Philippa, Priscilla, and Charlie Sloane in the little pavilion in the harborside park:

> To their left lay Kingsport, its roofs and spires dim in their shroud of violet smoke. To their right lay the harbor, taking on tints of rose and copper as it stretched out into the sunset. Before them the water shimmered, satin smooth and silver gray, and beyond, clean shaven William's Island loomed out of the mist, guarding the town like a sturdy bull-dog. Its lighthouse beacon flared through the mist like a baleful star, and was answered by another on the far horizon.
>
> "Did you ever see such a strong-looking place?" asked Philippa. . . . "Look at that sentry on the summit of the fort, right beside the flag. Doesn't he look as if he had stepped out of a romance?"

Revision has tightened the description of the sky and the water, and more significantly has expanded the gendered sense of the island in the harbour.

"George" becomes "William" (retaining the allusion to male monarchs) and the emphasis on strength, menace, and impregnable defence has been increased by the simile of the "bull-dog." Adjectives "clean-shaven" and "sturdy" ameliorate the frightening "baleful" male quality in the description, but the alternative terms "stainless," "chastely," "maiden," and "pure" have disappeared.

Anne returns to this place in the Kingsport park, overlooking the harbour, two years later on a rainy day when she wants "to feel alone and free and wild." Instead, she meets Royal Gardner, Prince Charming, while "a burst of pale November sunshine fell athwart the harbor and the pines."[47] The words "burst," "pale," and "athwart" foreshadow Anne's ultimate trammelled response to this princely suitor. Naturally, Royal takes Anne to this same scene to propose to her a year later. In her wild and desperate refusal of him, Anne may remember (as readers may also remember) the ominous word in the first description, "shroud."

The links between the original description and the sequence of fictional scenes reveal Montgomery's skill in narrative drive and continuity. The two passages are also a reminder of what a good writer she was, even as a college student—and of how much better a writer she became, after learning to excise some materials and to inject others.

In contrast to Anne's frantic reactions to the proposals of marriage is her happy response to the peaceful idyllic central scene—literally in the middle of the book—at Patty's Place. Not on the "Alpine Path" of painful growth but in the warm domesticity of this "homiest spot," four young women sit by the fireside with their comfortable chaperone, three purring cats, two china dogs, and a bowl of chrysanthemums that shine "through the golden gloom like creamy moons." The sounds and the brush strokes of colour and shape offer perfect satisfaction. Four college friends can make a comfortable nest for themselves, "the fun of homemaking without the bother of a husband," as Phil says. Their chaperone, Aunt Jamesina, comfortable, domestic, is ready to ask, "Have you learned anything at Redmond except geometry and dead languages and such trash?"

Verbal echoes of that idealized scene at Patty's Place are heard in Gilbert's final—successful—proposal. He offers an autumnal dream of "a home with a hearth-fire in it, a cat and dog, the footsteps of friends—and you!" But ambiguity enters again. Anne's earlier queasy attitude to proposals and invitations to marriage has been dispersed, not by any logical change in Anne's reasoning but by the sudden threat of Gilbert's death. The "happy ending" is also qualified by Montgomery's establishment of the setting of his proposal, in Hester Gray's garden, a place where Anne and her young girl friends once held a "golden picnic" (*Anne of Avonlea*, Chapter 13). The deserted garden is haunted by the memory of a woman who died young.

Her first name "Hester" may recall the passionate heroine of *The Scarlet Letter*, but her surname, her married name after her abandonment, is ominously "Gray." This garden is suggestively "rimmed by fences bleached silver gray." Montgomery emphasizes that in the day of the girls' Golden Picnic it was spring, a time of narcissus and violets. Now the long hills are "scarfed with the shadows of autumnal clouds," a description that perfectly pulls together all the wintry allusions to veils and shrouds touched into earlier proposal and wedding scenes.[48] Although she had ostensibly given "all the girls all over the world" what they wanted, Montgomery had revealed a deep level of doubt about "happy endings."

Montgomery underlined her own dubiousness by adding three contrary story elements. None of these three motifs had any source in her college memories. But all three relate to Montgomery's own current situation. They add richness to the texture of the book.

First is the theme of death. The first happy college scene takes place not in the classroom but in a graveyard. Midway through the novel, Ruby Willis, introduced first as a spur to jealousy because of her friendship with Gilbert, suddenly and without preparation emerges as a tragic *memento mori*, a warning of the impermanence of pleasure. A further encounter with the thought of death comes when Anne visits her birthplace, and hears stories of the early death of her young mother. (The name assigned to the mother, in an interesting echo of "Ruby Gillis," is "Bertha Willis.") The theme of death is here sweetened by thought of the mother, who died young, but had known the joy of motherhood. In a general sense, these dark shadows were cast by Montgomery's terrified response to the threat of war, hanging over the world when she began her book.[49] But a more personal experience is also in force. In her first pregnancy she had believed she might die in labour, a reasonable fear, given her age (thirty-seven) and the general prognosis at the time for late primaparta. In the second pregnancy (at age thirty-nine), so much more uncomfortable, these fears doubled.

Almost simultaneously, she suffered two dreadful shocks. On August 4, 1914, the First World War broke out; on August 13 her baby was born and died. She went back to work within two weeks, on August 31. She wrote on, through terrible news of the war. On November 20, 1914, ten days before her fortieth birthday, she wrote in her journal, "I finished 'Anne of Redmond' today" (November 20, 1914). "Never did I write a book under greater stress," she added. The thought of death had been present throughout the writing of this cheerful, funny book.

A second unexpected swing comes near its end, when Diana is presented "in the wonderful glory that comes to a woman when her first-born is laid beside her." Mrs. Allan, the minister's wife, adds a touching memory of her own loving mother. Montgomery left this paean to motherhood in the book, even when enduring overwhelming grief. There was no hint of such an emphasis in the college journal, although later in life Montgomery admitted that the hope of motherhood was a major incentive in accepting Ewan's offer of marriage.

The third surprising element is the story of Philippa Gordon. Montgomery made no lasting friendships at college, but Anne at Redmond finds a new alter-ego and kindred spirit. This lively girl, encountered first in the old graveyard, has come to college to escape her suitors and her mother's insistence that she get married. "Philippa" is derived from a man's name (like "Josephine" and several other names assigned by Montgomery to strong characters—the converse of the use of girlish names like "Bev" and "Hilary" for gentle sympathetic young men). The surname "Gordon" (which had earlier had been assigned to Kilmeny), echoes that of Montgomery's influential and challenging teacher Hattie Gordon. Flighty and frivolous at first, Philippa proves to have a good brain. One grumpy math professor "who detested co-eds and had bitterly opposed their admission to Redmond" succumbs to Philippa's mathematical prowess. She also has the good luck of falling fervently in love, unlike hesitant Anne. Her choice is a young visionary minister. Jonas Blake is unpolished in manner, but inspiring in his religious convictions. Philippa's fate is a hopeful version of Montgomery's choice in marriage.

The increasing discouragement that her own marriage was actually bringing to Montgomery at this time led her to distinguish between herself and the character of Anne in one significant way. During Montgomery's own college year she not only won an invitation to submit the article on women in education by the Halifax *Herald* and a prize for poetry in the Halifax *Evening Mail* but also experienced success abroad. As "Maud Cavendish" she sold "Our Charivari," and "Apple-Picking Time" to *Golden Days*, a Philadelphia magazine, "In Spite of Myself" to *Chicago Inter Ocean*, and "Fisher Lassies" to *The Youth's Companion*—"which uses only the best things" (March 21, 1896). All were composed during her college year. The money she made by her writing was not enough to support her for another year at college, but it was enough to encourage her to go on writing furiously after she returned to the Island and took up work again as a teacher.

The story of Anne as a writer is different. She appears as a potential author in the first chapter of *Anne of the Island*. Alone on her private place, which is named "Victoria Island" for an empress, she can withdraw into dreams, "curtained with fine-spun, moonlit gloom, while the water laughed around her in a duet of brook and water." Anne still has "budding literary dreams" at the end of the novel, but the two stories she has published sound feeble. "Averil's Atonement" is a stereotyped domestic romance. Rejected by a sensible editor, it is twisted by Diana into banality (and profitability).

Gilbert rationally sees the sale of the mangled story as a proper way to pay for college tuition, but for Anne it is a travesty on her art. Anne's second successful publication is a delicate sketch, dismissed previously in *Anne of Avonlea* as something no editor would accept because it has no plot.[50]

Anne's two publications can be seen as Montgomery's mocking bow to those who had criticized her own work as sentimental or thin. She offers through Anne's creations a parodic version of sentimentality and persiflage.[51] One could argue that the dialogue which takes place in the sketch between wild flowers and garden blooms, canaries and lilac bush, confronts the serious question of freedom and containment that is a hidden theme in the containing novel. Nevertheless, whatever hidden values Anne's compositions add to the text, in themselves they do not suggest commitment to a serious career as a writer.

Montgomery's own career was at a crucial point. She had ended her previous novel with the ominous saying, "The Story Girl was gone." Anne's diminution perhaps reflects uncertainty on Montgomery's part about the strength of her own continuing inspiration and addiction to writing, given the constraints of her new domestic life.[52] She externalized that worry about her powers by showing the dimming-down of Anne's "flash," her potential as a serious writer.

On the contrary, the subtlety with which Montgomery traces the stages of Anne's conversion from academia to matrimony shows no diminution of her own power. Precise, evocative, funny, with a sense of recurrences and echoes, symbolism and metaphor that add to the sharp focus of individual scenes, Montgomery had created an effective study of the gendered direction of a young woman's life.

Montgomery had fought against her publisher's notion that this book should be called "Anne of the Island" instead of "Anne of Redmond." In the end, Page was right. In spite of going to college Anne is indeed "of the Island," caught in the convention that romance and marriage and motherhood constitute the proper sphere and glory of women. Anne, who began by saying "I'm going to study and grow and learn about things," proves to be (as Milty Boulter's mother suspected) destined to spend her college years drifting down a staircase, with orchids pinned to a dress of cream silk and embroidered chiffon, and then finding a mate and a home.

Some young adult readers—maybe "all the girls"—would love this emphasis, and maybe would be impelled by it to think "If this is college, I must go there too." Older readers could continue to appreciate the subtler undercurrents in this curious, challenging novel.

Anne's House of Dreams

(Toronto: McClelland & Stewart, 1917)

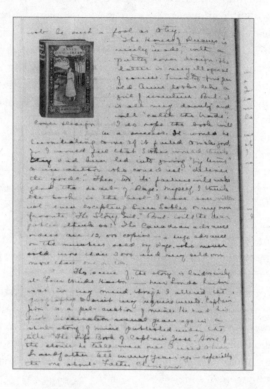

The first house of Anne Shirley's dreams was Green Gables. Rigidly neat on the outside, it had space within for a room of Anne's own, where she could dream of "a white velvet carpet with pink roses all over it . . . pink silk curtains . . . gold and silver brocade tapestry . . . mahogany . . . a couch heaped with gorgeous silken cushions, pink and blue and crimson and gold. . . ." *Anne's House of Dreams*, the fourth "Anne" book, begins with Anne and Diana in the garret of Green Gables, the storage place under the roof where books of geometry and other textbooks can be dumped. One attic window looks north over Lover's Lane and the "munificent" old orchard of rosy apples, the other looks at a "distant, white-capped blue sea." Marilla is downstairs in the kitchen of "the old gray-green house." Anne is telling Diana that she is going to live at Four Winds Harbour in a little house o' dreams, already furnished in her imagination, not a marble hall but "a tiny, delightful castle in Spain."[53]

Montgomery was right, both in a personal and in a general sense, to emphasize the connection between houses and dreams. Nest-building is an activity shared with animals, but for every human, particularly every female human, the choice and adorning of a particular home is deeply individual and tense-making. Being "house proud" means being proud of one's attitudes and taste. Like most women of her time and class, Montgomery had a sense of her home as being both a private haven and also a public demonstration of her personality.

In Montgomery's case, the house she now occupied in Leaskdale, Ontario, certainly made manifest her inner life. There was no fireplace or hearthside in the manse, so Gog and Magog, the large china dogs she had purchased (in duplicate) on her honeymoon had to be placed on either side of her bookcase. Appropriately so, since books were still so central in her life. Among her newly purchased books stood treasured old friends, including the American poets Whittier, Bryant, Longfellow, and Holmes, whose poems had shared the pages of her schoolbooks, along with Tennyson, Keats, and Browning. "Build me more stately mansions, O my soul!" Holmes's voice had counselled in "The Chambered Nautilus." Not a stately mansion but a comfortable yet stylish manse was the object of Montgomery's intentions. She photographed and carefully described almost every room in the little house.[54] The library (which was ordinarily the domain of the minister) housed her new desk with many pigeon holes. In the parlour were "four high narrow windows" veiled in lace curtains and "green brocade over-curtains." In the less attractive dining room, a single window "gives a view of several ugly back yards including our own." (October 24, 1911). "It was our home and I was its mistress," she wrote in her journal.

In that first year in this home, her cousin Frederica Campbell had brought sympathy and companionship, and helped Montgomery entertain on New Year's Eve (including among their guests Reverend John Mustard, her long-ago teacher—and suitor—in Prince Albert). "Never, before I was married, could I ask friends to my home and have things nice for them."

Montgomery had been mistress of the manse four years when in November 1915 she worked on the little story that would launch her into *Anne's House of Dreams*. "The Schoolmaster's Bride" was the tale of an Island man who experienced a vision in which he saw himself sitting by his own hearth-fire with his bride, after months of believing she was lost at sea.

Anne is the bride in the novel that Montgomery spun around that initial germ of a story. Married at last to Gilbert Blythe, she is destined to sit in happiness at her own hearth side, with the china dogs, Gog and Magog, a wedding gift from Patty's Place, on guard in the house of dreams, near Four Winds Harbour.

Life there begins with the recognition of four houses, to match the four winds, and to match the four personalities that Montgomery now began to create out of her own experience of self and others. Anne may have left the geometry books behind in Green Gables, but this is a book very geometri-cal in its mathematical symmetries and balances.

The four houses are described in the order in which Anne sees them. First is the light house, signalled by the "great revolving light," flashing "warm and golden against the clear northern sky": a star of good hope, com-ing from the tower that Captain Jim tends.[55] In *The Poetics of Space*, Gaston Bachelard postulates that in the verticality of any house of dreams, the tower rises from earthly depths to the height of reasoning and imagining (24).

Second, travelling towards their home, Anne and Gilbert see a large house, neat and bare, painted vivid green.[56] It is the home of Miss Cornelia Bryant, whose name combines a blurred version of Anne's old dream name of Cordelia and that of the "woodland poet" William Cullen Bryant—a double irony for a thoroughly down-to-earth woman.

Then they pass a gate and see Leslie Moore, the mysterious owner of the third house, later described as "surrounded by huge willows through which its windows peered, like shy, seeking eyes, into the dusk."[57] Significantly, Montgomery gives the woman entrapped in this house her own initials, "L.M."

Finally, Anne delights in the first glimpse of her own house, "like a big creamy seashell" (a chambered nautilus) "stranded on the harbour shore." Lombardies line its lane, sentinels, protectors of privacy. Fir trees stand behind the house, "enfolding secrets." As for the inside of the house, the description begins upstairs, in a room with two windows, like those in the garret at Green Gables, but they are touched into the story in reverse order, and with significant differences. The dormer window looks out to the har-bour and the sand-bar, rather than directly to the sea, and the seascape, thanks to the familiarity of Anne's quotation from Keats' poem, now trails a suggestion of being "perilous" and "forlorn." The gable window looks out to the brook, the harvest-lined valley, and the shy, rambling, old gray house among its huge ("weeping?") willows. Downstairs, friends gather around a supper table by the hearth fire, while the sweet sea breezes blow in through the open window of the dining room.

Four houses and four lives, each of them reflecting some part of the way Montgomery had been living before and during the early stages of compo-sition. Her creative "flash," like Captain Jim's hopeful star, had lighted the way through the start of another novel. Her daily life, like Miss Cornelia, had brought village gossip and also an undercurrent of anger at living in a situation that her husband blithely assumed was acceptable to her ("just like a man!"). Like resentful Leslie, she felt her days invaded, since a monstrous war now dominated her community and her home. Like Anne herself, Montgomery felt the joy of living in a home of her own—something she had dreamed of for many years before coming to the manse as a bride.

By late 1915, the manse had witnessed both sorrow and joy. Although haunted by the infant death of little Hugh, it was gladdened by three-year-old Chester, showing his "affectionate little heart in very dear little ways." And although Montgomery devoured the wartime newspapers, agonizing every day over details of the battles in Europe and on the seas, her kindred spirit Frederica Campbell could come from her college job near Montreal to bring laughter and courage (January 1, 1915). Montgomery's journal reflects the power of Frede's personality, and awareness that that power is hidden from many observers.

In the novel that was beginning to stir in her imagination, Leslie Moore, like Frede, will be a woman who "walks by herself." Leslie is constrained by the presence in her house and her life of her husband, a man felled in a terrible accident twelve years earlier, who lives on as a mindless, dependent, demanding hulk. Leslie's horrible dilemma, more tragic than anything Montgomery had ever introduced into her stories up to this point, shows among other things the darkening vision inflicted by the war. Captain Jim and Miss Cornelia, like loving guardians, invoke Anne's help for Leslie, the passionate young woman with "lips as crimson as the blood-red poppies she wore at her belt" and "splendid, resentful eyes." In a moment of impulse, Anne will dance, whirling like a child on the shore as she approaches Leslie and begins the careful development of a crucial friendship.

The friends who come to the open-hearted and hospitable house of dreams fill the first half of the book with their talk. Each is a story-teller, each with a limitation. Captain Jim, marvellous raconteur of sea stories from around the world, needs a polished writer to bring his stories into form. Miss Cornelia's tangy gossip often belies her kind heart because of her insistent scorn of men. Locked-in Leslie, thwarted in her womanhood, has great difficulty in revealing her jealousy, her resentment, and eventually her passionate friendliness toward Anne.

That jealousy will be sharpened when Anne reveals that she is pregnant. Again the connection between life and art is clear. Very early in 1915, Montgomery, now forty-one years old, discovered that she had become pregnant again. Physically miserable with nausea, she rejoiced in the hope of another baby. A month after Stuart Macdonald was born in October 1915, she was blocking out the happy story of "The Schoolmaster's Bride." When she went on to work out the full-length novel, the joy of Stuart's birth no doubt made it possible for her to revisit in fictional form the earlier tragic birth and death of little Hugh. As author, she retained the joy for Anne but deleted the nausea and also the journal's clear statement of facts. Euphemistically, Anne refers to pregnancy as the promise of "a mystic shadow" or "a thought too dear and sacred to be put into words." The first half of the novel contains the elation of Anne's expectant period and the devastation of loss.

Anne will question the pseudo-consolation of accepting "the will of God," in phrases like those that scorched the author's journal two years earlier after "little Hugh's" death. At that time, Montgomery wrote furiously about people who offered "threadbare assurances" that "'the baby is better off.' I do not believe it! Why should it be born at all—why should anyone be born? . . . And I do not believe that it was 'God's will' either. Why blame every sorrow on God's will? . . . And it is no comfort to me to be told that I shall meet my little son 'some day'" (September 4, 1914). Montgomery uses almost these exact phrases when Anne's baby girl dies, as the book nears its mid-point, its nadir.

While she was in the midst of the blocking-out period, however, Montgomery had two strange psychic experiences, one in February 1916 and one in March. One was a dream, the other a waking vision. Both trances began with unbearable tension but both ended with a sense of wonderful peace. The February dream begins in a storm and a frenzy of terror. Clinging to Ewan she sees a soldier dashing boldly into her house. At its climax the dream is broken by baby Stuart's cry. She tends to him, returns to sleep and resumes the dream—now completely changed into a springtime world. "I was walking down the hill beyond the church—nay, not walking but dancing, as a child might dance, and I wore a wreath of white blossoms in my hair. I danced the whole way home and I felt inexpressibly lighthearted and jubilant.[58] Then I awakened again." The second experience, a kind of daytime trance, began when an agony of mind and spirit assaulted her at the end of a long day of illness and worry, connected with despair over the ongoing battle at Verdun, where the fate of Paris and of France seemed to hang in the balance. "Suddenly the agony ceased." She was flooded with a sense of calm, peace, emergence, victory.

Both of these psychic experiences connected with the novel she was writing at the time, as well as with the war-torn world she lived in. She toyed with two explanations of the visions, one cosmic and one personal. According to her first interpretation, "as a priestess of old" she had "some strange foresight." She assumed that the vision foretold a turn in the fortunes of the war. The presence of the soldier perhaps rose from recent news that her halfbrother, Carl Montgomery, was about to go overseas. She needed consolation for fears about him. In general, she had long assumed that such mysterious foresight was possible. Indeed, she had assigned "second sight" to the Schoolmaster, in the little story completed just before beginning *Anne's House of Dreams*. That tale, offered by Captain Jim in his first visit to the little house, was in fact a completion of an old sketch, begun in 1911, just before her grandmother's death. At that time Maud Montgomery needed to believe in a bridal future and a hearth-side. Though put aside in 1911, it had no doubt remained in her subconscious as a vision of a "happy ending."[59]

Her second explanation was "I was as a woman from whom some evil spirit had been driven." She was enabled by these dreams to shift from despair to hope. In terms of her embryonic novel, she was able to pass from the tragedies of the first half of the book to the solutions of the second half.

The connections of cause-and-effect and life-into-art are mysterious. Perhaps in both these visionary moments, because she was working on a novel about a basically happy time of home-building and motherhood, Montgomery experienced in her dreams the shift from despair to joy even at that time of deep trouble personal and universal, and believed that the shift was prophetic. Or perhaps, conversely, the psychic experience of shifting from darkness to light in her dreams permitted her to work out that story in terms of the same essential shift to optimism.

Montgomery moved into the second half of her book, and by great self-discipline managed to finish it within a very short time, pushing ahead with the book at a pace she had not equalled recently. The entire book was completed between June 16 and October 5, 1916. Such a brief span of writing resulted in concentration and control unlike anything in her earlier work. At the exact mid-point, again with mathematical precision, the novel moves from problems to solutions.

Anne announces "I find I can go on living," her new confidence partly the result of the appearance of a new strong character in the house of dreams. "Susan is at the helm!" the new household worker announces.

Two other affirmative events ensue. Captain Jim responds to Anne's sad cry, "'I'm done with dreams!'" by unlocking his heart and revealing his own dream of love, still powerful although "Lost Margaret" had drowned many years ago. In the next chapter, Leslie responds to Anne's grief by baring her own secrets and revealing the love of family that was at the back of her mistaken acceptance of a loveless and increasingly dreadful marriage. "The barriers are down," and Leslie and Anne can clasp hands and "talk it all out" (like Maud and Frede "rinsing their souls"). In life as in art, kindred spirits can declare, "We are both women—and friends forever." A more dramatic shift comes when Miss Cornelia decrees that Owen Ford, a writer from Toronto, should come as a boarder to Leslie's house. Here is a recurring figure in Montgomery's fiction, a successor to the Story Girl's father Blair Stanley and to Stephen Irving in *Anne of Avonlea*. Owen, whose name surprisingly sounds much like "Ewan" plays a more complicated role in this novel. As a professional writer, he is enticed by Anne into solving Captain Jim's problem as a story-teller blocked on the way to publication. As a lover, he also brings a renewal of hope into Leslie's life.

Another bit of unexpected but satisfying plot management is the use of Gilbert's profession as a plot hinge. Gilbert insists that his duty as a doctor forces him to urge Leslie to agree to an operation on her husband Dick.

This operation may either kill him, or release him from his loss of memory. Dramatically, it turns out that there is a third alternative outcome. "Dick Moore" turns out to be in fact George Moore, an identical "double cousin," child of the brother and sister of Dick's parents. Montgomery mocks the melodrama when she quotes Miss Cornelia, "one of the freak resemblances you read of in novels." It is indeed like the melodramatic revelations in the novels Montgomery had revelled in all her life: *The Prisoner of Zenda* by Anthony Hope; *The Prince and the Pauper* by Mark Twain; and *A Tale of Two Cities* by Charles Dickens. But as in those old favourites, this plot works. Dexterity and a clever use of logic and the planting of clues (e.g., the dog Carlo's antagonism to the substitute Moore) make this denouement acceptable.

Having freed Leslie from her burdensome marriage, Montgomery went on to provide happy endings all round. Most obviously, she provides Anne with a healthy baby and endows her with the haze of happiness that the births of her own children had brought.

One more current part of Montgomery's life story played a part in this buoyancy. In 1915 her contractual bond to L.C. Page came to an end. In 1907 she had signed over to him the right of first refusal of her books for the next five years. In 1913, she had refused to renew a similar clause for her next books, so she was now free to discuss her plans with other publishers. During the time of writing *Anne's House of Dreams*, Montgomery tangled with her former publisher in a series of threatening letters and irate responses. She got into touch with other authors over the question of Page's honesty or otherwise: Mrs. Johnston of the "Little Colonel" series, and Marshall Saunders, who had already withdrawn from the Page stable of authors.[60] She emerged from this long-drawn-out battle triumphantly. She came to an arrangement with the Canadian publisher McClelland, Goodchild & Stewart to replace American Page as her publisher. Published in August 1917, *Anne's House of Dreams* was the first Montgomery novel to come in its first edition from a Canadian press.

One minor result of switching to a Canadian publisher was the introduction of a purely Canadian political sub-plot into *Anne's House of Dreams*. A previous election between the Liberals (Grits) and Conservatives (Tories) has led Captain Jim's friend Marshall Elliott to vow never to shave or cut his hair until the right party is restored to power. When the Tories are thrown out, triumphant Grit Marshall Elliott goes to the barber in the middle of the night. Now that he is no longer a perambulating haystack, Miss Cornelia staggers Four Winds by deciding to marry him. Miss Cornelia's rabid feminism has been one of the joys of the first half of the book. Her pace and pitch and tempo were perfect there, as she recounted for instance the way the women built a church in six months, after the men wasted two years talking about it. "It was fought out in bed and at board, and in church and at market." She was down on men in general and on some of her neighbours in particular. "His pigs are the best pigs available, while his children don't amount to much." She glibly spoke of someone who was "a wicked, fascinating man. After he got married he left off being fascinating and just kept on being wicked." She called a minister "a reverend jackass." Montgomery reports her opinions in a *tour de force*, a wonderful catching of the rhythms of gossip (perhaps facilitated by all those dreary parish visits in Leaskdale).[61] Among all the happy endings Miss Cornelia's decision that Marshall Elliott can come to live at her place is a neatly handled surprise. "I reckon I can manage Marshall Elliott," she announces.

In contrast with the deft handling of salty Miss Cornelia, Montgomery's sentimental ending of the Leslie/Owen story strikes several false notes. This is the only scene in the book where Anne is absent. She is lucky. Owen says some dreadfully precious things, such as, "Some evenings, a strange odour blows down the air of this garden, like a phantom perfume . . . I have never been able to discover from just what flower it comes. It is elusive and haunting and wonderfully sweet." But he does kiss her—or as Montgomery, relentlessly euphemistic again, puts it, "their hands and lips met." Nevertheless Owen communicates genuine passion (something never part of the Gilbert/Anne conversations).

For Captain Jim, happiness is having his collection of travel stories transfigured by Owen Ford's editing into a "real printed book," so that he can now sail, in a phrase that recalls once again that "ship of pearl," the chambered nautilus, "over the sunrise sea of pearl and silver, to the haven where lost Margaret waited." The orthodoxy of that phrase (let alone its sentimentality) seems to belie Captain Jim's honest avowal earlier, "I believe what I was brought up to believe. It saves a lot of bother." Montgomery, who had a strong streak of heresy herself, gave Captain Jim another aphorism, "Heretics are wicked, but they're mighty int'resting."

Whatever pathos Montgomery evoked with the sentimentality of Captain Jim's death, she countered quickly. When Captain Jim's beloved golden cat, First Mate, finds a new home in the house of dreams, Susan comments, "Cats is cats" and threatens, "If I find that yellow beast lurking near our baby, I will whack him with the poker, Mrs. Doctor, dear."

One last change looms at the end of the book. Gilbert proposes moving to a new home. He tallies the house's charms. It is up the Glen, handier for his work as a doctor; has a big lawn, magnificent old trees, twelve acres of wood grove, fine orchard; garden with a high brick wall around it; a house with a big garret and an attic window with a view of the lighthouse; a distant view of the sea, a closer sight of the Glen pond (replacement for the Lake of Shining Waters). Susan adds her two cents' worth: an appreciation of splendid pantries and closets and a cellar.

But Anne checks the charms of her own first house, down to "the two tiny quaint glass cupboards over the chimney-piece in the living-room"—a feature not mentioned at the outset; perhaps they duplicate Anne's present sense of eyes just opening.

Like many others, Montgomery mocked the convention of a "happy ending," but she believed in providing one for her readers. At first glance happy endings abound in *Anne's House of Dreams*. On second glance—well, maybe the old streak of irony is still providing a subtext. The marriage of Miss Cornelia to Marshall Elliott, for instance: the idea that a man-hating spinster like Miss Cornelia can absorb even a clean-shaven and well-barbered man into her stark green house seems preposterous. Leslie, married to Owen, will have to listen to him telling her pompously that red roses "hold all the warmth and soul of the summer come to fruition." Captain Jim has died with a smile on his face, but death doesn't seem like an ending happier than living on with his First Mate and his duty as light-keeper. As for Anne, the birth of her son is glorious (though who knows what her future as a mother may hold?) But her move to a more stately mansion is a change necessitated by Gilbert's professional life, not by her own desire. She is leaving a creamy seashell of a house for a distant view of the sea, seen over the bricks that wall in her new property.

For Montgomery herself, however, the ending is without flaw. She had been able to enter again her own house of dreams, her edifice of art, where she could control, decorate, and dance to her heart's content. And she could shut the door on it, knowing that her skill as a writer was unabated, whatever difficulties she might face in practicing her talent while living in the real manse in Leaskdale.

The plot of *Anne's House of Dreams* takes a final affirmative twist when Leslie offers a consolation. Owen will buy the little house and use it for a summer vacation place. "The old house would still be there." For now it is left to "winds . . . gray rain . . . white mist . . . the sea . . . the moonlight . . . silver sand-dunes . . . red rock-coves." Montgomery's sense of the beauty of her Island had been reinforced during the trip in the summer before she began writing the book. Her journal showed a renewed awareness of the Island's beauties, particularly the beauty of its seascapes. The descriptions in the new novel outpace those in *Anne of Green Gables*, for now the descriptions are focused not through the vision of a child but through the adult Anne.

When Owen Ford tells Anne, "Miss Bryant tells me that you write," she demurs. "Oh, I do little things for children." Montgomery must have chuckled as she wrote this version of critical attitudes to her work. She knew she was now writing a book well beyond the reach of most children. Like the house, her novel would "still be there" when the critics were gone and forgotten.

Rainbow Valley

(Toronto: McClelland & Stewart, 1919)

*R*ainbow *Valley* deals with religion—not religion in the sense of theological beliefs, but in the sense of the institutions in which beliefs manifest themselves: the church that is the outward and visible sign of the inward and spiritual grace. Many of the tensions in *Rainbow Valley* reflect those of the old-time Presbyterian community in which Montgomery grew up. Others illuminate her tussle with her own beliefs in the years when she was growing, perforce, into the role of minister's wife.

For readers of the *Selected Journals of L.M. Montgomery* that cover the years around the publication of *Rainbow Valley*, a frisson of horror rises from the first chapter. Susan Baker is passing along the local gossip to Anne, who has just returned to her Island. Anne asks, about a neighbour, "What is wrong with Harrison Miller?"

Susan's hair-raising answer is: "There are days when he growls at everybody because he thinks he is fore-ordained to eternal punishment. And then there are days when he says he does not care and goes and gets drunk. My own opinion is that he is not sound in his intellect, for none of that branch of the Millers were. His grandfather went out of his mind."

In 1917–18, when Montgomery was writing this book, her husband Ewan was increasingly seized with this same obsession. He didn't take to drink, but his state of mind was just as devastating for his wife—who every morning firmly left him to his delusions, and settled into writing a new book, with this bit of throw-away black humour at its outset.

Ewan Macdonald believed himself doomed to an eternity of punishment not for his own sin but because a just God must mete out eternal punishment to most of mankind. This doctrine was already being set aside in modern Presbyterian discussions, but Ewan Macdonald had been educated in earlier times. Furthermore, he had a temperamental readiness to accept the outmoded doctrine and to apply it to himself. Ewan had endured a succession of deep depressions, to culminate in breakdown in 1919. In childhood, in a backward, Gaelic-speaking community, he had heard sermons on predestination, hell fire, and election. The obsession lay dormant during the early years of his marriage and fatherhood, but in the time that Montgomery was writing *Rainbow Valley* it began to re-emerge.

This theology of predestination and eternal punishment is voiced humorously at the outset of the book. But as these opening chapters unfold, more general views on the church and its ministers are voiced by two strong down-to-earth women. Susan Baker is the cook and general factotum of Anne's family, and Miss Cornelia—more properly Mrs. Marshall Elliot—marshals the village and her husband. Susan and Miss Cornelia, invented by Montgomery as she moved through her circumscribed life as a minister's wife, voice all the negative and sceptical and sarcastic comments that sweet Anne (and well-controlled Montgomery) dared not make. One of Montgomery's major devices, increasingly, was putting negative comments, similar to those in her journals, into the mouths of comic characters—an old maid, and a late-married bossy old biddy.

They are discussing the choice of ministers. We may remember Anne's comments on the aspirants to the Avonlea pulpit early in *Anne of Green Gables*. After a sequence of comic clergymen preach for a call to Avonlea, Mrs. Lynde says about the successful candidate, "He isn't perfect, but . . . we couldn't expect a perfect minister for seven hundred and fifty dollars a year." When she wrote this, Montgomery was considering Ewan Macdonald as possible husband. In *Anne of Green Gables*, the ultimate incumbent in Avonlea is kind Mr. Allan. But now hilarity with respect to ministers bubbles up again in irreverence.

Married to Ewan and living in Leaskdale, whenever Ewan had a bad spell, Maud would have to listen piously to the incompetent men who filled his pulpit as substitute preachers. She would learn to chat feverishly in parish visitations to cover her husband's glumness and to arrange supply ministers when he couldn't mount the pulpit stairs because of his sense of sin and inadequacy. Some prescience of that parade of incompetents is in her mind, along with old memories, when Miss Cornelia and Susan, in Chapter 2 of *Rainbow Valley*, describe the temporary occupants of the pulpit in Glen St. Mary's:

> "Mr. Folsom . . . a good preacher, too, but somehow people didn't care for his appearance. He was too dark and sleek."
> "He looked exactly like a great black tomcat, that he did, Mrs. Dr. dear," said Susan. "I never could abide such a man in the pulpit every Sunday."
> ". . . Some thought we ought to call Mr. Stewart, because he was so well educated. He could read the New Testament in five languages."
> "But I do not think he was any surer than other men of getting to heaven because of that," interjected Susan.

That is heresy, of course. Each congregation hoped to be proud of its minister for his learning, as well as for his devout dedication to the word of God. Ministers were college-educated men, trained in Latin, Greek, and Hebrew as well as in theology and rhetoric, so as to be the most learned people in the church. Fine in theory, but Montgomery recognized the true result: isolation, frustration for the minister (for who can expect a congregation of farmers to listen avidly to expositions of the abstruse meanings of Hebrew and Greek theological terms?).

Rainbow Valley portrays a general fact about many churches, that the minister was separated from his community. His only hope for serenity would be to remain scholarly, abstracted from common life. That is precisely the chief character trait of the minister Montgomery creates for *Rainbow Valley*, Reverend John Meredith. His story is central in her new "Anne" book.

Ostensibly this novel is a continuation of the saga of Anne Shirley Blythe. Anne is now a mother, a permissive woman who leaves her children free to enjoy themselves and each other in a private hideaway. The youngest ones, Shirley and Rilla, are at home under the watchful eyes of faithful Susan Baker; while in Rainbow Valley, out of sight of the grown-up house, the older children, Jem, Walter, Nan, and Diana, can fry the fish they catch in the stream, roast potatoes, play games, swap stories, and enjoy the company of the children who have just come with their widower father, the new minister of Glen St. Mary.

Jerry, Faith, Una, and Carl Meredith will horrify the staid Presbyterian congregation by their ragged clothes, their inappropriate behaviour in church and their "sacrilegious" games in the cemetery. "Why did they ever build that manse beside the graveyard in the first place?" Anne asks. Miss Cornelia answers, "They got the lot cheap. And no other manse children ever thought of playing there." But the young Merediths, to our delight, do think of playing there, and of doing other disruptive things.

The division between the godly powers-that-be and the little children is one line in the novel. This disconnect culminates with the strange doings of the Meredith daughter called "Faith." Faith writes a letter to the editor justifying some of her misdoings in terms that further horrify; Faith takes over the church and preaches an impromptu sermon on charity, "to stop old cats from talking about how dirty the manse was." The bulk of *Rainbow Valley* will consist of a series of incidents like the scrapes that Anne got into in the first book, picaresque, not developing from small to large, petty to insignificant, just a series of funny tangles. True Faith will confront and confound the merely sanctimonious. Her sister, timid Una, will set out, like Una the red-cross Knight in Spenser's *Faerie Queene*, to fight the frightening evil.

But the central plot, the story with a beginning, a climax, a set-back, and an ending, will be the romance involving their father, the befuddled minister, Reverend John Meredith. The lovely cover on the first edition of the book is not of the children, but of sweet Rosemary West, with whom this other-worldly man is falling in love. His romance will be conducted, of course, in full view of the Miss Cornelias of this world; and connected, of course, to the major theme of religion, especially as it filters through to the community via a male leader.

"And for all he is so abstracted and dreamy he has a very good opinion of himself, man-like," says Miss Cornelia. But she is happy with the man Glen St. Mary has chosen as its minister. "Chosen": for the Presbyterian Church is essentially democratic.[62] Its ministers are chosen by the individual congregation, rather than being selected by a bishop, as in Roman Catholicism and in many Protestant sects. Church business is conducted by elected Elders in session; ministers and lay delegates meet in a General Assembly to elect a Moderator. The Moderator, during his term of office, will act as chairman rather than as ruler as the assembly hammers out church policy.

Notably, all these officials—minister, Elders, Moderator—were male in Montgomery's time. A bright little girl, as bright as Montgomery, was still subject to gender assignments; the best she could do was marry a minister, rather than develop her own theology and take her place in the pulpit. Reverend John Meredith represents the young Montgomery's many friends and relations in holy orders: Uncle Leander, John Mustard, Ed Simpson, John Stirling, and finally Ewan Macdonald, who preached successfully for the call to Cavendish Presbyterian church.

Now at the age of forty-three she was married to a minister, and the church dominated her everyday life. Indeed it dominated the life and work of many other women writers: the Brontës, Mrs. Gaskell, Marian Keith,[63] as it dominated the life of most small villages in the late nineteenth and early twentieth century. So the book Montgomery wrote in the village parish of Leaskdale in 1917–18 is not about college and the education of girls, but about the church and the ministry of men.

By the end of the second chapter the story has veered away from church-men in general to the romance of one particular minister. Clearly the man needs a wife. And Miss Cornelia places her begrudging and amusing stamp of approval on Rosemary West as a possible mistress of the manse: "My own grandmother was an Episcopalian." So was Montgomery's English grand-mother. Readers of the *Selected Journals* hear nothing of Lucy Woolner Macneill's beliefs, but maybe a little Episcopalian scepticism was part of the unspoken attitude in the Macneill household. Certainly the opening of the book alerts us to some amusing undercurrents about religion, in this funny book by a minister's wife.

Macdonald now had to fit her own writing into the interstices of the church's needs: in the Sunday school, the Sunday school concerts, the women's mission society, the choir, the organ, entertaining visiting minis-ters, visiting bereaved families, not to mention attending the church services twice every Sunday.

Here was material for a strong novel. Many a minister married, often in college, a clever and sensitive young girl. Many a young woman, so chosen, wound up in misery in a community that underestimated her talents, or absorbed so much of her energy that her talents remained buried. Curiously, however, Montgomery concentrates not on the wife's position, but on the man's feelings. *Rainbow Valley* offers a rare insight into a man's feelings and his sufferings.

At the same time, this book also mocks the man's abstraction from every-day life. John Meredith, over-godly and ineffectual, is so absorbed in his the-ological concerns that he never notices the unhappiness of his children or the slovenly state of his own house.[64] He leaves his children to work out their own lives, in a poverty imposed by his carelessness. He is typically unaware when his youngest daughter Una has brought a strange, rough-spoken little girl into the manse. "In the study below Reverend John Meredith walked the floor with rapt face and shining eyes, thinking out his message of the morrow."

John Meredith's story is a rounded study of abstraction. It counters the marginal portrait of Jonas Blake, an idealized, homely, funny minister, who marries one of Anne's friends in *Anne of the Island*. How long will Reverend Jo withstand the pressures of his exalted position? To an impudent question,

"Can't a man laugh and laugh and be a Christian still?" Aunt Jamesina answered, "A man, yes. But I'm speaking of ministers, my dear." Luckily, Montgomery's husband never read her whimsical novels, for they continued to make similar sly digs at ministers.

Ewan Macdonald harboured a recurring conviction that although many of his congregation might be elect, chosen by a merciful God for salvation, he himself was among the damned. One way Montgomery coped with Ewan's ideas about eternal damnation was to turn them into a funny child-ish version. Mary Vance exclaims,

> "Hell? What's that?"
>
> "Why, it's where the devil lives," said Jerry. "You've heard of him—you spoke about him."
>
> "Oh, yes, but I didn't know he lived anywhere. I thought he just roamed round. Mr. Wiley used to mention hell when he was alive. He was always telling folks to go there. I thought it was some place over in New Brunswick where he come from."
>
> "Hell is an awful place," said Faith, with the dramatic enjoyment that is born of telling dreadful things. "Bad people go there when they die and burn in fire for ever and ever and ever. . . ."
>
> "Do you mean to tell me," demanded Mary, "that I'd be sent to hell for telling a lie now and then? Why, I *had* to. Mr. Wiley would have broken every bone in my body one time if I hadn't told him a lie. Lies have saved me many a whack, I can tell you."
>
> Una sighed. Here were too many difficulties for her to solve. She shuddered as she thought of being cruelly whipped. Very likely she would have lied too.

Una's creator, Montgomery, lived a life of avoiding whacks by moving into the world of lies, known as fiction.

Meantime the church, as represented by Reverend Mr. Meredith, responds to such difficulties re human sin and eternal punishment, by thinking about St. Augustine. Yet Montgomery gives Mr. Meredith the kind of defence she probably longed to give her husband when Anne says, "We are *proud* of our minister and his family. . . . He is a faithful friend, a judicious pastor in all essentials, and a refined, scholarly, well-bred man." Words like this Montgomery no doubt wished someone would apply to poor beleaguered Ewan Macdonald. Anne's peroration is, "We *rejoice* in our minister and his splendid boys and girls!"

Much of the story of *Rainbow Valley* is presented from the point of view of Mr. Meredith. Not since *Kilmeny* was told from the point of view of Eric Marshall (related to Mrs. Cornelia Marshall Elliot?), and *The Story Girl* told from the point of view of Bev King, had Montgomery focused so much on male experience. Unlike the world of Patty's Place, where boys feature only as gentleman callers, or rejected proposers, boys carry social weight in the Rainbow Valley. Jerry Meredith is a dominant person in the minister's young family, setting up rules of conduct and enforcing discipline. Jem Blythe, though busy studying, is a sane element in the Blythe family. Gentle, visionary Walter is a subtle study. But the central, puzzling, convincing study is of Reverend John Meredith. In chapter after chapter we see the world through his eyes.

Maybe because World War was making the fate of young men so poignant to a woman who watched the young lads in the church sign up and had to take news of their deaths to parishioners. Her two little boys were aged six and three when she was writing this book, and they perhaps brought her new awareness of boys' interests. Maybe she was trying to cast off the trammels of being tagged a "girls' book writer," after three consecutive novels featuring a love story told from the point of view of a girl or a not-so-young woman: *Anne of Avonlea* (Miss Lavendar); *Anne of the Island* (Anne and Philippa Gordon); *Anne's House of Dreams* (Leslie Moore and Miss Cornelia). For whatever reason, Montgomery writes now a story hinging on a man's love, with emphasis on the changes in his emotions and perceptions.

John Meredith, though still wrapped in the memory of his dead wife, becomes entangled with two sisters, one clever and capable of stimulating theological argument, the other sweet and pretty. There is a fairy-tale quality here. Ellen West has cast a spell over Rosemary, suspending her life as in the Sleeping Beauty pattern. Ellen's interdiction of romance for Rosemary is derived from the failure of her own romance with Norman Douglas.

The focus swings back from romance to theology when Norman Douglas, now the village reprobate, demands from the gentle minister "a good rip-roaring sermon on hell once every six months—and the more brimstone the better. I like 'em smoking." Montgomery enjoys a theological chuckle at this talk of old-style preaching.

A more modern theological dilemma confronts the minister when he hears that Anne's son Walter, though terrified of fighting, is forced into combat. Mr. Meredith concludes, taking the position most Canadians accepted in war time, "My motto, Walter, is, don't fight till you're sure you ought to, and *then* put every ounce of you into it." *Rainbow Valley* was written near the end of World War I. Patriots on both sides of the conflict believed that God was with them. The young men in Ewan Macdonald's congregation had "flocked to the colours," and Reverend Mr. Macdonald (like most Canadian ministers) had encouraged enlistment as a speaker at rallies. The subsequent death of these young men was presented by the church as a glorious and righteous sacrifice. In her journals, Montgomery did not explore her reactions to the justification of that war, only reporting the endless dread of reading each morning's newspaper. She added an implicit comment when she photographed her little son Chester standing under the arch of flowers through which the men of the local battalion will march off to the transport trains en route overseas to Flanders fields. Montgomery watched those marchers, and she wrote *Rainbow Valley*.

Though she placed her story in a time before the war, she introduced a frightening premonition of the coming battles and losses at the end of the book, strangely out of tone with the story itself. In the odd, unexpected, prophetic final chapter, Walter foreshadows the coming of war. Readers are obliquely warned that the boys of Rainbow Valley won't live happily ever after.

As her life slipped into greater darkness, and the world stumbled through the First World War, destructive of faith for so many of her generation, Montgomery's faith in a benign God had dwindled and her sense of the mystery of evil had increased. Mary Vance, placed so firmly at the centre of the book, is an emanation of the new sense of evil that Montgomery picked up, along with so many of her generation, in the war years. This little waif, living secretly under Mr. Meredith's roof, is as close to an evil child as Montgomery had portrayed up to this point. Pale in appearance but bold and brassy in manner, with washed-out eyes and an exaggerated sense of her own importance, she comes into Rainbow Valley to inaugurate trouble. She is the opposite of Sara Stanley in *The Story Girl*, that vivid loner coming into a group of children to bring value and vitality. Adopted by a stiff-mannered elderly woman of the Marilla type, she seems like a parody of Anne, but she has none of Anne's winning optimism.[65] Mary Vance comes to Glen St. Mary—an unsaintly Mary, "ad-vancing" into the manse. Like "*Tann*is," the name "*Va*nce" seems to embed the name "Anne": a Jungian would say that all three characters are variants of the *anima* of Montgomery. Mary Vance, like Susan and Miss Cornelia, but in a darker, more ironic key, voices thoughts that Montgomery had to repress.

Mary Vance's concept of God, as explained to Una, is "I think He's an awful lot like your father—just absent-minded and never taking any notice of a body most of the time, but sometimes waking up all of a sudden and being awful good and kind and sensible." Here is a comic version of doubts expressed long ago to Montgomery's correspondents Ephraim Weber and George MacMillan and in dark musings in her early journal, "I feel tonight as if God were the cruel tyrant of Calvin's theology, who tortures his creatures for no fault of their own at His whim and pleasure" (December 24, 1909). Mary Vance enjoys horrifying the community; Maud Montgomery never did. Professionally, in her early days as a short story writer, she had set all these doubts aside and turned out light tales with conventional moral attitudes for Church papers and Sunday School magazines. This habit of tamping down her doubts would serve her, when she met and married a minister. But by 1917 some of the doubts erupted. Rather than by-passing her agonies of rebellion and disbelief, she touched them into the comedy of fascinating, funny, unpredictable Mary Vance.

Mary Vance's chief opponent is sturdy Faith Meredith. But Faith, too, has fun at the expense of ministers. Pomposity gets its comeuppance at the hands of Faith, who watches silently as a visiting minister's coat-tails catch fire. True Faith disrupts the godly by telling the unwelcome truth, in church and outside of it.

Faith's father suffers for the supposed sins of his children. But in the end, the novelist gives Mr. Meredith his Rosemary, sweet-spoken, sympathetic, ready for love. In fiction, for the abstracted minister, romance eventually warms and colours his life. For Montgomery and her husband, there was to be no such happy ending.

In the year that *Rainbow Valley* was published (1919) Ewan Macdonald's secret malady reached a climax. When the war was over, and so many young men did not return, he like other ministers who had spoken at recruiting rallies, seeing the war as a battle between good and evil, no doubt felt a new confusion and guilt. As he went down to the darkness of manic depression, Montgomery despaired. For her readers, however, she continued to strike light and happy tones in *Rainbow Valley*. "Thank God I can keep the shadows of my life out of my work. I would not darken any other life. I want instead to be a messenger of optimism and sunshine."

Miraculously, her bitter life continued to play into romantic funny books. In *Rainbow Valley*, written near the end of the war, whatever her own doubts, and whatever the darkness of her experience, she could still chuckle as she wrote in triple irony about poor young Faith Meredith's cry, "It's awful to be a minister's family. . . . I'll never, never *never* marry a minister, no matter how nice he is."

Montgomery continued to create people like John Meredith and Rosemary, and Norman Douglas and Mary Vance, celebrating the grandeur of human beings, and their foolishness and pettiness too. The title of the novel implies her ambivalence: the valley dips down, but the rainbow arcs upward.

Further Chronicles of Avonlea

(Boston: L.C. Page, 1920)

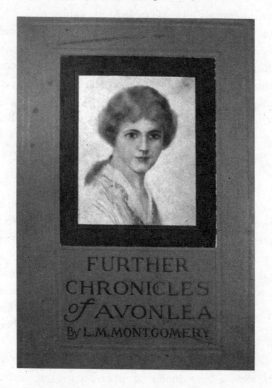

The publication of *Further Chronicles of Avonlea* was the climax of a bitter battle between Montgomery and her first publisher. At the time when *Chronicles of Avonlea* was under discussion in 1911, Montgomery had sent Page a big bundle of her previously published stories, for him to choose a few worthy of reissuing. After he established his choices, she instructed him to destroy those he had set aside. Secretly, he dismissed her instructions. Six years later, when she had decided she would no longer regard him as her publisher, she discovered that Page had not only retained the "culls," the stories passed over for the *Chronicles*, but that he now intended to bring them out as *Further Chronicles of Avonlea*. Montgomery came to the painful decision that she would have to sue Page, in order to protect her intellectual property.

The author was furious with the publisher for several reasons. He had cozened her into an unprofitable contract in the first place, and then had refused to adjust its terms when her book attained such unexpected success. He had short-changed her on royalties rising from the books published while she was under contract to him. Now, when she had switched to another publisher, Page was bringing out a new volume of her work, presuming that she would go back to the unfair royalty schedule she had just renounced. Furthermore, in the years since their composition she had reworked some of the stories and inserted them into novels published since 1911—a possible source of embarrassment now, if the public caught a glimpse of authorial parsimony, in recycled materials. These early tales lacked the complexity and finesse she had achieved in her most recent works, *Rainbow Valley* and *Rilla of Ingleside*. For this reason, too, she bitterly resented Page's unauthorized publication.

To these objections she would add another when the book actually came out, over her objections. The portrait of a "Titian-haired" young woman which appeared on the cover falsely suggested that this was part of the authorized "Anne series." Indeed, in 1911, here as well as in those used in *Chronicles of Avonlea*, Montgomery had inserted some often-awkward allusions to Anne Shirley as playing a minor part in each story, or had substituted place names (e.g., White Sands) and family names (Pye, Sloane, Blair) to accord with Anne's home village of Avonlea in a way that exploited the impression that this work continued the story of Anne Shirley.

Nevertheless, the stories warrant examination as part of Montgomery's published fictions. They are well crafted, like all the early writings that had passed through the hands of magazine editors. Furthermore, the changes made in 1911 show how often Montgomery's editorial emendations show a delicate sense of style. Thanks to the work of Donna Campbell, who has acquired copies of most of the magazines in which the stories originally appeared, it is possible to trace and analyze the changes introduced when Montgomery reworked her early stories. Even the changes in name are significant. In inserting the "Anne" and "Avonlea" allusions, she often deleted names that had deeper personal associations. *The Further Chronicles* are also important because they present motifs and characters that would reappear in her later productions.

The stories can be considered in seven groups, according to their use of these recurring motifs, in relation to stages of Montgomery's own life and to their re-use in her later writing.

(1) In childhood, Montgomery loved and admired her absentee father, even if her Macneill grandparents perhaps had less respect for him. A comparable hunger for a father's presence dominates Sara Stanley in *The Story Girl* and Jane Stuart in *Jane of Lantern Hill*. In both these novels, Montgomery will give the late-reunited father power as a successful artist. *Further Chronicles of Avonlea* presents "Her Father's Daughter" (first published in *Christian Endeavor World* in 1907) in which a girl insists on being married from her father's house, in defiance of her mother's wishes. Rachel's

father is a sailor, unwilling to fit into farm life, but bearded and handsome, like Montgomery's own father, Hugh John Montgomery—and like him unsuccessful in the family's eyes.

The characterization of the bitter, stubborn mother ("a tornado would hardly have caused her to swerve an inch from her chosen path") in "Her Father's Daughter" reflects Montgomery's memories of her grandmother's control over her clothes and her friends. Much later, *Jane of Lantern Hill* would present a fuller study of a controlling old woman's harshness, and of her contempt for a son-in-law considered a failure.

Another play on the theme of success and failure is "Sara's Way" (first published in *The Criterion*, 1904.) This young woman resists the suitor her sister presses on her, until it appears that he is a failure, whereupon she accepts him. One of the last stories in *Further Chronicles* returns to this first theme. "Only a Common Fellow" reveals unexpected nobility on the part of a man despised by the family of the girl he is to marry.

In yet another story, "The Brother Who Failed" (first published in *The Globe*, 1909), a family—called together like the family that readers will meet in *A Tangled Web*—comes to appreciate the man who has not succeeded in the world's eyes, but who has helped those in Avonlea who needed him. This version of true human success, written when Montgomery was burning with eagerness to climb the Alpine path, shows lingering resentment of the Macneill family's dismissal of Hugh John Montgomery as a failure.

A darker twist to the father-daughter relationship comes later in the book in "The Education of Betty." This girl is described in terms almost exactly like those Montgomery used to describe herself in her journal (December 13, 1920) with hazel ("grayish-blue") eyes, small and shapely hands and feet, and thick, nut-brown hair. She ultimately falls in love with a man old enough to be her father, and indeed a man who has played the role of loving guardian and mentor. This May and January romance told from the man's point of view has a happy ending. It will recur, totally inverted, in the later study of the strange relationship between Emily Byrd Starr and her older mentor, in the *Emily* series.

(2) In her twenties, Montgomery found one defence against unhappiness in the fun of friendship between girls or young women. "Aunt Cynthia's Persian Cat" (first published in *Reader*, 1904; also in *Canadian Courier*, 1914) presents a laughing narrator who claims that "men are a nuisance." The play between the narrator and her friend Ismay sounds like the giggly fun of days in Cavendish with Nora Lefurgey and the records of their mischievous attitude to young men, as recorded in their giddy joint diary.[66] In this first story in *Further Chronicles*, Max, a persistent suitor, is finally accepted, only because he can help solve the problem of an unwelcome cat. This white Persian, "blue-eyed and deaf and delicate" will reappear as the hated "Snowball" in *Jane of*

Lantern Hill. Montgomery was addictively fond of cats, as readers of her journals recognize.[67] But the cat in this first story in *Further Chronicles of Avonlea* is a complete complacent nuisance (like the men who come wooing).

(3) Later, as an unmarried woman in her thirties, Montgomery was well aware, in the lonely years before Ewan materialized, of the Cavendish attitude toward an "old maid." In "The Materializing of Cecil" (first published in *Home Magazine*, 1907; also in *Canadian Courier*, 1912), a spinster, "not at all homely," concocts an imaginary lover to ward off contempt and pity, and gives him the name of a maker of patent medicine. When the imagined lover materializes, he falls for her because she does not look like a lank old maid. He proposes to take her out west (like *Mistress Pat*, leaving beloved Silver Bush). Valancy in *The Blue Castle* will enact a fuller version of this story of late-life romance.

"In her Selfless Mood" (first published as "Eunice Holland's Sacrifice," *Springfield Republican*, 1904) concerns an old maid's possessiveness. Devoted to the brother she has looked after ever since their mother's death, this woman resents his marriage to one of the Pyes, long-time enemies of the boy's family. Small-pox strikes, restoring the care of her brother to his long-rejected sister. This melodramatic story, complete with two deathbed scenes, a disputed mortgage, and the sister's loss of her family home to a vulgar sister-in-law, seems in many ways to foreshadow *Mistress Pat.*

"The Little Brown Book of Miss Emily" (first published in *Farm and Fireside*, 1907; also in *Maclean's*, 1917) is a more sentimental "old maid" story. Little does a mocking young narrator know (until too late) that the faded spinster once fell desperately in love—only to be renounced by an artist because of his snobbish class-consciousness. In revising this story, Montgomery added Anne as narrator, and expanded this intrusion to include Diana Barry. The motif "Diana and I" recurs, suggesting that both these young people share the community's scorn of a spinster.

(4) Another group of stories, including "The Return of Hester" (first published in *Canadian Magazine*, 1909), dramatizes the conflict between two women. These stories draw obliquely from the years when Montgomery was held from marriage by her grandmother's needs. Hester, a proud older woman dominates and draws a promise not to marry from her younger sister. When death dissolves the pride of Hester, her ghost returns in gentleness to bring reconciliation with the younger woman's faithful suitor. The clash of female wills foreshadows the situation between the West sisters in *Rainbow Valley.* There the resolution will come not from a ghostly revenant but by a rueful change of heart on the part of the older sister, so that the younger one can marry a Presbyterian minister.

(5) "The Conscience Case of David Bell" (first published in *Westminster*, 1909) is a laughing commentary on life in the Presbyterian Church. Written

before Montgomery, as a minister's wife, became a part of the church establishment, it portrays the effect of evangelical revivalism on a staid Presbyterian congregation. This story is ironic toward the evangelist, with his grammatical errors and lapses into vulgarity; it is pitying toward the unsophisticated farmer who endures a torturing crisis of conscience under evangelical pressure. The tone of this story will later be assigned to minor characters like Miss Cornelia in *Anne's House of Dreams*. Earlier, Montgomery had expressed more directly her attitude toward church affairs, boding not too well for her future married life as the wife of a minister.

(6) "Jane's Baby" (first published in *Christian Endeavor World*, 1906) focuses on the force of "innate and denied motherhood." Montgomery averred that hunger for babies was one reason for marrying Ewan, even though she felt no passionate love for him. In this early story, written in her spinster days, Montgomery presents two tragi-comic sisters, warring over which one has the right to adopt an orphaned baby cousin. The two sisters are set against each other, like the sisters in "The Return of Hester" and like the mother and daughter in "Her Father's Daughter." In each case, the opposed women are distinguished from each other in fairy-tale fashion: one sister is "fair and tall and fat" (like Rachel) and her sister is small, dark, and thin (like Rachel's mother). The rivalry in "Jane's Baby" ends when the baby goes into convulsions, and one sister runs to the other for help (a forerunner of Diana's panic-stricken appeal to Anne for help with croupy little Minnie-May in *Anne of Green Gables*).

"The Dream-child" (first published in *Christian Endeavor World*, 1909) is another, ghostly story of "the holy passion of motherhood." In a small house by the harbour (very much as in *Anne's House of Dreams*) husband and wife face the death of a baby son. The grief-haunted mother feels the dead child calling her toward the sea, and as years pass her life becomes controlled by the haunting quest. This is a strange foreshadowing of Montgomery's agonies of grief at the death of her newborn second son, Hugh.

Contrasting with this tale in every way, "The Son of his Mother" (first published in *Canadian Magazine*, 1904) is a study in a mother's neurotic obsession with her son, named Chester. Ironically, of course, this was the name Montgomery would give her own son, the boy whose life and loves became the stimuli for terrible jealousy and anxiety. "Chester" was also the name of one of Montgomery's Macneill uncles, the successful one who went west, became a well-known lawyer, and satisfied, presumably, his own mother's ambitions and pride. In the *Further Chronicles* story, the possessive woman becomes jealous when her son develops a romantic interest in a young woman. Chester reacts by running away to sea and is presumed drowned, to his mother's unimaginable grief. When he is dramatically restored to life, the mother appears cured of her obsession.

(7) At the end of *Further Chronicles*, the publisher included a story that bore minimal reference to Avonlea. "Tannis of the Flats" (first published in *Criterion*, 1904; also in *Canadian Magazine*, 1914) could not conceivably be set in or near Prince Edward Island, although an Avonlea woman is affected by the events it records. But it is not to be ignored in a full study of Montgomery's work, or in a critical analysis of the ways—conscious or unconscious—in which she selected and worked her materials.

"Tannis of the Flats" is a different braiding of most of the themes that preoccupied Montgomery in the years before *Anne of Green Gables*. Besides its intrinsic interest, it has become a flash-point for critics who read its treatment of the mixed-race people of the frontier as racist.

This story is the late and only valuable literary result of the year young Montgomery spent in the Canadian north-west, in Prince Albert, Saskatchewan, "3000 miles from home" (August 20, 1890). A week after arriving at the new home of her beloved father—and of her sulky, unlovable, and five-months-pregnant stepmother—she was enrolled in the local high school. Of the eight boys who were her fellow-pupils, four were (as she wrote in her journal) "'nitchie'—which means that they have Indian blood in them." They seemed to her "detestable" and "as homely as stump fences" (September 3, 1890). She had picked up the local lingo quickly. "Nitchie" was a word drawn from the Algonquin language (nitchee, neche, neechee, neejee, nichi, nichiwa) simply meaning "friend."[68] Today it is tagged in encyclopedias as "a racial slur." The boys in young Montgomery's class were named Clark, McDonald, Maveety (McVitie?), and Oram. Unlike the Métis, whose parentage was mixed Indian and French Canadian, these boys were part Scottish. Strange sights for a young lady from Cavendish—to be noted in the September 1890-diary, consulted much later when the idea of writing a story set in that raw new world occurred to the adult.

At recess Maud and the other two girl students sat on the school verandah, watching "the passers-by—Indian for the most part—'braves' with their dirty blankets over their shoulders or chattering dark-eyed squaws with their glossy blue-black hair and probably a small-faced papoose strapped to the back" (September 19, 1890). Notably, in the journal, unlike the words "nitchies" and "braves," the word "squaw" is not set in quotation marks. Maud was simply using a term based on the aboriginal language, "derived from Proto-Algonquian et^kwe:wa (t^ represents a theta—a th sound)."[69] The term "squaw" has recently become central in the "language police controversy" regarding offensive words, but for the young stranger from the East in 1890–91 it was part of the lingo in common use among her father's friends. Her only other journal reference to First Nations or Métis was to a "Fannie McLaughlin, a 'breed' girl" hired as a servant to help with housework (March 7, 1891). Among her first publications while she was in Prince

Albert was an article on Saskatchewan which contained innocuous details about "the characteristics of the Indians" (June 6, 1891).

The spectacle of dark-skinned people, among the first of her impressions of her new life, would be the base for the only story she set in the West. Tannis Dumont is the daughter of a "French half-breed" and a "pure-bred Highland Scotchman." Tannis looks "as if all the blood of all the Howards might be running in her veins . . . [has] a somewhat whiter skin . . . ruddier bloom. But the dominant race was Indian." Tannis is fresh from the Prince Albert high school (that is, about the age Montgomery was in her year at the same academy).

Like Montgomery, Tannis is ready for love: Montgomery's journal is full of thoughts about boys at home, about friendly young Will Pritchard who slips her ring on his finger, and about the awkward teacher, John Mustard, from whom she receives her first proposal of marriage. For Tannis, there is no such proposal. The charming young Englishman, Jerome Carey, offers a flirtation that is misinterpreted as something more by the Aboriginal girl. He abandons Tannis when a woman from the East comes to reclaim him.

Montgomery's time out West proved brief. After the birth of her half-brother Bruce in March 1891, she was taken out of school to serve as household help, and ultimately, in August, packed off home to Prince Edward Island again by the troubled father, embarrassed and humiliated by his new wife's jealous attitude to this lively sixteen-year-old step-daughter.

A sad ending; but the end of "Tannis of the Flats" intensifies into tragedy. In darkness and storm, a deadly brawl ensues between the Englishman and a young man of Tannis's own race. Tannis caps the story of her own defeat in love by riding, perilously and selflessly, to bring her rival to Carey's deathbed. The operatic ending then reverses, and glorifies obsessive possession.

Nothing could be further from the parochial events of the other stories in *Further Chronicles of Avonlea*. Yet the themes are comparable. The loneliness of an unmarried woman opens the story, with Elinor Blair, changed by her trip west, "with a shadowed look in her eyes." The father/daughter theme recurs. Tannis's father, Auguste Dumont, is complacent about his daughter's affairs—perhaps a deep reflection of Maud's disappointment in her father's failure to defend her against her stepmother. The archetypal antagonism between two women, one light, one dark, becomes extreme here. Tannis is slender, with dark skin, delicate foot and hand, and blue-black hair; Elinor presents "the pretty, fair-tinted face, the fluffy coronal of golden hair, the blue, laughing eyes." The complexity of the theme of success and failure is forwarded, with a racial twist. Tannis is doomed to loss of love because of her inferiority in the eyes of society. In its recapitulation of themes, "Tannis of the Flats" is indeed an appropriate conclusion to the book of *Further Chronicles of Avonlea*.

Montgomery published this story in 1904, thirteen years after her return to Prince Edward Island. It is strange that she made so little use of her western experience. This was a country made familiar to readers by "Ralph Connor," a Presbyterian minister whose works were widely praised.[70] Presbyterian publications kept Ralph Connor's treatment of Western themes in her sight. "Tannis of the Flats" proves Montgomery would have been capable of continuing the story of the "great lone land" of the frontier. A good guess is that her year in the West with her father and stepmother was too painful to be treated directly, or even as directly as a Western tale would allow. But Prince Albert had released the deeper themes that would continue to consume her and to reappear in the lighter stories reprinted in *Further Chronicles of Avonlea.*

"Tannis of the Flats" inaugurated a thirty-two-year series of fictions with titles following the formula "A of B" from *Anne of Green Gables* through *Pat of Silver Bush* to *Jane of Lantern Hill.* Here, though, the place-name "Flats" is preceded by no propitious signifier such as "Green," "Golden," "Rainbow," "Silver," or "Lantern." "The Flats" fits both the photographs of the raw little frontier village Montgomery pasted into her journal, and also the mood into which she tumbled during this sad reunion with her dear father.

For many modern readers, the value of the story is cancelled by the implied racism. The narrator refers jocularly to "half-breeds and quarter-breeds and any-fractional breeds," and declaims, "Your true Indian is bad enough, but his diluted descendant is ten times worse." This posture rouses horror in some readers, who decry "stereotypical depictions of slovenly, ugly, vicious, scheming Native Americans and biracial people."[71] This commentator concludes, "It would be an act of mercy for the publisher to produce a library edition which omits the final story."

At the time of publication, however, the publisher had other worries to contend with. Montgomery had come to a boiling point in her exchanges of letters with L.C. Page. She heard more and more about his increasingly bad reputation among booksellers, other publishers, and other authors. Page had become notorious for his exploitation of American women writers, people like Annie Fellows Johnston, the author of *The Little Colonel,* and Eleanor H. Porter, author of *Pollyanna.* Montgomery heard nasty stories about the publisher first-hand from Marshall Saunders, the other Canadian woman writer tied to him by a long-term contract.

In the process of fighting Page, Montgomery carried her case first to law courts in Boston, Page's home area. She entered the courts of the State of Massachusetts as plaintiff against her publisher in two cases. The first concerned the original contract. She now believed that Page had defrauded her, withholding some of her royalties. In the spring of 1917, her distrust had intensified as she checked her royalties very closely, and found he had been withholding payment while differences were being thrashed out. She got in touch with the attorney of the American Authors' League and prepared to do battle with the man she now considered a crook, even if it meant going to Boston to tackle him in the courts of his own constituency.

Secondly, she fought him over the forthcoming *Further Chronicles*. Again the very competent lawyer of the American Authors' League helped her fight for her rights—and incidentally for the rights of other authors. She won the battle but lost the war. Even while she was preparing to shift to another publisher, Page was preparing to bring out, against her wishes, that curious book of stories that he had originally considered second choice. Montgomery renewed the battle, this time in the Massachusetts Supreme Court, arguing that in particular the use of a "Titian-haired" woman on the cover, and also the recurring unapproved uses of "Anne Shirley" and "Avonlea" breached her rights. Finally she carried another case to the New York State Supreme Court, in an argument involving Stokes, the American publisher who held the rights to cheap reprints of her books. She was supported throughout by the American Authors' League, who saw this as a test case for supporting authors' rights over their works.

She was supported more importantly by her own pride, her indignation at being exploited, and her innate sense of justice and fairness. The court trials were a terrible test of her courage and endurance.

In spite of this background of temper and resentment, *Further Chronicles of Avonlea* is a book worth cool reconsideration. In the years since Montgomery's death there has been a movement to reconsider her apprentice work in the short story form, and to rediscover her strength in the genre. In the 1980s and 1990s, her Canadian publishers, McClelland & Stewart, brought out a series of volumes, each grouping together a set of early stories clustering around a single theme: *Stories of the Sea, Ghost Stories, Stories of Love*.[72] These modern collections were interesting successors to that much disputed and furiously assailed collection, *Further Chronicles of Avonlea*.

Indeed, the collection as a whole illustrates the wide range of themes and tones and audiences that interested Montgomery in her apprentice days. "Tannis of the Flats" does more. It illustrates the alchemy by which Montgomery converted her youthful suffering in the year out west into an archetypal study of passion and jealousy.

~ Rilla of Ingleside ~

(Toronto: McClelland & Stewart, 1921)

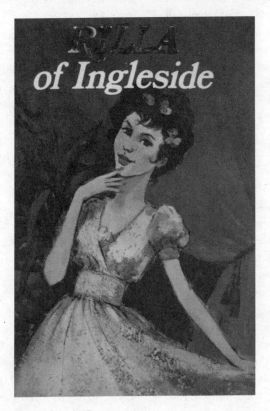

In Flanders fields, the poppies blow
Between the crosses, row on row,
That mark our place; and in the sky,
The larks, still bravely singing, fly
Scarce heard among the guns below . . .

John McCrae, "In Flanders Field," 1915

Colonel John McCrae's wartime poem uses two archetypal images—the scarlet poppy, suggesting full sensuous natural life, and the graveyard cross, suggesting geometric man-made death. In 1919, four years after the publication of "In Flanders Fields," Montgomery created *Rilla of Ingleside*, her own version of the poppies and crosses, larks and guns of wartime.

For her, poppies held personal significance. Before "In Flanders Fields," she had used this brilliant exotic flower symbolically both in *The Story Girl* and in *Anne's House of Dreams*. The hypnotic, articulate Story Girl's "large curving mouth was as red as a poppy," and Leslie Moore's "lips were as crimson as the bunch of blood-red poppies she wore at her belt" epitomizing her repressed passion. Like the poet McCrae, Montgomery used the poppy as a symbol of vibrant life.

Also, for Montgomery, as a late-Victorian girl brought up in the Christian tradition, singing hymns about "the old wooden cross," the "Cross of Jesus" that led Christian armies of missionaries "on to war," the cross "towering o'er the sands of time" in which Christians could glory—for such a girl the symbolism of the cross as signifying suffering and death was all-powerful. Her life as a minister's wife kept that old symbolism strong— until wartime events added new meanings.

World War I (1914–18) was just one of the "crosses" that history would add to those Montgomery already had to bear. Her journal entry for August 30, 1914, had recorded, "On August 13th a darling little son was born to me—dead." Then she had moved to the universal tragedy: "While I was lying helpless bad war news began to come too—news of the British defeat at Mons and the resulting long dreary retreat of the Allies which is still going on before the victorious rush of Germany's ready millions. Everything seems dark and hopeless" (August 30, 1914). On September 5 in an entry baring the private distress of going to the graveyard where her baby was buried, Montgomery also agonized over the German march on Paris.

How closely her intense response reflects the general instant absorption in the war can be seen by a look at contemporary newspapers. For instance, in the week the war began, the *Family Herald and Weekly Star* offered maps of the war zones to new subscribers; by September 4, 1914, 10,000 had been distributed. In her journal, Montgomery constructed a verbal equivalent of that map, touching in all the places and campaigns she would eventually use in *Rilla of Ingleside*.

Rilla of Ingleside, like life in the pre-war western world, and like Montgomery's life in Leaskdale, begins in idyllic happiness. Evil comes suddenly, undeservedly, and irrevocably. Beginning on the day the Austrian Archduke was assassinated in Sarajevo, the first eight chapters of the novel detail the events of August 1914, as people at home hear the terrible news of British retreat in Belgium, and boys begin mustering as volunteers in Canada. Rilla Blythe,[73] Anne's youngest daughter, is barely sixteen as the novel opens; she preparing for her first grown-up party, pretty, glowing, self-dramatizing, and is totally unready for the interruption of her pleasures by the news of the declaration of war in faraway Europe. She is unprepared also for the instant male responses: "We're cubs in a family row," "Some fun!" "Can't leave France in the lurch," "Hoist the flag," and "Call for volunteers." Local Island boys are in khaki a week and two days from the time they volunteer, and on their way overseas from Valcartier, without embarkation leave, within a fortnight.

For the next four years of the real wartime, Montgomery grabbed the newspaper every day to read of the great battles raging: the Somme, Passchendaele, Vimy, Ypres. She paced the floor night after night when the fall of Paris was threatened. Her journals also record how she went on with daily life in the face of that horrifying suspense and vicarious suffering. She rolled bandages and coped with bickering parishioners in her husband's church.

In October 1915 she gave birth to another son, another boy to make the loss of young men in the parish ever more poignant. That was the year when Colonel John McCrae published "In Flanders Field." Like most Canadians, Montgomery followed the Turkish campaigns around the Dardanelles, agonized when German armies captured Warsaw, and worried about pressures on Belgrade in Serbia and about President Woodrow Wilson's efforts to keep the United States out of Europe's war and to work as a peace negotiator.

In *Rilla of Ingleside*, the Blythe family in Glen St. Mary's reacts to each successive event, just as Montgomery had done in the vivid contemporary notes preserved in her diary. The quiet neighbourhood enlarges its horizons as it becomes concerned with Antwerp, Turkey, Serbia, Calais, Lodz, Warsaw, Szuro, Belgrade, and Prezemysl, a weird concatenation for the parochial minds in Glen St. Mary. Thanks to her wartime journal, Montgomery was able to lift into literary form the daily life on the home front between 1914 and 1918, creating one of the very few records of war from a woman's perspective. The accuracy of *Rilla of Ingleside* on the swift Canadian response to the call of "the dear old Mother country," the subsequent battles and losses of life, and also the shifting moods of the "home front" has led to its acceptance by modern historians in Canada and elsewhere for use in classes on World War I.

Montgomery obsessively recorded her impressions of the horrors of the trench wars in the north and the big battles such as the Somme. The war fronts expanded to Italy, Romania, France, and into the air—all to be revisited in *Rilla of Ingleside*. Before the Canadian war effort ended, as one of the characters records, "Four hundred thousand of our boys gone overseas—fifty thousand of them killed." There were only twelve families in Leaskdale, but there were twenty-one names of those on active duty: four Mustards, two Shiers, two Kennedys, two Colwells, two Arnolds, one Leask, and so on—six of them killed in action. *Rilla of Ingleside* would recapture that experience of a country raising "crosses, row on row."

For a successful novel, however, Montgomery needed to add some hint of warmer life, of poppies blowing between the crosses, of love in wartime. So at the outset of the novel Rilla Blythe falls in love with Kenneth Ford, the handsome son of Owen Ford and Leslie, the woman who in *Anne's House of Dreams* had tucked the scarlet passion of poppies into her belt. Charming as it is, however, Rilla's story carries no similar sense of passion. Montgomery was not in the mood to create a powerful love story. Her attitude to romance, always inhibited, had now turned cynical. Mockingly she wrote in her diary about the things she had left out of "The Alpine Path," the autobiography she had written in 1917. To that formal memoir she privately added a half-funny, half-sad account of her "love affairs" (January 5, 1917). She ended frankly with "I was never in love with Ewan."

Rilla's first experience of love is presented as touchingly innocent and naïve rather than as passionate. It is followed instantly by the departure of Kenneth, intent on joining up. As long as the war winds on, there is no flowering of romance for Rilla. Even in the final reunion with Kenneth, Rilla's response is childish, signalled by her relapse into a baby habit of lisping. That slight lisp is one thing that differentiates Montgomery's new heroine from articulate, exuberant Anne, and from the Story Girl—and from Montgomery herself. Rilla has no intellectual ambition, no desire to go to college like her sisters Nan and Diana. She doesn't write, except in a girlish journal. She certainly doesn't enjoy the kind of frank friendly exchanges that marked the development of Anne's love for Gilbert.

Yet this vision of romance, trammeled by insecurity of wartime, unsure about an outcome, seems appropriate and convincing. Like most women in wartime, Rilla's life has been put on hold. She dare not feel resentment, when she considers what young men are enduring. The pallor of her romance is the product not only of the writer's mature cynicism but also of her realistic vision of the relation of the sexes during war time. But the book was not written until after the war was over, and for a book published as the 1920s began, Rilla presents an old-fashioned vision of female abilities and rights. Accuracy again: her story precedes the major change in the status of women effected by the war. She also, however, reflects an oddity of Montgomery's attitudes.

As an unexpected consequence of the overseas experience of Montgomery's half-brother Carl, Montgomery herself was given the rare opportunity to vote in the national Canadian election, a privilege assigned only to women who had members of the immediate family serving overseas. Though Montgomery accepted the privilege, she was not eager to see the right to vote extended to all women. Her young heroine Rilla typifies an anti-suffragist stance. It was one very common in her time, in spite of the liberation that many women experienced during a war that opened new employment opportunities to them. Rilla is content to grow into "real" womanhood as nurturer and housekeeper and meantime she waits quietly for her man to return from the war.

At home in Ingleside, Rilla matures, as the foster mother of a "war baby." This is a development different from the poppies of passion. Coerced into accepting responsibility for a motherless child, Rilla's experience of pseudo-motherhood immerses her in a life force diametrically opposed to the killing.

Rilla's care for the war baby "Jims" also clinches Kenneth's recognition of her as truly lovable when he briefly returns to Ingleside. This scene, effectively handled, again pulls back from anything erotic, offering instead a gentle warmth and humour. This is one spot among many where Montgomery sharpened her effects by careful revision. The scene begins with a phone call from Kenneth Ford. Originally Montgomery had him ask, "Hello, is that Rilla?" to which Rilla answers "Yeth." Notes for revision, appended to the manuscript, show a change to "Hello, is that Ingleside?"/"Yes"/"That you, Rilla?"/"Yeth."[74] The change underlines Rilla's shyness and immaturity. Two lines later in the manuscript, Montgomery changed Rilla's anxious cry for someone to "attend" to the crying baby, into a more youthful, dramatic, and comic cry, "*Why* doesn't *somebody* come and shake him!" Small changes like these, which occur throughout the manuscript, show Montgomery's never-failing craft and particularly her sense of comedy.

The potential love scene is handled not as romance. Susan Baker takes over the lovers' reunion with comic remembrances of the childhood follies of both Rilla and Kenneth. Although *Rilla of Ingleside* offers a pale version of romance, it compensates by the richness of this kind of down-to-earth humour. The first half of the book ends with a travesty of a wedding, the abrupt, secretive marriage of Miranda and Joe, an unattractive young couple. The groom cries all through the ceremony and the bride's pet dog takes a fit and is sick.

Susan Baker, the strong-minded old maid who runs the Blythe kitchen, represents one aspect of Montgomery: the woman who copes and turns an ironic eye on the mess made by others. At the darkest hour of the war Susan says, "'I shall anchor my storm-tossed soul to the British fleet and make a batch of bran biscuits.'" Susan epitomizes the staunch response of women to the war. "Wait you till the Big Push comes in the spring and the war will be over in a jiffy," she says, and later declares, "The Hun will never set foot in Prince Edward Island as long as I can handle a pitchfork." Then, announcing the news of "Armageddon"—"The British line is broken and the German shells are falling on Paris," Susan adds, "I am afraid I let the potatoes burn." For Susan, there are two villains, one public, one private: President Wilson of the United States, who goes on writing peace-making notes instead of declaring war; and Mr. Pryor, "Whiskers-on-the-moon," the local pacifist and perhaps Hun sympizer. In the end there is a great church scene, where Whiskers-on-the-moon, like the German Kaiser, gets his come-uppance.

Both comic and poignant, the idiomatic voices of women fill this book, enriching the unending insistence on the facts of war. To quote Anne, "A good laugh is as good as a prayer, sometimes." Nothing in the grim and factual journals suggests this richness of talk. Montgomery's power to catch the sound of voices is a different gift from the dogged determination to get the facts down correctly. Surely lightness is one function of fiction, or as Miss Oliver says, "I am in that state of mind where even a lie is a comfort, providing it is a cheerful lie." Humour is like the "larks" in McCrae's poem, "half-heard among the guns below." Montgomery's comic trademark laughter soars still, in the face of battle.

As the war wound on, Montgomery's life had been far from comic. In 1917, the war had come close to her personally when her half-brother Carl was severely wounded at Vimy Ridge. One of his legs was blown off above the knee, and he was invalided home. Montgomery met him for the first time in Toronto and brought him to Leaskdale as a very visible war hero. At that time she was still writing *Rainbow Valley*, a story set in the halcyon pre-war days. She named one of the happy children in the Valley "Carl." This boy reappears in *Rilla of Ingleside*, crippled in a different way, blinded in one eye.

Throughout the war, at home in Leaskdale, name after name was added to the honour roll in the little Presbyterian church. Every time one of these deaths was recorded, Montgomery accompanied her husband on visits of condolence. *Rilla of Ingleside* would later wring tragic force out of these experiences. Jem, the boy born in the House of Dreams, is missing in action, then imprisoned. He escapes to Holland and returns, "with a barely perceptible limp." But Montgomery assigns death on the battlefield to Anne's favourite son, Walter, killed in action at Courcelette, that skirmish where Carl Montgomery was wounded.

Walter's story is linked with the John McCrae and his poem "In Flanders Fields." In the novel, Anne's reluctant soldier-son writes "the one great war poem," acclaimed all over the world for its beauty and for its power to stir civilians into supportive action. Walter is a fine and ironic study of courage and cowardice in wartime. He turns sick at the thought of a bayonet charge but he can write a poem that draws others to his fate and can die as bravely as any of the ranting heroes.

Montgomery knew the McCrae poem—everyone did. She had also met the poet, before the war. Dr. John McCrae was medical aide-de-camp for Earl Gray at the time the Governor-General made a special trip to Prince Edward Island, solely to meet the young author of *Anne of Green Gables*. Montgomery's journal makes no mention of the handsome Montreal doctor, who was about her own age at this time. But she eventually picked up the poetic torch from him. At the same time as she was working on *Rilla of Ingleside* she was also finishing a book of poems, *The Watchman*. The title poem, like Walter's imaginary one, echoes McCrae's themes and imagery.

But the novel shucked off the idea of the noble "torch" of remembrance. As her life drew into greater darkness, and the world stumbled through the First World War, destructive of faith for so many of her generation,

Montgomery's faith in a benign God dwindled and her sense of the mystery of evil increased. *Rilla of Ingleside* conventionally affirms resurrection for the war dead, life everlasting, but the novel catches the radical shift in faith that followed the end of the First World War. Throughout the novel she gives Reverend John Meredith fine words endorsing a righteous war (even when two of his sons go overseas), but her own reaction is clearer in Anne's grief and shock at the loss of her best-loved son Walter. The eldest son Jem returns, undramatic and unheralded. The drama is left to his little Dog Monday, frantically relieved that the war is over.

The real world war ended, in a sense, in October 1918, though armistice was not official until November. In the aftermath of war the terrible Spanish flu took a new toll. Among the victims was Montgomery's beloved cousin Frederica Campbell. On January 25, 1919, a date Montgomery would annually recall with agony in her journals, Frede succumbed to the influenza that ironically capped the death-toll of battles.

In the sad winter of 1919, Montgomery began copying out her early journals in a clear readable form, transcribing the entries into a series of legal ledgers. In part she undertook this "grim mechanic exercise" of recopying in order to reconnect with her life before Frede's death, the happy times when the two young women played with Maud's babies, and "rinsed their souls out together" in intimate talk. Now she was also no doubt aware of the value her journals had always been to her as a source for the *Anne* books and wanted to preserve them for her own possible future literary use. Perhaps she was convinced that the story of her own life, in relation to the stories in her novels would be of value to others, future readers and writers. Re-reading the most recent of her journals she found source material for a new book.

After six weeks of desolate mourning, Montgomery resolutely began writing *Rilla of Ingleside*, on March 12, 1919. She intended to begin the story of Anne and her family in "the green, untroubled pastures and still waters of the world before the war," before Montgomery's own walk through the valley of the shadow of death. At the beginning of her book she added a character new to the Anne saga. Miss Oliver, sensitive, rather sad, with almond-shaped brown eyes and a clever, often mocking mouth, a woman whose life had been a struggle, seems like a portrait of Frederica Campbell.[75] In the novel Montgomery ascribed strange visionary dreams to Miss Oliver, giving her the gift of second sight, psychic power, which she believed she herself possessed. When the book was finished, she dedicated it to Frederica, "a true friend, a rare personality, a loyal and courageous soul."

But Frede had died, and partly because of this devastating loss, *Rilla of Ingleside*, even in its happiest moments, is shadowed. As she finished her work on the novel, she had to pick up yet another cross. In May 1919, five months after Frede's death, Ewan Macdonald's first major mental breakdown occurred. In June he went to Boston to consult a "nerve specialist." Back home there was a brief remission of his mental distress when his old friend Captain Edwin Smith came to Leaskdale to preach for him, but by November, when Montgomery was nearing the end of "Book 10" (as she called *Rilla* during the writing period), Ewan was again enduring terrible fits of depression and religious phobia.

Furthermore, as a writer under pressure from her demanding public, her publishers, and her own ambition, her creative energy had been dragged down. Partly because of this professional tension, joined to the demands of her two very small boys and the growing pressure of war work, Montgomery lost most of the time she had always spent in the escape and solace of reading her favourite books. Instead, she obsessively read newspaper accounts, especially in the Toronto *Globe*, of the ongoing battles overseas. In 1916 she refers only to Rupert Brooke's poetry, and to Wordsworth as bringing repose of spirit and Kipling's *Kim* bringing refreshment (August 1; December 10; December 21). In 1917 she was charmed by Pepys' *Diary* but less pleased with Butler's *The Way of All Flesh* (February 25; April 1). She turned from war worries to Macaulay's less urgent *History* and Rawlinson's *History of Egypt* in 1918 (February 25; March 31). By 1919 she had returned to reading contemporary novels, though not with much enthusiasm, in the familiar tune up for her own writing.

Style and structure in *Rilla of Ingleside* show the absence of the enrichment she had previously drawn from books. The novel adheres closely to her journal, reproducing its depiction the war's events, and following its inexorable day-by-day time-line. She had simply to record the crosses, "row on row." There are very few descriptive passages of the kind that had given texture to the earlier Anne books. *Rilla of Ingleside* substitutes directness in reporting events for the prettiness of descriptions of nature, and adds the humour of Susan Baker's sturdy resistance to melodrama or pathos.

The relative flatness was part of the literary *zeitgeist*. One best-seller of the *Rilla* year was Sinclair Lewis's *Main Street*. She didn't read it (or at least didn't record references to it), but she was influenced as Sinclair was by a kind of lowering, an exhaustion, after the war. Miss Oliver says, "I wonder if things won't seem rather flat and insipid when peace really comes." *Rilla of Ingleside* offers values appropriate for its time: honesty, endurance, and pride.

Montgomery was buttressed against depression by her faith in her own work. In the post-war years, Canadian soldiers had been gradually demobilized and returned home, their stories keeping fresh the war they had lived through. For Montgomery, listening to the soldiers' recalling the events of wartime reassured her of the value of the novel she was finishing. Working on her own version of the war story also gave her an escape from the insecurities of the ongoing battle against that publishing giant L.C. Page.

As the overseas war came to an end, Montgomery's other war had revved up. In a Massachusetts law court, the judge had awarded her twenty thousand dollars, to cover her losses in royalties, as falsified by Page. Weary of the battles, in January 1919 she signed over to Page all rights on her books up to that point, for the sum of $18,000—a terrible bargain, as it would turn out. The legal battles would go on long after World War I was over. Soon Montgomery would be back in Boston, battling in court against his exploitation and deceit.

Of this battle there is no trace in *Rilla of Ingleside*. Indeed Montgomery never used her legal troubles or her experiences in court in any part of her fiction. She finished writing the novel on August 24, 1920. She had just returned from another session in the Boston court house, where she was suing Page for the unauthorized publication of *Further Chronicles of Avonlea*. Soon she would be embroiled in another case, when Page retaliated by suing her for "malicious litigation."

Yet on the very day she finished *Rilla of Ingleside*, she wrote that she already had a new story in mind. "And I want—oh, I want to write—something entirely different from anything I have written yet. I am becoming classed as a 'writer for young people' and that only. I want to write a book dealing with grown-up creatures—a psychological study of one human being's life. I have the plot of it already matured in my mind" (August 24, 1920).

This human being would not be a simple girl like Rilla, but one like herself, gifted beyond the average in her ability—her compulsion—to write. It would be about a person who writes not for pay or as a result of pressure from her publisher or fans, but because she *has* to write. Someone like the writer she knew herself to be: someone she would name Emily.

Emily of New Moon

(Toronto: McClelland & Stewart, 1923)

They flash upon that inward eye
Which is the bliss of solitude;
And then my heart with pleasure fills,
And dances. . . .

   William Wordsworth, from "I wandered lonely as a cloud"

Emily of New Moon is a book about power. Emily Byrd Starr is powerless
at the outset in the face of her father's death, powerless again to withstand
the decisions of her mother's family about where she is to be raised. All the
powers of adulthood are levelled against her. Everyone, from the woman
who kept house for her father to the aunts and uncles gathered at the New
Moon farmhouse, tells her the hurtful truth—that nobody wants her. Yet
as the novel unfolds, Emily finds within herself ways to withstand those

forces. Above all, she discovers the power of her "flash," the force of imagination that permits her to outface daily life.

Montgomery found a source for both major elements in *Emily of New
Moon*—the minutiae of adult powers ranged against a child, and the power
to withstand through imaginative escape—in her journals. Those diaries
reminded her that "*Materially*, I was well cared for. . . . It was *emotionally*
and *socially* that my nature was starved and restricted" (January 7, 1910).
Re-reading her journals, she also recalled her childhood discovery of a coun-
tervailing ability "to live that strange inner life of fancy which had always
existed side by side with my outer life—a life into which I have so often
escaped from the dull or painful real" (January 7, 1910).

For both the story of hostile power and that of the "flash" in *Emily of New
Moon*, however, Montgomery drew on sources beyond those recorded in the
early journals. Montgomery had changed during the war years, and so had the
world, especially the world of women. *Emily of New Moon* is an amalgam of
details drawn from the journals and from more immediate experiences. The
novel raises questions about duty, patriarchy, and heredity, pressing questions
in the 1920s, more urgent than in the days when young Maud Montgomery
lived and wrote her journal in Cavendish. It answers those questions with
humour and drama, in the form of the most powerful of all her novels.

Her memory of early years had been refreshed recently. In 1919 she had
begun copying (and probably reconfiguring) the old rough entries into new
ledgers, partly as an escape from the pressures of her adult life, her husband's
first major episode of mania, the sudden death of her beloved friend and
cousin Frede, and the legal machinations of her Boston publisher Page. In
the early jottings about her life as an ambitious, thwarted but unusually
gifted child, Montgomery recognized the germ of a new kind of story. At
the moment she completed *Rilla of Ingleside* in 1920, she envisioned with
relief a series of books about a new heroine. "[S]he has been christened for
years. Her name is *Emily*. She has black hair and purplish gray eyes" (August
4, 1920). In December 1920 she wrote, "I have begun to collect material for
my 'Emily' books" (December 13, 1920).

Much of the material for the first book in the series came not from the
direct journal account written in the 1880s when Montgomery was not
much older than young Emily, but rather from the long diatribes written
later in adult moods of depression. In the journal entry for January 7, 1910,
for instance, she found one such bitter reminiscent passage, recalling (and
perhaps exaggerating) all the hurts of her childhood, the early pains and illnesses, the humiliation of being mocked by sarcastic teachers and an unrea-
sonable and irritable grandfather. Again, just after she finished writing the
ninth chapter of *Emily* she remembered a "long unthought-of happening":
her grandmother making her pray for forgiveness—a prayer that she uttered

"with a soul filled with humiliation, impotent anger, and a queer sense of degradation" (October 21, 1921). She could use this memory when she wrote about a little girl chilled by unkindness.

At the time of writing *Emily of New Moon*, Montgomery was not only reassessing her own childhood; she was also thinking about the general question of child-rearing, reading Freudian material in the popular press, and pondering the theories of neurotic repression. A small footnote: one of her son Stuart's strongest memories was of pushing flowers through the crack under the door of the parlour, shut against him for hours to ensure his mother's concentration on her writing.

Within the fictional world of *Emily of New Moon*, Montgomery presented adults who have the power of withholding love. The Murray clan disapproves of Emily and she is powerless to resist. Adults cruelly lay guilt on children when bad things happen: "That's what comes of bringing [Emily] here" is a commonly shared conclusion. Many of the forms of exerting authority over children are subtle; the abuse of adult power is more often psychological than physical. True, Aunt Elizabeth physically incarcerates Emily in a terrifying death-filled spare room (an echo of many readings of the second chapter of *Jane Eyre*, perhaps), but her more common weapon is ridicule and coldness. Similarly, Dr. Burnley, father of her friend Ilse, withholds his love with very damaging results. Sheer meanness makes Miss Brownell the teacher taunt Emily and then punish her for answering back; Lofty John is "just teasing" when he pretends Emily has eaten a poisoned apple; small-minded malice makes Aunt Ruth remind her of her mother's shameful elopement. Throughout the early part of the book Aunt Elizabeth piles indignity upon outrage.

Montgomery, however, will show a later Aunt Elizabeth mellowing, defending Emily from the other aunts and uncles, apologizing to her for reading the letters she has secretly written to her dead beloved father, and reacting with terror to Emily's delirious illness. Maybe Montgomery was making amends, revising memories of her own grandmother, admitting how much she owed her.[76] Emily, to exorcize early ill feelings against Aunt Elizabeth, adds childish footnotes recanting the harsh descriptions she has written in her secret letters. To exorcize Montgomery's own bitterness, the mature author softens the portrait of harshness she has painted.

In most of the novel, however, the chill of duty rather than the warmth of love marks misapplied adult power. "Doing your duty" is a phrase that recurs throughout the book from the moment Ellen Green freezes Emily with the news of her father's imminent death. Aunt Elizabeth does not shrink from doing her duty, or from reminding everyone that she has taken in an unwanted child. Miss Brownell "did her duty" in reporting Emily's rebellion. In this focus on the way a sense of duty reduces individual freedom, Montgomery is again adding to the mix of memories a more present anger. All too much of her own time in Leaskdale had been usurped by the call of duty to the church and the community. The frustration of the duty-ridden wartime years lingers, and is transferred to Emily's story.

Montgomery, however, has a novelist's sense of drama. She uses the theme of duty to carry off a surprising conclusion. Old Great-Aunt Nancy Priest out of a sense of duty sends for Emily, treats her well at Wyther Grange, and eventually says, "I feel I've done my duty by you for this year. Go back to New Moon." But there has been a dereliction of duty during the visit. Great-Aunt Nancy has gossiped in Emily's hearing, forgetting that it was her duty to protect the child from knowing the story of Ilse Burnley's mother. Beatrice Burnley was thought to have run away with a lover, abandoning her baby, forgetting her duties as wife and mother. Great-Aunt Nancy regrets her gossipy slip-up, but for Emily this story of sin brings a drastic fall from innocence. Very soon, wandering in despair, she literally falls from a steep cliff. She is rescued by Dean Priest, the strange cousin who lives at Priest's Pond. So a fine, unexpected climax follows, as Montgomery exploits the "duty theme."

As forceful as the invocation of duty in the inter-generational struggle is the power of opinion. "What will people say?" is a weapon wielded against Emily at her father's funeral; later it governs decisions on manners, dress, and general propriety. At school her fellow pupils mock her assertiveness. Propriety prohibits certain kinds of reading, not only novels, but certain kinds of non-fiction including Dr. Burnley's books on anatomy. "Little girls do not read books like that," says Aunt Elizabeth. Of course, people will say nothing if men use words that are not "ladylike." "Bull" is a sexually loaded word that women cannot use; "dod-gasted," the euphemistic oath of Lofty John, is also taboo for a girl. Society restricts acceptable language; the range of permissible language reflects a denial of sexuality: "It is improper to talk about having children."

Within the larger community, whether the fictional village of Blair or the real hamlet of Leaskdale, patriarchy imposes the power of men over women. Tradition declares that women must learn to sew a hem that can't be seen, and no one expects a woman to be rational: Dean Priest pronounces, "Like all female creatures, you form your opinions by your feelings."

The indignity of these patriarchal comments would be obvious to the reader of the early 1920s. Since the war, young women had been bobbing their hair, shortening their skirts, and applying for jobs as bank tellers and filing-clerks, not to mention assaulting the male bastions of law and medicine. Montgomery's responsibilities as a minister's wife in a small rural community gave her a particularly sharp sense of the continuing power of patriarchal pressures on wives to conform to expectations, and sharpened her imaginative resistance to that socialization.

Significantly, in *Emily of New Moon* it is a female figure who is the major supporter of patriarchal rules and boundaries. Aunt Elizabeth announces, as she tries to deny Emily the chance to go to high school, "I do not believe in girls going out into the world." Uncle Wallace counters, "Teaching is a genteel, lady-like occupation." His comment embodies the conventional male attitude to women; its force illuminates the overbearing power of male opinion over even so staunch a woman as Aunt Elizabeth.

Many of the scenes in *Emily of New Moon* focus on women's discreditable ways of gaining power. Rhoda Stuart, doll-like and smiling, offers Emily a snake in the box. Ilse Burnley is disruptive in her defiance of society, Aunt Nancy, cruel in her mockery of dependent Caroline. Teddy Kent's mother is neurotic in her possessive hold on her son. Forced into positions without real power, these women strike back in destructive ways.

In a male-dominated society, the only power a woman had was ultimately her physical presence. Women in *Emily of New Moon* are conditioned to see that their destiny depends on their ability to attract men. On her first day in school, Emily is asked, "Have you got a beau?" and told, "Everybody in our class has a beau." The dark side of this vision of a world in which women's only function is to be beautiful and attractive to men appears late in the novel. Great-Aunt Nancy Priest is presented as "yellow-skinned and wrinkled and shrunken . . . withered and shriveled," yet still concerned with memories of "beaus," still proud of a pretty hand, a slender ankle, still ready to discuss "come-hither eyes." The power of this emphasis results in a plot in which young Emily and her friends Ilse Burnley, Teddy Kent, and Perry Miller become involved in an early dance of attraction and rivalry. Montgomery recalled, and used in her fiction, her own insecurities as a child. She remembered the force of resistance to change and openness. She gives Emily a stronger self-assurance, partly because of her personal attractiveness.

Out of a sense of fairness, Montgomery also introduces in her novel many men willing to encourage Emily's ambition and to admire her writing: Cousin Jimmy, Father Cassidy, Jarback Priest, and Mr. Carpenter. Montgomery remembered supportive men like them in her own early life, such as Professor Anderson, back in her Charlottetown days. Her Canadian publisher "Mac" McClelland had backed her in her fight against L.C. Page, and her new confidant Edwin Smith had become "a companion of intellect and sympathy." Over the years, the two men who had been her faithful correspondents, Ephraim Weber and George Macmillan, had encouraged and praised her, and shared honestly in debates about authorship and about love and theology. She would dedicate this book to George Macmillan for his "long and stimulating friendship," whatever her dismayed awareness of the general power of patriarchy.

In *Emily of New Moon*, money has power that outweighs male preponderance. At school, Emily is welcomed by Rhoda Stuart. "Your Aunt Elizabeth will likely leave you all her money . . . so . . . I love you." Great-Aunt Nancy, the old crone of Wyther Grange, can make her clan dance at her will, because of the wealth and property she has at her disposal. Montgomery knew this kind of money-power well. She had always kept scrupulous score of her earnings, and now they were large enough to support her family in a style beyond the reach of a minister's salary, a situation that may well have exacerbated Ewan's depressions. With two sons reaching the age where she felt she should send them away to a good boarding-school,[77] Montgomery was becoming more than ever absorbed in the race for money. Her profession was one of the very few in which women were well enough rewarded, relative to men.

In the more revered field of theology, there was no such inversion of the hierarchy. Patriarchy in Emily's world is based on the Presbyterian belief in an all-powerful, austere, father-god. Reverend Mr. Dare is daring indeed when he tells Emily that God inheres in everything beautiful. His congregation would not agree: Presbyterian theology premised that beauty is a snare and a temptation. Community force is used to discredit imagination, nonconformity, art and poetry. "Don't you know that it is wicked to write novels?" Aunt Elizabeth asks, continuing the Puritan attack on human creativity that once led to Emily's burning of her first book. Young Teddy Kent suffers equally for his gift of painting, and cousin Jimmy's poetic gift confirms the community's assumption that he is "not right in the head." On this point, an unorthodox position could be safely, and subtly, proffered by Father Cassidy. The priest who welcomes Emily ("And a very nice little Protestant you are") praises her beauty and encourages her creativity. Montgomery trims the whimsical Roman Catholic priest's influence, however, by giving him a bit of a comic Irish brogue.

In real life, Montgomery got no obvious support from the principal theologian in her life—her husband. While she was writing *Emily of New Moon* she unleashed in her journal a list of the things about the church and about Christianity itself that appalled and infuriated her (October 21, 1921). She contradicted the Presbyterian catechism that Stuart was learning and substituted her own unorthodox notion of God. Her God was somewhat like herself: he created all things not "for his own glory" but "for the love and pleasure of creating them—of doing good work—of bringing beauty into existence" (October 21, 1921). She could not openly question orthodox positions, except in a novel.

"I won't be prayed for!" says Ilse, perhaps voicing the resentment of the much-prayed-for minister's wife. Emily voices heterodox ideas in a more romantic way, repeating what Ellen calls "your father's awful notions." That unworldly artistic father had warned his little daughter against Ellen's (Presbyterian) God. He argues "God is Love itself" but when her father dies, Emily declares, "I don't like God any more." Early in the story she hears of Dr. Alan Burnley, who "doesn't believe in God. . . . Not in any God."

But Montgomery was not an iconoclast. Late in the novel, Emily unearths the true story of Dr. Burnley's lost wife—not lost in adultery, not abandoning her motherly duty, but accidentally fallen to her death in a deep well. After this revelation Dr. Burnley recants, goes to church every Sunday, and the village gets used to seeing him in the old Burnley pew. The minister's wife in Norval performed the same ritual of appearing in church even on the Sundays when her husband was too filled with the terrors of predestination to get up into the pulpit and preach.

The church preached against pride, but family pride was a source of power in fiction and in fact. Montgomery gives to Emily many of her own certainties as well as her doubts. Pride in heritage is one. The New Moon Murray family is reduced to two old maids and their lovable but ineffectual brother. Yet family pride persists, as a weapon against the rest of the world. "'She is not a Murray, that is plain to be seen'" is Aunt Elizabeth's first reaction to Emily. In the face of Murray pride, Emily is bolstered by memories of her gentle nonconformist father. Yet she is indeed a Murray, and even Aunt Elizabeth cannot stand up against the "Murray look" levelled against her by Emily Starr. Cousin Jimmy early recounts all the family history, and the local community watches to see what qualities of the Starrs and the Byrds will manifest themselves in Emily. Conversely, the village assumes that someone like Perry Miller will never amount to anything, because of his lower-class family background.

As a child, Montgomery had lived in a society with a similar set of attitudes. Although most Canadians officially scorned snobbery, her family took pride in being set above others. The Macneill pride was proverbial and the Montgomery family had boasted its connections with the Scottish Earl of Eglinton, and Maud's grandfather Montgomery had been a member of the Canadian Senate in Ottawa. But the war had swept away some of the snobberies of earlier colonialism. Furthermore, an Ontario society had no memories of Montgomery or Macneill glory to match the respect common in Prince Edward Island. Now, in Leaskdale, she was torn by the contradiction between her sense of her worth as a member of two proud families and the attitudes of her present world.

With her wonderful sense of humour, Montgomery could turn family pride into a matter of comedy. Even the conundrum of heritage could be dissolved by laughter, at least in fiction. When Emily's newly acquainted aunts and uncles consider which members of the family she looks like, Emily bursts out indignantly. The Murrays are shocked into silence; but

Cousin Jimmy laughs "a low chuckle, full of mirth and free from malice." That kind of chuckle is waiting again when Great-Aunt Nancy Priest takes up the catalogue of features, "There's something of your grandfather Murray about your eyebrows. . . . " To Jarback Priest Emily summarizes the catalogue, "I've got Father's forehead and Grandma Starr's hair and eyes, and Great-Uncle George's nose, and Aunt Nancy's hands, and Cousin Susan's elbows, and Great-great Grandmother Murray's ankles, and Grandfather Murray's eyebrows." Emily's response to such catalogues is, "I don't like to be told I look like other people. I look just like myself."

Emily, in fact looks just like Maud Montgomery in many ways other than family heritage and personal independence. Both scrambled to find paper and a place to write. Each of them lacked models to follow, as well as living (or near-by) parents to foster their talents. In both cases there was no memory of a nurturing mother; in both, although a father was alive during the child's first phase, the emotional core was a feeling of orphanhood, a sense of being unimportant and unwanted. While writing about Emily, Montgomery confided poignantly to her diary how much she regretted knowing so little about her mother, "gay, lively, mischievous, . . . 'fey' . . . delicate." One of the moments when Emily experiences her "flash" comes when she takes possession of her mother's old room. Her sense of its consecration draws one of Aunt Elizabeth's most cruel comments: "Your mother . . . ran away—flouted her family and broke her father's heart. She was a silly, ungrateful, disobedient girl." Perhaps there is an echo here of the Macneills' criticisms of Maud's mother, long-dead Clara, for her choice of Hugh John Montgomery, older, and not very successful. Expanding Emily's story, Montgomery probed deeply into the secrets of her life. So doing, she created a recognizable girl with widely-shared family and societal problems.

Emily shares with Montgomery, however, one highly uncommon experience. Montgomery calls it "the flash." The word recalls William Wordsworth's poem, "The Daffodils." The movements of once-seen flowers in that poem "flash across the inward eye/Which is the bliss of solitude."[78] Emily's experience is initially not reflective, like Wordsworth's, not something that happens when a sensual experience is recalled later. Emily's "flash" is a sudden heightening of the senses in the presence of nature. In a "glorious, supreme moment" she catches a glimpse of a realm beyond the natural world. She is intensely stirred by something physical, "the dark branch boughs against the far-off sky, a high wild note of wind in the night, a shadow wave over a ripe field, a greybird lighting on a windowsill," or a hymn sung in church, or firelight in the kitchen. Her "flash" represents an excess of consciousness, a radiant surge of response to stimulus.

The flash is sometimes but not always connected with the urge to write. It can come with the recognition of a felicitous word. Many times, of course,

Emily writes without experiencing the flash. Conversely, it may come when she is not writing, though there is still a connection with creation. In the chapter "Trial by Fire," Emily is asked by the hostile girls at school if she can sing and dance, sew, cook, knit lace, or crochet, to which she answers "No." When taunted with "Then what can you do?" she answers, "I can write poetry." She hasn't meant to say this, but as soon as she does, the "flash" comes: "Right there, surrounded by hostility and suspicion, fighting alone for her standing, without backing or advantage, came the wonderful moment when soul seemed to cast aside the bonds of flesh and spring upward to the stars. The rapture and delight on Emily's face amazed and enraged her foes."

Montgomery is very careful to catch the exact nature of this intense moment. It was an experience she knew and treasured. George Bernard Shaw saw it as "the true joy of life, the being used for a purpose recognized by yourself as a mighty one." Another of Montgomery's contemporary writers wrote of human ability to experience "near bliss when we are in the throes of creation . . . a baby making a mud-pie, . . . or Gibbon writing the last words in his History . . . more for the sake of the thing itself than for applause and profit."[79] Psychiatrists offer a colder scientific explanation of such an experience. Montgomery, like many creative people, moved into a "hypomanic" phase when she began composing, an elevated, grandiose sense of racing thoughts. In this intense mood a veil seemed to lift between her and another world.

Emily of New Moon offers a precise description of the flash, and a recognition of the linked moment when super-sensory intensity leads to writing. This account has been of supreme interest to later writers. Many testify that this account gave them essential reassurance and encouragement. Canadian authors who have acknowledged the way this book ratified their own early sense of power include Jane Urquhart and Alice Munro.[80]

For readers without that gift, the novel has the typical Montgomery panoply of other charms: humour, drama, perception, surprise, a sense of natural beauty, and of family and community life. The settings are haunting: the little brown mushroom of a house where Emily lives at first with her father and the Wind Woman; New Moon itself, no mushroom growth but "a big white house peering whitely through a veil of trees;" the clapboarded Tansy Patch, the Disappointed House, Wyther Grange with the "chessy-cat knocker" on its parlour door; the bayshore cliff, where Emily reaches for a "farewell-summer" and feels the earth give way beneath her feet; the mossy narrow ledge from which she looks at "the boulder-strewn shore thirty feet below."

Emily of New Moon, finally, has the power of strangeness, the mystery of the "flash" reinforced by another paranormal element—Emily's experience of second sight. She has been obsessed with the mystery surrounding the disappearance of Ilse Burnley's mother. In a delirium brought on by near-death sickness, Emily envisions the truth and leads to the re-opening of an old well. Beatrice Burnley's body is discovered there, and her innocence is proven. Emily has no memory of that "fey" vision, but her value in the community is elevated by this mysterious power. No part of this story of the finding of Mrs. Burnley's body has any direct source in the journals, yet it seems connected with Montgomery's recurrent experience of intensely vivid dreams, which she believed were prophetic. The psychic experience is carefully discriminated, both in the journal and in the novel, from the creative "flash."

The story of Ilse's mother also carries allusions to adultery that mark Montgomery's exposure to the new frankness—critics called it "muckraking"—of novelists who were her new contemporaries, such as May Sinclair of England, and Sinclair Lewis of the United States. In recording her reading during the time she mentions May Sinclair's two bestselling novels, dismissing *Mary Olivier* (1919), but nevertheless going on to read *The Romantic* (1920). Both were sensationally frank. *The Romantic* begins with a monologue by a woman whose lover has just ended their adulterous relationship. Montgomery sandwiched these Sinclair books along with a book about cats called *The Tiger in the House* (1920) among her books by old favourites, the Brontës, Dickens, Hugo, Sarah Orne Jewett, and Mark Twain, all within six months. Once again she had fed her own imagination by gorging on the work of others.

Refreshed, aroused, amused, Montgomery the author—known to her community as Mrs. Ewan Macdonald—could shut herself into the parlour in the Leaskdale manse and close the door. As memories flash across "that inward eye," they shift into a new image. . . . A little girl, whose purplish-gray eyes turn black as she prowls in confusion along the bay shore, reaches for a vivid flower—an aster; no, call it a Michaelmas daisy—and the earth beneath her feet gives way. Emily looks down in terror at the dark boulder-strewn sands, thirty feet below.

Montgomery is on the Island—in her island, in the "bliss of solitude." Her fountain pen drives across the page, stops, crosses out a colourless phrase, pounces on a felicitous word. Not an aster or a Michaelmas daisy: no, she substitutes "a farewell-summer." Her heart "with pleasure fills, and dances. . . ."

Emily Climbs

(Toronto: McClelland & Stewart, 1925)

*E*mily Climbs seems farther from Montgomery's own life than the other two books in the Emily series. *Emily of New Moon* had been very closely tied to Montgomery's childhood, as recorded in a series of long reminiscent passages in her journals. In *Emily's Quest*, the last in the series, Montgomery's would draw closely on her own experiences as an apprentice writer, and would also echo the series of emotional entanglements that disturbed her as a young woman. In contrast, *Emily Climbs* bears little obvious resemblance to Montgomery's life in her adolescent years. *Emily Climbs* records life in a high school rather than (as in Montgomery's case) a period of study at an urban college. When, in *Emily Climbs*, an admiring writer offers young Emily a job in New York, the novel has clearly moved far from the story of Montgomery's life as she "climbed the Alpine Path" in Prince Albert, Saskatchewan.

Yet parallels exist, not to the surface of Montgomery's life, but to the psychological truth of her development. One way to perceive some of the deeper layers of meaning and feeling in a book is to listen to the sounds of names, and to watch the recurring shapes of things. The poet James Reaney called this level in any art "Babble and Doodle," the apparently meaningless sound of words, and the apparently meaningless shapes drawn without control. Turning off the rational mind and reading the names in an *Emily* book as a kind of babble, or looking at its recurring patterns, regarding shapes and forms and directional signals as revelatory doodle brings a new experiencing of the book and of Montgomery's state of mind in 1922, as author of *Emily Climbs*.

The first kind of babble inheres in names. Names of people and places taken merely as sounds, or as echoes of other names, trigger involuntary responses. Some names trail with them meanings established in the first volume of Emily's story. Emily's first name still appropriately echoes that of Emily Brontë, one of Montgomery's favourite authors, epitome of wild genius. There is pathos in the name too. Little Em'ly, charming in childhood, tragic in love, lingered from memories of Charles Dickens's *David Copperfield* (1850). This book is mentioned in Emily's journal, as it had been in Montgomery's, and Dickens was cited in Montgomery's list of favourite novelists, second only to Scott. Emily Dickinson comes to mind, too. Near the time of writing *Emily Climbs*, Montgomery quoted Dickinson as a poet of bitter honesty (January 23, 1923). But the name also brings a memory of Montgomery's Aunt Emily, a young woman when baby Maud came into the Macneill house, and later the wife of Uncle John Montgomery in Malpeque, to the west of Cavendish. That Emily could be critical, with more than a little of the Macneill sharpness in tongue. The fictional Emily will not be all pure poetic spirit; she will share that tartness. Finally of course, "Em," or "M" is a significant initial for Maud Montgomery Macdonald herself.

Emily's other names are ambivalent. "Byrd," her grandmother's maiden name, suggests the "gift of wings" that Emily will share with her creator, but also carries an implication of vulnerability. "Starr," her father's surname, suggests brilliance and light, but it is a brilliance of the night, of distance from the ordinary daylight world.

Names of other characters, familiar from *Emily of New Moon*, are almost obtrusively suggestive. "Mr. Carpenter" still acts as builder of Emily's intellectual development. Dean Priest's doubly ecclesiastic name suggests male authority, academic and theological. Old Kelly, like an antique soothsayer, warns against marrying "a Praste," a warning perhaps drawn from Montgomery's own experiences with Ed Simpson, John Mustard, John Sterling, and Ewan Macdonald.

"Teddy Kent's" first name was Jo March's nickname for Edward Lawrence, the boy next door who longs to be part of the *Little Women* circle. At the time of writing, "Kent" probably drew on the image of the young Duke of Kent, handsomest and most popular of the royal British princes in the 1920s. "Perry" is a variant of Peter, the name of the other attractive but scorned hired boy in *The Story Girl* and *The Golden Road*. This hired boy's last name is "Miller." The miller is part of a farming community, a hard worker. The mills of the gods grind slowly, and Perry Miller will rise in the world. He seems to draw something from Montgomery's memories of Herman Leard, suggesting the perilous possibility, and the ultimate value, of settling for an imperfect farm lad.

"Ilse's" name sounds like "Ipse," the Freudian other self. Montgomery was well steeped in the current and hotly debated theories of Freud. The name also sounds like "or else," another suggestion that she is the other self of Emily and Montgomery. Ilse's surname carries other appropriate suggestions: Ilse "Burnley" burns with ferocious energy.

Most of the action in *Emily Climbs* takes place in "Shrewsbury," where shrewish older women watch and criticize the teen-aged writer. While attending a big High School, with its assemblies and stiff regulations, she boards with her Aunt Ruth Dutton, who buttons her into formal propriety. Emily's school life bears no trace of Montgomery's short, exotic, free-wheeling sojourn out west in Prince Albert, Saskatchewan, where her school was a in a hotel that also housed a dance hall, a Free Mason's Club room, and a jail, where drunks could be stashed in a row of cells located behind the schoolroom. Maud's classmates included three girls and eight boys, the sons and daughters of ranchers, trappers, and Mounted Policemen. Perhaps memories of her step-mother's hostility colour the portrait of Emily's ruthless Aunt Ruth.

Emily is denied a chance to go on to "Queen's," the Charlottetown college featured in *Anne of Green Gables*. "Queen's" was the interestingly feminine name substituted for the real, masculine name of Montgomery's academy: Prince of Wales College. Montgomery—and Anne—found friendships, the admiration of classmates, and the encouragement of professors at the post-secondary college. For Emily, family and money dictate that there will be no study at Queen's. Emily does not experience the benign influence, the royal femininity of Queen's. The portrait in Aunt Ruth's house of Queen Alexandra becomes a focus for her hatred of Shrewsbury.

Like Anne and like Montgomery, Emily remains addicted to writing in spite of Shrewsbury. From this second book the darkening force of Miss Brownell is absent, but "brown" turns to "black" in a new enmity. At Shrewsbury, hated Miss Brownell has a niece. "Evelyn Blake," evil and black-hearted, an enemy at sight, a rival in school, turns out to be a trickster, a plagiarist, and a cheat.

Other new names appear in *Emily Climbs*, sometimes with a strange foreshadowing of Montgomery's later work. An early reference to "old Sarah Paul" at whose funeral all her relations speculate about what they will get from her will, suggests the plot of *A Tangled Web*, where the name "Paul" will expand to "Penhallow." Mrs. Peter DeGeer demands an obituary poem for her husband, foreshadowing an incident in *Anne of Ingleside* and mingled there with the story of another loathsome Peter. "Jason Merrowby" is a merry old boy who sneaks a swig of whiskey while sawing wood, not unlike Abel Gay in *The Blue Castle*. The name of "Miss Royal," the successful novelist, trails meaning from *Anne of the Island*. In that novel, Royal Gardner offered a spurious charm and an apparently glamorous future on the mainland. Similarly, Miss Royal seems to offer fame and fortune, but only if Emily agrees to leave the Island. Emily rejects the beguiling royal offer.

Turning from "babbles" to "doodles," readers should consider the patterned drawings of an abstracted moment, a moment of free-wheeling imagination, externalized in lines not controlled by the rational mind. Most of Montgomery's novels, like any complicated artwork, include unintentionally significant motifs. One recurring "doodle" in *Emily of New Moon* is the recurring image of entrapment. Emily is trapped in an empty church. Later she is trapped in a boot closet. A little lost boy is trapped in a closet inside an empty house. Still later in the story, a snow storm traps Emily and her friends into spending an unchaperoned night in a deserted house. Each time, suggestive details illuminate hidden meanings.

Emily is trapped in the church because of her dangerous writing. She has gone back to pick up a scrap of paper filled with mockery of the minister (Mr. Sampson, a tower of false strength) and of a choir member (Miss Potter). The menace in the church comes from a madman, hunting for his dead wife, accompanied by his "demon hound." Mad Mr. Morrison, searching for his long-dead wife, tries to catch Emily. To a modern ear this sounds like child molesting. Placing this frightening incident in a church may imply Montgomery's reaction against an oppressive, patriarchal, degrading religion that seems to repress female creativity and ambition. Emily is rescued from the church by Teddy. He comes in response to her psychic cry to him, carried across a distance of a mile.

This coheres with another recurring pattern, in which Emily is saved by male admirers. In *Emily of New Moon*, she owed a first debt for her life to healthy young Perry when he saved her from a bull. Dean Priest has saved her from a deathly fall over a cliff, in a situation connected to her horror at the thought that Ilse's mother "fell," losing her reputation for virtue. Now Teddy, saving her from a madman's passion, will also have a psychic claim on her.

Returning to entrapment, Montgomery shows Emily hiding from neighbours because of vanity: she is wearing an unbecoming "Mother Hubbard" smock. Two women, "scrawny Miss Potter," the choir member, and Mrs. Ann Cyrilla—how much that sounds like "Anne Shirley!"—provide the menace this time, the menace of mockery, deflation, and pity. Emily rescues herself by bursting out of the boot closet. She has been trapped this time by the convention of female beauty. In domestic scenes, women self-decorate. Later, when Evelyn Blake adds a moustache to Emily's sleeping face, her horror attests to her entrapment by the conventions of female attractiveness.

The next example of entrapment and release is more complicated. Emily has spent an exhilarating night outdoors, sleeping on a haystack with Ilse. Next morning she sees and is possessed by the sight of a small brown-shingled house with beautiful casement windows, one of them set above the door under the eaves, "glowing like a jewel . . . out of the dark shingle setting." She and Ilse move on toward another house, white as marble, set against an emerald hill, and under a black sky. Here they hear of a lost child, mourned by three women, a stricken screaming mother, a talkative neighbour, and a grandmother, incapable of mourning but prepared to tell her one and only story over and over. This old woman, Old Mistress McIntyre, recognizes that Emily has the gift of "second sight." In the night, Emily's gift produces a drawing of the little house where the lost child is trapped, shut in an upstairs closet where the walls are now all scratched where he tried to get out. The little boy was locked in, behind the jewelled casement window.

In the fourth case, being caught in an empty house with Perry and Teddy brings added terrors for the two girls. Ilse becomes drunk on a medicinal dose of whiskey, and Emily is intoxicated first by the nearness of Teddy, and then by the sudden exhilaration of thinking out a full-length story about dreams. The sexual overtone in this particular story of entrapment is unlike anything Montgomery had attempted in her earlier work. She had recently been released from some inhibitions partly by the spirit of the jazz age of flappers, short skirts, "boyish-bob" hair, and cocktails. This new power to face the full range of sexual freedom had also come into her life with the new friendship of a sophisticated and articulate friend. In February 1922, when Ewan was away, Captain Edwin Smith came to Leaskdale to preach in his place. She wrote:

> It is such a delight to have a real conversation with a companion of intellect and sympathy. Captain Smith is one of the few people I have met with whom I can discuss with absolute frankness, any and every subject, even the delicate ones of sex. Sex is to men and women one of the most vital subjects in the world—perhaps *the* most vital subject since our total existence is based on and centres around it. Yet with how few, even of women, can this vital subject be frankly and intelligently discussed. It is so overlaid with conventions, inhibitions, and taboos that it is almost impossible for anyone to see it as it really is. (February 28, 1922)

Montgomery, like many people in the 1920s, felt stimulated by the influence of the Freudian theories of which she had been reading. She felt herself freed by the new concepts from the conventional silence she had long been locked into. Some of that delight spills over into the "naughtiness" of *Emily Climbs*.

Opposite to "locked-in" is "locked-out." Emily is "bean-balled" to keep her out of the Skulls and Owls society. More dramatically, she is locked out of the Shrewsbury house by Aunt Ruth because she has taken part in a play. Later, when Perry kisses her, he is forced to scramble out of the window, which is shut behind him.

Another set of recurring motifs concerns eaves-dropping, spying, and gossip. Emily, trapped in her boot closet, overhears malicious neighbours, with humiliating results. She in turn is overheard, watched, spied on. Her moonlit petticoat swim with Ilse is noted, reported on as impropriety—"without a stitch on!" She overhears Aunt Ruth's criticisms of her slyness, and of her "making eyes." Aunt Ruth accepts a false story that is "all over town" about Emily on the main street, "with a man's arms around you, kissing him." Aunt Ruth jumps to a scandalous conclusion when she finds Emily and Perry in a compromising situation. All these incidents create the sense of a Puritan community, repressive, prying, over-concerned with propriety.

Sometimes eavesdropping is good, however. Emily overhears Aunt Ruth saying something about her to Mrs. Ince (a "nice" anagram): unexpectedly nice things about her, her mother, and her father. Cousin Jimmy also fortunately eavesdrops when Aunt Elizabeth, promising Emily the chance of attending high school, attaches the unacceptable condition that Emily give up writing. Jimmy, having listened in, can suggest a compromise: give up writing fiction, but go on with poetry and essays.

Ilse's anti-social trick of telling the story of her drunkenness rouses the worst round of scandalous gossip. Emily's Aunt Ruth quells the storm by exploiting the Murrays' social position, and by remembering all the old scandals that could be attached to the local gossips who are damaging Ilse's name. This defence is reminiscent of Montgomery's experience years earlier, when her Aunt Annie Campbell defended her against the critical others in her extended family. The accusation then was that young Maud was "a flirt," over-interested in boys.

Many undercurrents in *Emily of New Moon* suggest a similar uneasiness about burgeoning sexuality. Mad Mr. Morrison, searching for his dead wife, leads into the moment when Teddy notes Emily's "fringed, mysterious eyes and the little dark love-curls clinging to her ivory neck." This erotic moment is interrupted by his neurotically jealous mother. Another hint of sexuality involves Dean Priest noting "how perfect the white line of her throat—how kissable the sweet red curve of her mouth." Later he will continue, "Your skin is like a narcissus petal." In return, when the four young people are marooned in the old John house, Emily is thrilled with awareness of Teddy's "tall, boyish straightness, his glossy black hair, his luminous dark-blue eyes," aware too of "that wave of unimaginable sweetness that seemed to engulf her, body and spirit," a "fetter of terrible delight that so suddenly and inexplicably made her a prisoner." This erotic spell is quickly succeeded by a desire to write out a story. Everyone blames Emily's brushes with sexuality on her inheritance, the fact that her mother Juliet eloped. Perhaps this reflects Montgomery's own disturbance about the loss of her mother. Perhaps, on the other hand, it comes from the worry that as Chester's mother she will be blamed for her son's increasingly troublesome behaviour. A good deal of the plot of this novel revolves around that terrifying question, "What will people think?"

Besides recalling that past terror of gossip, *Emily Climbs* also invokes a current trouble in Montgomery's life. It was written at a time when Montgomery was terrified of the possibility of finding herself the object of local spying, because of her knowledge that the young woman who was the current maid at the manse was an inveterate gossip. She knew that her growing friendship with Ewan's old classmate Edwin Smith was likely to set tongues wagging.[81] She dreaded the false interpretation that could be put on her friendship, knowing the small-minded prejudices that people were prey to. Montgomery felt herself set apart from the pettiness of the parish gossips by her own background.

A similar assumption of class differences appears in the novel. The Murrays' social status means that the Murray name carries over from Blair Water to Shrewsbury, and to distant Malvern Hills. The other side of this status is the snobbery that despises Perry Miller for his Stovepipe Town origins. Even Emily is contaminated. When Perry goes to dine at the grand house of Dr. Hardy, Emily is horrified at his social gaffes.[82] Ilse's snobbery, displayed in her fury at Perry's ambition, is complex; Aunt Ruth's is a simpler snobbery. Her exploitation of the Murrays' superiority can however help Emily out of the social difficulties consequent on Shrewsbury gossip.

Finally, the story returns to the "locked-in" motif. Emily has a chance to go to New York with Miss Royal, to a guaranteed successful career as a sophisticated writer. Instead, she stands under the stars at New Moon and decides to tie herself to her own homeland. Janet Royal is an example of what Emily (or even Montgomery herself) could become, an eccentric success, perhaps like her acquaintance and literary rival Marshall Saunders, or Montgomery's first literary pen-pal Miss Zieber, or her long-time friend Marjory MacMurchy.

Emily's rejection of Miss Royal's offer reveals a puzzle of motivation in Montgomery, an emerging uncertainty about the dream of literary success. As a very young writer, Montgomery had believed, and made her readers believe, in the success of a "Story Girl." In both novels about Sara Stanley, the gifted story-teller is acclaimed by her contemporaries and by the adult world too. Maybe this reflected Montgomery's early pleasure in the fuss that was made about her, when she so early published poetry and stories. Maybe it just revealed the naïveté of a young achiever, thinking all will always go easily for a gifted woman who dreams of success as a writer.

How different is the view in Emily! In this late vision of what it is to be a talented artistic girl, obstacles will arise much greater than those faced in *The Story Girl*, such as Felicity's jealousy or Dan's stolidity. The portrait of Miss Royal suggests that there is something unfeminine, something unsatisfied, in success for an unmarried woman. So Emily rejects what modern feminists might see as a proper journey, made under the guidance of an older woman, to a country of liberated desire and female authenticity. As Marie Campbell says, "Emily receives the message that she cannot be an artist, creator, from a myriad of sources in her patriarchal society. Yet nowhere is the silencing of the female voice more effectively accomplished than when these messages are internalized."[83]

Locked into her own star, however, in rejecting Miss Royal's offer, Emily proceeds to lock herself away from the easy acceptance of the conventional fate for a young woman. She turns down her cousin Andrew Murray, and all her clan's hopes of roping her into family traditions. Then she laughingly turns down Perry Miller, with his promise of professional success and wealth in Charlottetown. No need to turn down Teddy. He is so absorbed in his own hope of success that he doesn't ask her, an outcome that finally brings her a great sense of relief and freedom. The Shrewsbury years are over; she returns to being "Emily of New Moon."

All these babbles and doodles both reinforce and undercut the surface meaning by oblique techniques of connotation and metaphor. These devices suggest the ambivalence of the author's concepts of womanhood, artistic calling, the force of sexual attraction, and the stabilizing force of an established social system. *Emily of New Moon* adds a further complexity through the use of an imagined diary, based largely, but not entirely, on Montgomery's own journals. Emily's diary, begun when she is thirteen as replacement for letters to her dead father, can be read intertextually with Montgomery's diary, begun at the age of fourteen, at the time of her father's re-marriage. Points of psychological comparison emerge. Both reveal mood swings between warmth with friends and the cooler pleasures of solitude; between high aspiration and hope, guilt and shame. The same concern with style emerges, the same concern with class, the same stated preference for the rose garden rather than the pig sty.

The constant literary allusions emphasize Emily's similarity to her creator in tastes and influences. Emily's journal, like Montgomery's, mentions Scott's poems, Viking sagas, Emerson's essays, Tennyson, Irving's *Tales of the Alhambra* (1832); George Macdonald's *At the Back of the North Wind* (1871), Byron, Macaulay, Dickens's *David Copperfield* (1850), Mrs. Browning, Mrs. Hemans, the historical works of Francis Parkman, and Bliss Carman's poetry.

In a final puzzling complexity, Montgomery acts not only as source, but also as interpreter of Emily. As an intrusive narrator, she discusses the shape of this book and the meaning of Emily's choices. After a slow start when Emily meanders through discussions of her life and hopes in self-conscious diary entries, the second chapter breaks into an odd and awkward intrusion, which seems to scorn the work the author has been doing so far:

> This book is not going to be wholly, or even mainly, made up of extracts from Emily's diary; but, by way of linking up matters unimportant enough for a chapter in themselves, and yet necessary for a proper understanding of her personality and environment, I am going to include some more of them. Besides, when one has material ready to hand, why not use it?

An odd comment, apparently showing fatigue, or disinterest. Other intrusive authorial comments often contravene the indirect positions established by allusions, connotations, and recurring motifs. The narrator criticizes Emily for deeds which all the sub-texts support as valuable. She praises her for a conformity that the whole tenor of the book derides, and explains in simple terms deeds that a build-up of allusions have presented as inexplicable. Yet the intrusions, awkward as they are, serve to remind the reader of the fact of creation, and to keep the author in mind as part of the overall focus on writing. The object of the book, after all, is to explore a creative talent in its chrysalis stage. The stylistic device of authorial comment keeps this objective in focus, even when the story veers away into an opposite interest: the depiction of youthful sexuality braided into Emily's character along with her literary aspirations.

Montgomery said that Emily was the most like herself of all the characters in the fiction. Later writers have found in Emily a model of a young woman as apprentice writer, a portrait of the artist as a young woman, fit to inspire and encourage other young women aware of their own interest in authorship. But Emily as she "climbs" is in fact less like Montgomery as author, more like Montgomery as woman. She is a study of a young person moving into sexuality while opposing the force of a gossiping, unsympathetic community. Unlike *Anne of Avonlea*, where Anne becomes thoroughly absorbed into the community, *Emily Climbs* features a young woman alienated by gossip and meanness. The most significant change of Montgomery's direction appears in this novel, as compared to *Rilla of Ingleside*, in the emphasis on a sexual awakening. When she was writing *Emily Climbs*, Montgomery was on her way to a study not just of conventional romance, but of sexual passion. She reveals in this second Emily book how much she is changing and developing as she moves toward the magic of her own "Blue Castle."

The Blue Castle

(Toronto: McClelland & Stewart, 1926)

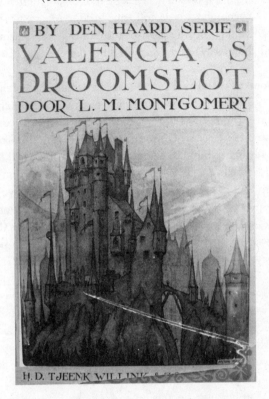

BY DEN HAARD SERIE
VALENCIA'S
DROOMSLOT
DOOR L. M. MONTGOMERY

H. D. TJEENK WILLINK

The Blue Castle is about a different island, not Prince Edward Island, but Mistawis. The name "babbles" of mist and awe, and—whisper? wish? wistful? It is the island of dreams and love, found late.

In a 1922 journal entry, Montgomery reported seeing an island, a miniature version of the place that she always held in her mind as *the* Island. That summer, her family had foregone traveling to the old, beloved Island for their annual summer holiday because of the pressure of legal problems. Added to her lawsuits against exploitative publisher Page in Boston was the more locally humiliating new suit brought in Toronto by Marshall Pickering, a Methodist who lived in Zephyr (where the Presbyterian church was part of Ewan Macdonald's charge, along with Leaskdale). Instead of taking the train to Prince Edward Island, she drove with husband Ewan and little sons Chester and Stuart northward from Leaskdale into the Muskoka district, cottage country for thousands of Ontarians.

Here, away from the frets and restrictions of life as a village minister's wife (always under the eyes of parishioners, not to speak of the domestic sur-veillance of the maid at the manse), freed suddenly from domestic duties, relieved at last from the constant needs of very small children (for now her boys were old enough to go off on little trips with their father), Montgomery could sit on the lawn of a summer hotel. Gazing at a misty island just off shore, she could dream of a life there.

> I picked out an island that just suited me. I built thereon a summer cottage. . . . I peopled it with summer guests—Frede, Aunt Annie, Stella, Bertie [Bertie McIntyre, the dear Charlottetown cousin who had recently resurfaced in Toronto], Mr. MacMillan [the Scottish pen pal seen only once, during the honeymoon visit to Berwick] (to whom I engaged Bertie!). . . . [W]e swam and sailed and fished and read and built camp fires . . . and always we talked—the soul-satisfying talk of kindred spirits, asking all the old, unanswered questions. . . . Sometimes we varied it by going out to dinners and dances (for in my dream Ewan was *not* a minister!) . . . but always glad to skim back home . . . to our own dear bit of an island. (July 31, 1922)

A day of dreaming, and the germ of her next novel was established.

Almost two years would pass before Montgomery recorded another dream—a sleeping dream this time, of the kind she always took very seri-ously, since she believed they presaged some change in her life. In March 1924, she recorded dreaming that she encountered her long-dead mother, who turned out (in the dream) to be not dead, but dying. This dream marked a shift in her own depression and a determination to try her hand at adult fiction. Within a few days she entered the first reference to a new story. *The Blue Castle* would be the story of a youngish woman who, through facing the thought of death, escapes a dreadful, binding life and finds an island of her own. There the old bitter life will indeed die, and Valancy Stirling will revel in the "soul-satisfying talk of kindred spirits" of the Muskoka daydream.

But *The Blue Castle* is a remarkably bi-polar book. It begins not poeti-cally on a misty Island but realistically, in the family circle of the awful Stirlings. At twenty-nine, unmarried (read "old maid") Valancy, "cowed and subdued and overridden and snubbed," lives with a mother prey to "sulky fits," and with a whiney elderly cousin named Stickles. She is belit-tled by her successful clan: three aunts, four uncles, plus cousins—not jolly ones like the Park Corner Campbell crew, Clara, Stella, George, and Frede, and not like the imaginary King cousins and aunts and uncles in *Story Girl*. In the *Emily* books Montgomery had recreated the aunts and uncles of her own youth as circling around a defenceless girl—defenceless except for her ability to imagine, and her gift of words. Valancy Stirling has no such gift; she is doubly defenceless because she also lacks Emily's spunk, her dark colourful beauty, and her memory of a loving father. Valancy is nicknamed "Doss." She is assumed to be dross, and docile.

Valancy's true name signals Montgomery's knowledge of a real-life spinster repressed by society. Isabella Valancy Crawford, creator of passionate poetry, had been doomed in the 1880s to support her mother and sister by hack work for Toronto papers.[84] Montgomery had made this late-Victorian poet the subject of talks to the Uxbridge literary "Hypatia Club." Along with other members of the Canadian Authors Association, Montgomery mourned the loss to Canadian literature from the early death in poverty of this virtuoso poet, victim of a patriarchal unreadiness to acknowledge genius in an unmarried woman. But although, like Isabella Valancy Crawford, Valancy Stirling is valiant, she has no literary ambition. Unlike Crawford and Montgomery, Valancy does not escape from an ugly and frustrating life by writing books. Instead she reads, escaping into a dream of wild places through the preachings on nature and freedom found in books by her favourite author, "John Foster."

Valancy's addiction to reading echoes Montgomery's own. In 1903 she had written, "My only guard against misanthropy this past week has been the re-reading of four old favourite books." When *The Blue Castle* was shaping itself, Montgomery immersed herself in a wide range of books, reading fiction and non-fiction with the kind of absorption she imputed to Valancy. The books Montgomery read when beginning *The Blue Castle* included Scott's *Waverley*, (1814) "a blue moorland hill swept clean by the winds of heaven," and *The Blind Bow-Boy*, (1923) a horrible example of the "putrescence" she wanted to avoid. Re-reading *Zanoni* (1842), she remembered her girlhood fascination with the "dream lover" in this highly charged early Victorian melodrama. *The Gods of Pegana* (1905) by Lord Dunsany wove a spell of Celtic twilight. On March 16, 1924, she reported recent readings of old and new fiction, from Austen's *Emma* (1815) and *The Gayworthys* (1865), to Conrad's *Youth* (1902) and *Flaming Youth* (1923). More seriously, she studied "a book on neurasthenia," Stanley Hall's *Life and Confessions of a Psychologist* (1923), and "a book on how glands regulate personality." *The Diary of Marie Bashkirtseff*, like Marie Corelli's *Ardath*, reminded her of youthful passionate longing for fame; Mrs. Gaskell's *Life of Charlotte Brontë* brought Rochester and Heathcliff back to mind, providing macho models for Barney, the man Valancy will marry. Montgomery read for escape and sustenance and enlargement, but the reading determined shifts in her professional and personal direction.

In early sections of her journal (which she no doubt checked during the period of composition), she could find other sources for Valancy's initial characterization. In 1905 she had confessed, "There isn't the least likelihood I ever shall have a house of my own" (November 24, 1905). Next page: "I know how I would like to be married—and never will be." Long dreary passages penned around 1905 provide parallels to Valancy's ennui, depression, anxiety, and worry. But the journal also presents sources for other aspects of Valancy's life, especially her sense of humour: "The only fun of the evening was a drunken fiddler. It sounds awful, but he *was* drunk and he *was* funny" (December 6, 1905).

The first fourteen chapters of *The Blue Castle*, which foreshadow Valancy's breakaway, besides presenting a case study of depression which makes everything look ridiculous and ominous, create also a comic study of a dysfunctional family. Then Valancy leaves her depression behind.

Escape begins with a threat of possible death. A doctor's letter warns her that because of a weak heart she has one year to live. The letter adds that any sudden shock will kill her. At this warning of imminent death, Valancy does not go into a "decline" as a Victorian woman in fiction and also often in reality would have done.[85] She opts not to languish, but to live her own life, a mark of her modernity. In an existential moment she moves into the realization that she is going to die, soon, and then she moves on. The death motif initiates a plot of considerable intricacy, new in Montgomery's work.

A wildly funny scene dramatizes Valancy's break with her domineering clan. She hides from them the doctor's diagnosis and also her response to it, setting up the standard dramatic trope of secret truth, the "hidden-behind-the-screen" device, where the audience knows something of which the actors remain unaware. No one but the reader knows what has set Valancy free to say outrageous things about the Stirlings' "little snobbocracy."

Valancy will escape first into a world of people unimaginable in the standard Montgomery stories: an unmarried mother, a roaring drunk, some randy country fellows, and a disreputable hard-bitten hermit, with whom Valancy will fall desperately in love. Concocting such a story constituted shock tactics for an author revered for her whimsy, her delicacy, and also for her tendency to shy away from romantic endings.

Montgomery was tired of seeing her work relegated to the "children's books" section of libraries and bookstores. She had just finished the two *Emily* books, which bore her old trademark in their presentation of an imaginative, whimsical child who copes successfully with hostility and exclusion. Revision of *Emily Climbs* had been hard going, yet "whenever I forced myself to sit down to it, I found solace and escape—I was free from my bonds and torments and roamed in an ideal world—coming back to reality at the end of my three hour's 'stint' with renewed courage and 'grit'" (March 9, 1924). Now she was ready to take a new path to solace and escape, focusing on an adult rebellion against conformity.

The first phase of Valancy's apostasy is her friendship with "Roaring Abel" Gay. The huge, red-bearded, bible-quoting village drunkard gives Valancy a chance to flout conventions, and permits her author to have fun with Presbyterianism. Roaring Abel can quote scripture, define predestination, enjoy sin, and despise ministers and church-goers (for, "What's the use of going to church if it's all settled by predestination?"). Montgomery was throwing over as many traces as was Valancy when she created Abel. (Norman Douglas in *Rainbow Valley* was a paler advance version, red-bearded, strong-minded—everything but drunk.)

Defiance is compounded when Valancy actually moves into Roaring Abel's house, to look after his outcast and dying daughter Cissy. Abel's house is no Blue Castle: the adjectives applied to it are "faded," "dreary," "leprous," "patched," "askew," "dwindling," "ragged," "crone-like." Each term evokes the Valancy of the first chapters. She has moved into a transitional phase, keeping house for Abel Gay. In the Gay place, she cleans and gardens and cooks, and looks after Cissy.

Poor pretty Cissy Gay is much more the victim of patriarchal convention than Valancy. Seduced by a summer tourist, shunned by a pious village after giving birth and losing her "nameless little baby," left to the care of a drunken father, Cissy has nothing to look forward to but death. Valancy, on the other hand, can outface death, emerge from her old-maid shell, put on a green and crimson outfit and go dancing. (Part of Montgomery's Muskoka dream had been of dancing; her early journals record how much she loved to dance—before she married a minister.) Valancy's escort is Cissy's patron and friend, Barney Snaith.

Barney's name is, as his father later reveals, short for Bernard. Perhaps a powerful contemporary author was behind Montgomery's choice of the name. Brilliant, contentious George Bernard Shaw was setting the English-speaking world on edge in the 1920s. Montgomery read Bernard Shaw's *Saint Joan* (1924) as an example of a woman's determination and force during the year she was writing *The Blue Castle*.[86] Linda Jackson-Hutton has also suggested that "Barney" may link with "Blarney Castle."[87] Fleeting references to Barney Snaith as a man with a "whimsical grin" have been deftly introduced early in the novel. He will eventually emerge as the major figure in Valancy's new life. With him she will find a home of her own.

Longing for a house of one's own is another motif deep-rooted in Montgomery's life and her fiction. Homesickness recurred as a desperate debilitating state in her early days. After she married and moved to Ontario she was doubly assailed: by homesickness for Prince Edward Island, and by frustration at having to live, inevitably, as the wife of a Presbyterian minister, in a house owned by her husband's church. With similar yearning for home, Anne longed to be "of" Green Gables, to belong to Marilla and Matthew and Avonlea. Emily missed New Moon when she was away at high school, though happy in pursuing her quest, the drive to become an author. Unlike the little girls in the earlier books, Valancy has run away from her first home, and is not in quest of a career, but in search of a mate.

In *The Blue Castle*, Valancy Stirling moves toward her dream in an erotic drive through the night, after fleeing with Barney Snaith from the disreputable dance at Chidley's Corners:

> she was enjoying herself—was full of a strange exultation—bumping over that rough road beside Barney Snaith. The big trees shot by them. The tall mulleins stood up along the road in stiff, orderly ranks like companies of soldiers. . . . She was not in the least afraid, with Barney at the wheel. . . . She ceased to feel anything except that she was part of a comet rushing gloriously through the night of space.

Valancy recognizes that she is in love—"justified" (a powerful theological term!) by love. "She had exchanged her shopworn soul for a fresh one."

Cissy's quiet death forms the next plot hinge. This death will free Valancy for a second rebellion against convention. She proposes to Barney, marries him and moves with him to his island. It is the island Montgomery had dreamt of that Muskoka morning.

Perhaps a whispering echo of "real-life" romance was part of the creative force of that Muskoka day-dream. Montgomery had been freed to enter this new dream world, in part, by the re-entry into her life of a man who had played a small role in her maturing sexuality. The day before drifting into her dream of an island, Maud and her family had paid a visit to Reverend John Mustard in his Muskoka cottage. Now a successful minister in Toronto, "Mr. Mustard" was the man who had long ago proposed to sixteen-year-old Maud, out in Prince Albert, Saskatchewan. Now Montgomery wrote that, left alone with him while Ewan and the boys and Mrs. Mustard went fishing, "I was rather distressingly conscious of the [time] when he asked me to marry him." To her vast amusement, John Mustard made no reference whatsoever to their long-ago encounters (July 30, 1922).

She herself gives no description in her journal of the charming rustic cottage John Mustard and his sons had built. But when she came to write her novel, she incorporated many of the details of the Mustards' cabin into Barney's house on the island of Mistawis.[88]

In Valancy's earlier life she had been "islanded" in her desperate separation from her family's beliefs and intentions. Now she is enisled in a different sense, separated from ordinary social conventions, but deeply involved with Barney Snaith. Like her creator who in 1922 had revelled in a dream of "youth, mystery, delight: . . . I lived it all out in every detail," Valancy relishes every detail of her new life.

In the novel, unlike Montgomery's first dream, there is no crowd of friends on the island. Just two lovers, Valancy Stirling and Barney Snaith. This is part of the iconography of the island as a fortress, walled by the sea. Here there is time for "the soul-satisfying talk of kindred spirits," the kind of talk Montgomery dreamed of, at first sight of the Muskoka island.

There is the echo here of another crucial part of Montgomery's recent experience. In February 1922, she had written in her journal of the charm of frank discussion of every imaginable subject with an intelligent and sympathetic man like Captain Reverend Edwin Smith, Ewan's friend from college days—now solidly married and father of six children. In July, three weeks before the Muskoka holiday, the Macdonalds had taken a little trip to Niagara Falls and on the way home "reached Oshawa where the Smiths are living now and stayed all night there" (July 8, 1922). When he first came back into the Macdonalds' life in 1919, Maud had written in her journal, "He is by now fifty years old. But he looks about 35 . . . not a trace of stoop or stodginess in his slender, upright figure" (September 21, 1919). In 1920 she added, "There seems to be something infectiously healthful about his personality—you simply *catch* optimism from him" (July 24, 1920). This soul-satisfying kindred spirit joined Bernard Shaw as one of the originals leading to the creation of outspoken Barney Snaith.

At first sight of Barney's island, the novel, like Valancy and Barney, leaves behind "the realm of everyday and things known and land[s] on a realm of mystery and enchantment where anything might happen—anything might be true." From this point on, improbabilities pile onto coincidences and move toward a fabulous conclusion. A magic mirror; a ring of jewelled islands, emerald and amethyst; a masked ball; a silver forest in winter, "a spell-bound world of crystal and pearl": all seem like features of a fairy-tale. There is even a motif from the Bluebeard tale, a secret room which Valancy must never enter and never question. As in a fairy-tale, there is metamorphosis: Valancy is given a new name, "Moonlight," and a new appearance, so charming that a great painter wants to do her portrait.

The fairy tale comes to a halt, again with the entry of the death motif. Valancy is trapped in the path of an oncoming train. At the point of death she is saved by Barney. In a reversal of the Cinderella story, he tears Valancy's shoe off her foot, to save her life from the thundering train. The sudden possibility of her being killed leads to his recognition and announcement of the strength of his present love for her.

For Valancy, the experience brings a different revelation. Surely such a shock should have killed her, if the doctor's diagnosis of her heart condition was correct. Another plot twist unravels: Valancy discovers that the doctor's letter went to the wrong "Miss Stirling." It was another woman who was doomed to die. Valancy will live. But the thought that she is not to die leads her to guilt and shame for having married Barney under false assumptions. The whole perfect island life appears to have been founded on a falsity.

Finally, in a fairy-tale ending, Barney's father comes to Mistawis and tears the veil from Barney's true identity. Behold Bernard Snaith Redfern, son of a millionaire. Cinderella has married a prince. Montgomery however mocks the romance tradition when she makes this a comic revelation. There will be untold wealth for the heroine, happily married to a great fortune; but the maker of the fortune is ridiculous, a comic little man, unpretentious, even humble in his desire for reunion with his wilderness-loving son. Old Doc Redfern is a gnome-like medicine man. One of the best comic moments in the book comes when he is revealed as suffering all the ailments and disadvantages that his "Purple Pills" and other remedies are supposed to cure.

The moment has its tragic shadow, given that for all her mockery, Montgomery was beginning to slip into an endless circle of ailments, and to treat them, not with the "Redfern's Purple Pills" but with an equally meretricious round of pain-killers and soporifics (all now known to be addictive, with dangerous side-effects).

Doc Redfern puts a new obstacle in Valancy's path, with a story of Barney's earlier love life, a tale that consumes her with jealousy and despair. She flees the island, though not before she discovers yet another of Barney's secrets. Braving the Bluebeard secret chamber he has barred her from, Valancy discovers that Barney Snaith Redfern is also the man behind the nom de plume of "John Foster." It was he who authored the books that sustained her in her Cinderella days. The author's surname underlines the fostering role that literary art can have in the life of a lonely and insecure reader. His first name is also suggestive. "John" had seemed like an obvious name for the minister in *Rainbow Valley*. Now it was freshly connected with another minister, the "Mr. Mustard" who had suddenly reappeared not as a comic young man but as a successful and effective member of his profession. "John" was also the first name of another well-remembered minister. Reverend John Stirling came to Cavendish soon after Montgomery had settled for engagement to Ewan, and married Margaret Ross, who was once perceived to be Maud's rival for Ewan as a suitor. The memories of early courtship clustered around the name "John" add power to the notion that Valancy has married, unbeknownst to herself, the ideal man.

As with Barney/Bernard Shaw, another real author is shadowed in "John Foster." Bliss Carman, a powerful figure for many Canadians with his bohemian beliefs and his celebration of a vagabond life and fervent response to nature's moods, wrote very much in the style of "John Foster."[89] Many readers beside Montgomery had found that Carman's poetry could sustain a sense of identity, beauty, truth, and courage. A volume of his essays, *The Making of Personality*, had been Ewan's first gift to her, many years earlier. More recently, the handsome poet had crossed her path in public appearances.[90]

Whether or not Carman is remembered here, the use of a successful writer as the culmination of all dreams is undercut ironically in *The Blue Castle*. Snaith chuckles sardonically when Valancy quotes his work to him. Montgomery might well laugh at herself too, as she shows Barney's modesty about literary fame. Feeling irate at Canadian critics' preference for work by male Canadian writers like Morley Callaghan over her own kind of writing, she had protested privately and in public speeches. Now she backs down and presents Valancy, happy to enjoy the glory reflected from her husband. Unlike the Story Girl, the young Anne, and Emily, Valancy has had no desire to climb the Alpine Path to authorship herself.

First, though, Valancy must return in chagrin to her old home, believing that she is not her husband's true love. This flight is frustrated by Barney's masterful rescue, which in turn is greeted with applause by the Stirling family, now that they know about his enormous wealth. The tone of the ending reverts to the comic social realism of the novel's opening. Then finally Valancy's husband proposes to take her (as Montgomery's imagination had always taken *her*) to the Alhambra, to Rome, and Samarcand. As jealous cousin Olive Stirling says, at the end of the novel, "We can believe *that* or not, as we like, I suppose."

The journals at the time of the writing of *The Blue Castle* reveal why Samarcand held such allure. On April 10, 1924, Montgomery mentions *The Blue Castle* by name for the first time, but then a single entry on March 9, 1924, begins a litany of troubles. This was the darkest time for Ewan, "sitting there, a handkerchief tied round his head, his eyes wild and terrified, his face repulsive with the vacant almost imbecile expression so characteristic of these attacks at their worst." His conviction of his "lost" condition had intensified. "A curse on the devilish theology that implanted such ideas in his consciousness!" (March 9,1924). Furthermore, money worries rose from disappointing royalties, reflecting "general rotten business conditions." There were extra parish visits ("torture") to make, before the spring roads around Leaskdale became impassable. Chester was worrying his mother with upsetting signs of "early maturity." Other cares piled up during 1924 to 1925, the years of composing *The Blue Castle*: the lingering decline and death of her Aunt Annie Campbell, the mother figure from Park Corner days; ongoing lawsuits against L.C. Page; tiresome church work such as drilling the young people for a Sunday School concert; and more seriously, the current urgent discussion of the "Church Union Question." This proposed negotiation of a union with the Methodist Church seemed to foreshadow the end of many

Presbyterian parishes, and hence the narrowing of Ewan's professional expectations. Montgomery also suffered bouts of tonsillitis and cystitis, and endured the antics of a neurotic maid servant. Final aggravation came in the form of a comment on her novels in MacMechan's *Headwaters of Canadian Literature*, which declared that her work lacked "deftness of touch."

As always, writing offered a defence against troubles. On February 8, 1925, she told her diary: "On Wednesday I finished a novel, *The Blue Castle*—a little comedy for adults. I have enjoyed writing it very much. It seemed a refuge from the cares and worries of my real world" (February 8, 1925). She had achieved, to quote from the imagined work of John Foster, "a few minutes of transfiguration and revelation."

"Transfiguration and revelation" are indeed appropriate terms for the gifts of good fiction.

Emily's Quest

(Toronto: McClelland & Stewart, 1927)

"Quest" is a double-sided term. Traditionally, it suggests the chivalric romances of Lancelot, Galahad, and their fellow knights, searching for the Holy Grail. Emily's quest fits this definition. Her Grail is the chalice of literary achievement, not imagined in terms of financial reward or critical acclaim, but as the production of something that measures up to her own standards of style, form, and content. Like James Joyce's *A Portrait of the Artist as a Young Man*, published in 1916, *Emily's Quest* is primarily a *künstlerroman*, the story of growth as a creator. A portrait of the artist as a young woman—a *künstlerin*—had been painted in 1868 by Louisa May Alcott in *Little Women*. In 1924 Montgomery repainted the picture with more force and intensity. The third book in the *Emily* series, like Montgomery's own journal, records the details of inspiration, revision, refinement, submission, rejection, subjugation to some of the formulas of publishers, and finally acceptance for publication. Emily's literary quest is that of a young person obsessed with words and with the power of crafting words into stories.

But Emily, besides being an artist, is also a young woman. For her there is a second quest—the quest explored in courtship stories. She is in search of love, questing for a mate. The novel, again like the author's journal, is replete with details of suitors, entanglements, true and false lovers, engagements and jiltings, affinities and revulsions. As Montgomery dealt with this romantic quest, she touched on details that recalled her favourite books, playing ingenious changes on the literary tradition of courtship. In Jane Austen's *Pride and Prejudice* (1813) she found three aspirants for Elizabeth Bennet's hand: comic Collins, false Wickham, and proud Darcy. Charlotte Brontë's *Jane Eyre* (1847) furnished other stereotypes to play with, in cold domineering St. John Rivers, and Mr. Rochester with his powerful psychic pull. Montgomery twisted echoes of all these suitors into the story of Emily's quest for love.

The two quests, for fame and for love, are uniquely intertwined throughout this heavily-, cleverly-plotted novel. Of all the novels, this one most closely parallels Montgomery's own flirtatious growing-up years and the perils and pleasures of her aspiring authorship. It also distorts the facts, consciously adding climax, suspense, and an unexpected conclusion.

Emily's Quest begins with a seventeen-year-old who realizes that she belongs to the "ancient race of story-tellers." As a young adult, she can shut herself off in her room, stay up all night, prowl alone through the "Tomorrow Road"—and write. Rejection slips come, but acceptances come too, and these partly reconcile her family and her community to her literary avocation. Here is the first of the correspondences. At that same young age, Montgomery, flushed with her first publications had the pleasure of writing in her diary, "Lieutenant Governor Schultz of the Territories [the northwest Canadian areas now comprising Manitoba, Saskatchewan and Alberta] . . . read my article on Saskatchewan and admired it very much" (July 17, 1892). In fact as in fiction, this is a story of early successful production.

But Dean Priest, long Emily's mentor, warns her not to dream of being a Brontë or an Austen, and cautions her to count on "those eyes—that smile—" rather than on her pen. Dean is personally impelled by possessiveness, but he also speaks for her community, which assumes that a female's entry into adulthood must mean setting aside personal ambition and turning attention to the other female quest: the search for an acceptable suitor.

Emily's courtship story begins as comedy. A lady-like young minister and an adoring man full of high-flown phrases appear and are dismissed with despatch. Because of her rejection of both, Emily is considered "fickle." Yet the newcomers demonstrate to her community that Emily is properly in quest of love as well as of professional success. That swift sequence of men wanting to marry Emily in the early part of the book is like the parade of equally smitten young men pinned in Montgomery's early journals. Nate Lockhart told her he loved her when she was only fifteen. Will Pritchard gave her a ring when she was sixteen. John Mustard, Lou Dysant, Lem McLeod all proposed marriage when she was still very young. All attest to the fact that Montgomery, like Emily, was attractive to men during the years when she was first finding her strength as a writer. The parade of suitors is not just a comic sequence but a report of normal developments in a community focused on marriage and generation.

Emily's long-time attachment to Teddy Kent is still smouldering, but Teddy has left Blair Water for a year of studies away from the Island. This is comparable to the opportunities open to Nathan Lockhart, the boy who shared Montgomery's schoolgirl dreams and tastes. Nate left the Island to study at Acadia College in Nova Scotia, an adventurous exit that Montgomery could not hope for.[91] Emily, after Teddy's brief return and abrupt second departure, flings herself feverishly into her work. She sets aside her "pot-boiling," rescues the draft of an old story which "seized hold of her imagination and called forth all her creative impulse" and writes a novel entitled *A Seller of Dreams*. In Montgomery's case there could be no such quick accomplishment of a major work. In her years of teaching in a series of one-room rural schoolhouses, by dint of writing very early in the morning and late at night, she had produced and sold a goodly pile of short stories and poems in the 1890s. But in fiction she can let Emily glory in a book which is a fully-developed expression of her youthful self, her setting, and her values.

Montgomery continues the "Emily" plot beyond this happy moment. To Dean Priest, long her mentor, Emily submits "A Seller of Dreams" for judgment. Dean's verdict: "cobwebs—only cobwebs. . . . Fairy tales are out of fashion. . . . And your characters are only puppets." This contemptuous comment brings the temporary death of Emily's self-assurance as a writer. She burns *A Seller of Dreams*. In her consequent despair, she literally falls and pierces her foot on a pair of scissors—Aunt Laura's needlework scissors, a double omen of spinsterhood and domesticity. In the resultant weakness of her recovery, Emily accepts Dean's proposal of marriage. The metaphors of a fall and a wounding that precede her acceptance of Dean and of marriage signal Montgomery's reservations about this "happy ending." Montgomery is following the formulas of romance, the patterns in Austen and Brontë. Before Emily finds true love, she must experience an anti-romance.

Dean Priest, the false lover, recalls the chilly Anglican priest St. John Rivers in Charlotte Brontë's *Jane Eyre*. Again, however, Montgomery presents something besides a literary echo. Like Emily, Montgomery at the end of her apprentice period accepted one of her suitors. Her fiancé, Edwin Simpson, was in fact a "priest," though of a Baptist anti-priestly congregation, and he was a "dean" in his subsequent prominence as a national leader of the Temperance movement of the early twentieth century. Ed was a distant cousin, but like the Murrays and the Priests, the Macneills and the Simpsons had been at odds ever since the two families arrived together from Scotland, almost 200 years earlier. The young people, though locked into a neighbourly situation of mutual dislike and distrust, became engaged. Edwin Simpson, blandly self-assured (like Dean Priest and St. John Rivers), created from the beginning a sense of entrapment which grew stronger as the engagement continued because of his need to possess exclusively. His visit to Montgomery in Bedeque, when she lived in the Leard household, proclaimed his ownership. Handsome Ed Simpson was not physically crook-backed, but had an odd personality, as part of a very eccentric family. Maud's journals never specified how he regarded his fiancée's vaulting ambition as a writer, but years later she combined her memory of him with her reading of Brontë's domineering St. John Rivers to create a subtle portrait of the way a man may limit a woman, under the guise of protecting her.

Dean Priest's indifference to Emily's writing, or his dislike of it, had another source in Montgomery's life story. The minister that she eventually married was no "Jarback," but a pleasant, good-looking, easy-going man. As her husband, however, Ewan Macdonald took no interest in her work, never read her books, was somewhat jealous of the attention they brought to her, and resented her decision to go on using her maiden name, "L.M. Montgomery," on her books. In his attitude to her professional power, Ewan Macdonald, as well as Ed Simpson, contributed to the portrait of Dean Priest.

Because "Jarback" Priest derides Emily's ambitions, the "flash," that mysterious power of vision that had set her on the path of her art, departs. The artist as a young person seems to have disappeared from the story, just as, long ago, in *Anne of Green Gables*, the story of Anne's literary ambitions veered away into the traditional path of a courtship tale. The marks of male dominance over Emily are clear. She feels that her emerald engagement ring is a "fetter;" less dramatically but more ominously, Dean says he must get a dog to keep Emily's cats in order.

Emily sets to work with Dean in furnishing a house. Emily's happiness in arranging furniture reflects Montgomery's excitement at the time of writing this book. Because Ewan had received a call to a new church, the Macdonald family prepared to move away from Leaskdale to a new home in Norval in February. Montgomery enjoyed deploying her belongings, both the books and pictures and ornaments she had brought from Cavendish and also the elegant new furniture bought with the royalty money earned by her ever-popular books. In *Emily's Quest*, in contrast, most of the furnishings of the little house are the fruit of Dean's world-wide wandering. Emily, who has never ventured beyond New Moon and Shrewsbury, can only contribute some bits and pieces inherited from her long-dead mother and grandmother, and a curious "gazing-ball," a present from eccentric old Nancy Priest, who was related to both Emily and Dean. The irony of the disparity of belongings brought to the shared house destabilizes what seems at first to be the conventional ending of a courtship story.

The fun of setting up a house acts as a pivotal mid-point in the novel. Significantly, this pleasure balances the fact that Emily is not in love with her fiancé. The little grey house means more to her than Dean does. In terms of the archetypes of romance fiction, Dean is the false lover. His high-flown speeches should have signalled to Emily that there was something meretricious in him. "'Think of the music penned in this fragile, pale-blue wall,' said Dean, touching an egg." He announces that he needs, "Not the music of the moon perhaps . . . a loom for the weaving of dreams and a jar of pixy-brew for festal hours." Montgomery gives him these turgid speeches, as if in mockery of her own propensity to purple passages, and also as an indication of something spurious about him.

Emily breaks off her engagement to Dean when she belatedly recognizes the depth of her bond to Teddy Kent. In Montgomery's real life, she broke her engagement to Ed Simpson partly because of her sense of his strange frigidity. Partly, also, according to her journals, her connection to Ed was disturbed by her passionate feelings for another man, the seductive Herman Leard. Here the journals obliquely suggest the dark-eyed young charmer, Teddy.

Though far away, Teddy is revealed as Emily's one true love, in a strange psychic experience. This twist in the plot was foreshadowed in the earlier novels, when Emily's psychic call brought Teddy to rescue her from Mad Mr. Morrison, and when her power of "second sight" led to the discovery of the body of Ilse's mother, and to the rescue of a lost boy. Now because of this strange power she is able to wing a silent message to distant Teddy, saving him from a terrible death, and proving to herself how deep is her connection with him. The phenomenon of second sight links with Montgomery's belief that she herself had abnormal powers, a fey ability to "see" distant events. Certainly a remarkable level of sensitivity was related to her art, her creative gift. The mysterious tie to the true love, however, again carries echoes of Charlotte Brontë's *Jane Eyre*. The heroine there feels a strange psychic pull to Mr. Rochester, the man she has fled before entering St. John Rivers's home. Emily Brontë, too, had imprinted on her readers' minds the possibility of an irrational tie between lovers—in this case, Heathcliff and Catherine of *Wuthering Heights* (1847). In Montgomery's novel, psychic experience opens Emily's eyes: she cannot marry Dean after all.

The break with the demon lover connects with the resumption of the literary quest. Emily's rejection of Dean leads to his revelation that his judgment of her work was falsified. *A Seller of Dreams*, he now admits, had genuine value. He had lied about it, demeaning it in order to bend her to his will. "Because I hated the book. You were more interested in it than in me. You would have found a publisher."

Once the engagement is broken, Emily feels free, though "freedom is bitter." She returns to her journal-keeping, writing of the miracle of the rebirth of the "flash"—"my old, inexpressible glimpse of eternity." The result is a period of professional success. The second half of the book begins as Emily climbs the "Alpine Path." Acceptances come in from many magazines. Visible successes connect with a sense of inner fulfilment. "Not all the dreams of Eden . . . could have been as sweet as those I am dreaming tonight, because the power to work has come back to me." It is a pronouncement exactly like those Montgomery made again and again in her own journal, about the blessed fullness of the joy of literary creation.

She too, like Emily, entered a period of frenzied literary production after breaking her engagement to Ed Simpson in 1898. Her grandfather's death in the same year had led to her return home to keep house with her grandmother. Freed of teaching responsibilities, she could focus most of her energy on her writing. To read Montgomery's journal around the turn of the twentieth century is to feel exhausted by the scope of her enterprise, and exhilarated by the number and range of her successes. A preliminary bibliography of her publications between 1898 and 2006 includes the titles of 237 short stories and 204 poems.[92] In spite of this astonishing professional achievement, the turn of the century was a period of increasing loneliness.

Many years later, at the time she was writing *Emily's Quest* in the 1920s, terrible loneliness assailed Montgomery again. Her husband was becoming more and more remote as a result of mental illness. In trying to shield the nature of his illness from his own children, and from the church and community, she had become more and more strained. She was caught in her Scottish clan's valuing of aloofness and dignity. Pride isolated her and drove her deeper into her own suffering.

This current loneliness, reinforced by reading her own journal account of long-ago isolation, surfaces in the early part of the second half of *Emily's Quest*. Emily pours into her diary a tortured sense of rejection and solitude, along with the counter theme of professional success. In one sense the inclusion of these long sections of Emily's journal slows the movement of the plot, apparently acting as make-weight or filler. In fact, however, these sections are essential to Montgomery's central purpose: to tell the whole story of the life of a writer. For her, periods of lonely introspection, times of writing up her own response to nature and recording local voices and gossip, along with her meditations on faith and astronomy, were all essential parts of her growth as an artist. Emily's journal, like Montgomery's, is central to her life. Realizing how this lonely period had fuelled her as a writer, Montgomery assigned a comparable period to Emily. The inclusion of self-pitying sections of the imagined journal reflects Montgomery's insistence on telling the exact truth about the artist's quest.

As the story of a double quest, the second half of the novel might be expected to unfold quickly, now that Emily has recognized the depth of her love for Teddy Kent. Indeed, Teddy's old whistle begins the second half of the book. "He was still her master." The plot does not however move immediately to a romantic "happy ending." A delaying action begins with a second parade of suitors. Again, in a real-life parallel, a succession of men began to pursue Montgomery after the breach of her engagement to Ed Simpson and the sudden death of Herman Leard in 1899. More dangerous than the parade of young men from earlier days came a handsome widower, cousin Oliver Macneill from a far western State, and an older supplicant, Will Houston, already married to a beloved cousin. Emily's mid-novel romances provide scandal for the community. In the novel, unlike the tortured journal, they also provide comedy for the reader, to balance the emphasis on the writer's loneliness.

Both Emily and Montgomery make cutting remarks about the suitors— in private. Both are circumspect, showing the female virtue of propriety. In the novel, the only people who can be outspoken are Ilse, who is motherless but has good social standing and is beautiful, her brusque father Dr. Burnley, Perry, the young man who came only from Stovepipe Town, and simple Cousin Jimmy. But gossip swirls around Emily's dealings with possible husbands. Gossip is a form of social control, and the middle part of *Emily's Quest* is accurate as social history. The small community has a stake in continuation and therefore in courtships. Cavendish in the 1890s and the fictional Blair Water are equally fixated on the need for a young woman to marry.

As if in passive denial of society's fiat, Emily lets slip the chance of turning to Teddy. Rather, she moves through a series of repressions and rejections of his love. She refuses to answer his whistle, pulls her hand away from him, and allows Ilse to break up a serious moment of closeness. When Ilse tells the truth about Teddy, identifying his egoism, his need of adulation, and his acceptance of being chased by many women, this reinforces Emily's self-restraint. She will never "chase" him—that offends a taboo: it is unladylike. The social convention prevents happiness and love, and the Murray pride makes her stand alone.

Montgomery's journal of 1898 had recorded a comparable control of her passionate love for handsome Herman Leard. Montgomery's relationship with Herman was complicated by the fact that she was at that time engaged to Edwin Simpson, who kept a jealous eye on her while she was in Bedeque. Perhaps there is an echo of this situation in the presence in *Emily's Quest* of Teddy Kent's mother, whose jealousy "coiled in her soul like a snake." Mrs. Kent, crying in the dark, rejected by her husband because of her own temper, is a fine portrait of a neurotic jealousy.

This jealousy gives the plot a melodramatic twist. Late in the story, Mrs. Kent admits that she has tampered with a letter written by Teddy, declaring his never-diminished love for Emily. It is too late for Emily to profit from Mrs. Kent's gift. Her repulse has led Teddy to set his passion for her aside, and become engaged to marry beautiful Ilse Burnley. Although the Montgomery journal includes no such conclusion to the Herman Leard story, local evidence now reveals that there was indeed a comparable situation in real life. Herman was in fact engaged to a Bedeque girl at the time he was trying to make love to Montgomery. In the novel, a happy solution comes when Ilse breaks off the engagement. But no romantic ending ensues.

Instead, Emily, walking in a loveless autumnal world through newly ploughed fields, discovers a lost treasure. With her heel, she spikes a family diamond. This constitutes a reprise and reversal of the wounding of her foot, which connected with the burning of her first book and her acceptance of Dean. Immediately following the discovery of the lost diamond, Emily's Aunt Elizabeth undergoes a major change. No longer the martinet of earlier days, she now enjoys Emily's literary work. This encouragement leads Emily to "an instantaneous vision of the new book, as a whole—a witty, sparkling rill of human comedy." In *The Moral of the Rose* Emily has indeed "spiked a diamond," as Montgomery did in writing *Anne of Green Gables*.

"How does she do it?" Cousin Jimmy asks (as many would ask of Montgomery's magic). "Those folks are alive!" Jimmy sends off the manuscript to a publisher, after Emily becomes dejected by a series of rejections. Montgomery too had expanded a little sketch, into the full fun of *Anne of Green Gables*. She too, of course, experienced glorious success. Montgomery delighted in copying into her journal all the reviews her books received; Emily, in the same way, delights in receiving the world's opinion of her work. Most of all she relishes Aunt Elizabeth's opinion, expressed in Chapter 22, near the end of the novel: "Well, I never could have believed that a pack of lies could sound as much like the real truth as that book does." Emily's first quest, to climb the Alpine Path, and inscribe at its height a woman's name, seems satisfactorily ended.

The story returns less happily, however, to the second path, the courtship quest. There is a curious air of Sleeping Beauty in the last part of the book, an over-long wait for the prince to return to claim his bride. Teddy's long absence, after Emily has admitted to herself her love for him, may echo the trauma of Ewan Macdonald's absence in the years after Montgomery had to undergo a long waiting period. Ewan went to Glasgow right after the engagement was established, then to far-away Island parishes, and finally to Ontario. Ewan's absence was not, like Teddy's, a deliberate separation, but the emotional effect was the same. Emily's journal entries near the end of the story echo many of those penned in the dreary years when Montgomery was waiting for Ewan, working at her writing but without pouring into her journal any of the élan of her earlier memoirs. Outwardly an exciting period because of the amazing success of *Anne of Green Gables*, this was a time of suspension for her.

In the last quarter of *Emily's Quest*, the drama in Emily's life lies in her journal, her writing, and her lonely walks. Yet Emily is not a static character, although her development is not indicated in action. Her development is in integrity and discipline, as reflected in her journal and her creative writing. But the happy romantic ending with Teddy Kent seems blocked.

Resolution of this knot comes neither from Emily nor from Teddy but from someone "else," provocatively named Ilse. When impetuous Ilse suddenly hears of a disaster threatening the life of Perry Miller, she leaves Teddy in the moment before she is to marry him, jumps out a window with the train of her wedding dress wrapped around her shoulder, and joins Perry.

In a conventional story, this situation would be resolved if Teddy now rediscovered his love for Emily, and swept her away in turn. Instead, concentrating on his own hurt pride, Teddy leaves once again for Montreal. In the damp chill dusk after his departure, Emily goes to the Disappointed House, still furnished with Dean's belongings, reminders of the travels she never made.

Montgomery now gives her audience what it wants, or at least what she accepts as what it wants. With no visible motivation, Teddy returns, calls to Emily, and bridges the years. He whistles, and Emily comes to him. In this long-delayed love scene, Teddy does most of the talking. "I was lonely." "I was furious." "I hated women for a while. I was hurt." He vents his resentment of Ilse, who "made a fool of me—me, who fancied I was beginning to cut a figure in the world." Presumably, he will go on cutting such a figure. "I was too proud" is Emily's single comment before Teddy indulges in his long rant of vanity and self-absorption. As a heroine of romance, Emily is signalling to the reader as well as to Teddy the submissive role she is prepared to play. Jarback Priest would have destroyed Emily through his possessive absorption in her life, leaving her no room to breathe. Teddy will be the opposite: he will never be truly involved in her concerns because he is so absorbed in himself. Emily will replace the mother for whom he was "all in all."

The final chapter does not suggest that Emily will continue her writing career. Though Teddy began with handicaps like Emily's, he is now able to quit commercial illustrating and do more significant portraits. Emily will remain an inspiration for his art. The life Teddy now offers will probably leave her still marginalized. "Writing beyond the ending"[93] of romance, Montgomery implies a tamping-down of Emily's ambition. Here the fiction departs radically from the author's experience. For Montgomery, marriage barely slowed down her professional work.

manse, with an outlook onto the Credit River. Montgomery herself would be nearer to the city with its literary world, its museums and art gallery and shops and theatres. There was a quick rail service from Norval to Toronto. Montgomery could take a more active part in the Canadian Authors Association meetings, and there she would hear lively talk about the emergence of new fads and fashions in publishing circles.

Such talk had a too-real meaning for her. In 1925 she had had the unpleasant experience of having four short stories she had written at the request of the *Delineator* set aside, because the magazine's new editor felt that they were out of date, not sophisticated enough for the new readership he hoped to attract. A year earlier, the previous editor of the magazine had happily published four stories, titled "What's in a Name?," "The Magic Door," "The Bobbing of Marigold," and "Her Chrism of Womanhood."[95] The four had brought in $1600—a very satisfactory sum (October 30, 1925), and a request for a further four stories, with the promise of $2000 (January 7, 1927). Then came the note, rejecting them as old-fashioned, and insulting her (as she felt) by paying for the stories but refusing to print them.

In her wrath, she picked up the little "Marigold" sketches and in 1926 and 1927 defiantly enlarged them into a whole novel. Doing so, she accepted implicitly the modernizing suggested by the insulting editor. She began her story with an echo of James Joyce's experimental *A Portrait of the Artist as a Young Man*. Joyce had begun his "stream-of-consciousness" novel with, "Once upon a time and a very good time it was . . ." Montgomery started *Magic for Marigold* with "Once upon a time—which, when you come to think of it, is really the only proper way to begin a story—"

Literary fashion of the time might well encourage Montgomery to focus this new story on the consciousness of a child much younger than any of her previous subjects. A.A. Milne had turned such a topic into a best-selling series of books as he moved from *When We Were Very Young* (1924) to *Now We Are Six* (1926). Readers responded enthusiastically to the child's bravado as presented by Milne:

. . . When I was Five
I was just alive.
But now I am Six, I'm as clever as clever.
So I think I'll be six now for ever and ever.

The best part of Marigold's story will take place as she climbs from babyhood to the age of six.

Related to this whimsical emphasis on the early stages of life was the general mid-twenties interest in developmental psychology.[96] Responding to the taste of the time, Montgomery concentrated on the development of a child, from infancy until she reaches the age where Anne and Emily's stories began: a good idea for marketing a new kind of "L.M. Montgomery book." She emended and polished the little stories that had been so wrongly (she thought) dismissed by *The Delineator*. Like the short story "What's in a Name?," *Magic for Marigold* begins with a four-month-old baby, not yet named. This focus reflects a general interest in infancy, no doubt related to the current drop in infant mortality.

Discussion of her name erupts into fierce family arguments. Readers in the mid-twenties, fascinated by changing family dynamics, would note with interest that Marigold's nuclear family is all-female. This is a recognizable picture of family structure in a world still reeling from the huge loss overseas of a generation of men.[97] The one exception in Marigold's circle is a lively adventurous uncle named "Klon," short for "Klondike," come home from the far west; perhaps he was drawn from loving memories of Montgomery's father. With Uncle Klon as an amused bystander, the Lesley family will emerge as a fighting combination of mother, aunts, grandmother, and great-grandmother, each with a different idea about raising a child. Montgomery was ready to chuckle over current controversies about early childhood education.

Marigold's mother adheres to the now old-fashioned theories of German educator Friedrich Froebel. In the 1890s Froebel had designed a "kindergarten," where each child would grow like a flower, in a setting filled with gifts, nature, folklore and games, and mother love. This baby's mother wants to give her child a flower name, signalling a hope that her nature will unfold in a world like a Froebelian kindergarten.

Ultimately, the baby is named as her mother desires, although not because of that desire but because of the family's gratitude to a "lady-doctor" named Marigold, who saves the infant's life—after male doctors gave up hope for her. Here the book pays tribute to a real "lady doctor," Dr. Helen MacMurchy, one of an emerging group of women professionals. Neither the real Dr. Helen nor the fictional Dr. Marigold "had any children of her own" but each "knew more about mothercraft than many women who had." Now that Montgomery was in Norval, she was more closely in touch with Dr. MacMurchy and her sisters than ever before. Dr. MacMurchy, who had given Montgomery good advice during her late-life pregnancies and also when Chester and Stuart were babies, was Chief of the Division of Child Welfare in Canada's Department of Health. She was an authority on genetics, and had also published five "Little Blue Books" in 1923, offering directives for newborn and infant care, and emphasizing the need for a rational structured system. In spite of her admiration for this "lady-doctor," however, Montgomery would emphasize the opposite value of imagination, "magic" in other words, in the raising of Marigold.

Marigold's Young Grandmother, stately, with sharp steel-blue eyes, was on Dr. MacMurchy's side. Her distrust of imagination accorded with what was now standard practice in schools. Old fairy tales had been replaced in 1920s school texts with pictures of real children performing ordinary useful tasks. Again, Montgomery's closeness to Toronto had strengthened her ties with the whole MacMurchy family, including sister Bessie, a teacher, and the father, who was Principal at Jarvis Collegiate. Following the direction of the Chicago theorist John Dewey, these professional teachers worked to prepare children for practical citizenship. In reaction, Montgomery eschewed such "social realism," and created in Young Grandmother an unsympathetic disciplinarian, unable to comprehend Marigold's needs.

Marigold's Old Grandmother, still eager for life in her nineties, favours yet another way of child-rearing. She finds Marigold amusing, watches her slyly, and talks to her as if they were contemporaries. She enjoys teasing and chuckles when Marigold reacts fiercely. She seems to share some of the views of an educational innovator named Dr. William Blatz. Toronto was buzzing over the experiments of Dr. Blatz, who in 1925 had established a nursery school on the University of Toronto campus, "where a child can be a child." Parents and teachers could watch through a one-way window as the "Blatz babies" played their way into self-concept and socialization. Montgomery gave her readers the same sort of experience when she put little Marigold on display. Dr. Blatz believed emotions such as anger, jealousy, and shame are stimulating and exhilarating forces in infants. Fear and anger seemed to his followers to be strong driving forces, not necessarily negative ones, since they energize responses. Marigold is certainly energized by Old Grandmother's outrageous taunting and challenges in her earliest days. Old Grandmother draws from a source other than the arbiters of child rearing. Feisty old grandmothers were in literary style. Mazo de la Roche's *Jalna* (1927) had shown the world what a domineering matriarch could be. Marigold's Old Grandmother has a lot in common with Adeline Whiteoak of Jalna. She is also a trial version for the portrait of Aunt Becky in *A Tangled Web*, Montgomery's next book.

Old Grandmother dies when Marigold is seven. But before that happens, Marigold climbs slowly the steps from babyhood. Again Montgomery picks up on a stylish innovation. James Joyce's much-talked-of opening in *A Portrait of the Artist as a Young Man* used baby-talk to suggest the infant's stream-of-consciousness: "There was a moocow coming down along the road and this moocow that was coming down along the road met a nicens little boy named baby tuckoo."[98] Marigold's equally random and illogical first responses to her environment run along similar lines, but Montgomery slips in a suggestion of imaginative, metaphoric transformation seen in Marigold's baby-talk:

Sometimes it was just lilac-bush. And sometimes, especially in the twilight or early dawn, it was a nodding old woman knitting. It WAS. . . .
It was so nice and thrilly to stand down on the wharf and see the trees
upside down in the water and a great blue sky underneath you. And
what if you couldn't stick on but fell down into that sky? WOULD
YOU FALL THROUGH IT?

How would a rational Young Grandmother cope with such a child?

After the two preliminary chapters about Marigold's naming, there is a
first glimpse of a small girl laughing, and dancing. Then flashbacks recount
her development, tabulating the emotions she has experienced: pride,
shame, jealousy, grief, fear, daring. Montgomery's charmed but clear-eyed
analysis of these passions stands in contrast to tradition. Earlier romantics
like William Wordsworth had idealized baby emotions as trailing clouds of
heavenly glory, while Puritans had assumed that original sin is a birth gift,
and Freudians had suggested dark taboos as the source of childhood passion.
Montgomery's interest is still, as it had been in the writing of the *Emily*
books, concentrated on the peculiar gift of certain children, whether it is
called the "flash," or "ecstasy," or paranormal intensity.

Montgomery assigns to Marigold her own ecstatic response to seasonal change, times of day and night, stars and wind and fire, which had
all been renewed and intensified in the new beautiful Norval setting.
Writing these early chapters, Montgomery in her new work-space in the
Norval manse was beginning a long-to-be-continued habit of gazing at
the "Hill o' Pines" on the horizon, "god-like trees rising majestic out of
the white sweep of snow with the pale fallen banners of sunlight between
them" (December 11, 1926). "Cloud of Spruce"[99] is described as a poetic
environment. Montgomery devotes a full chapter to the sensual stage of
the little girl.

Then Marigold, like Montgomery, having prowled alone, responding
first to the real world of light and water, adds an imagined "Hidden Land"
over the hill. Here is the precursor of the "island" which an imaginative person can reach after ecstatic response to the sensual world.

Marigold's emotional world is enriched by the play of mystery and folklore. Fiddle music by the French Canadian hired man Lazarre and his stories of death and bewitchings introduce the kind of folk wisdom that
Froebel considered important, a position later re-emphasized on psychological grounds by Bruno Bettelheim. Montgomery had already demonstrated her fascination with traditional tales in *The Story Girl* and *The
Golden Road*. In *Magic for Marigold* she lessens their respectability by
assigning them to a "hired hand." But Old Grandmother adds another
kind of narrative—family anecdotes, funny, grotesque, poetic.

In her last pre-school year, Marigold's life expands to include imaginary friends. At five, she encounters "The little white girl" and "the little girl in the spring." To reach them, she must "make magic" by following a ritualized procedure. Marigold's magic is perhaps a variant of Emily's "flash." Montgomery is still pondering the mystery of imagination, tracing it to its earliest manifestations. At five, Marigold feels the pull of something beyond the family home.

At six, she finds Sylvia, a beloved imaginary playmate.[100] Conversations with her preview the state of absorption in which a writer broods up moments of imagined talk, dialogues concocted in the "bliss of solitude." Sylvia is to be found beyond the Green Gate, and to be summoned by reciting a magic rhyme. (In the early story version Montgomery uses the more evocative word "rime.") So intense is her love for Sylvia that some members of her family become alarmed.

With a real child named May Kemp as companion, Marigold breaks a prohibition that has been laid against playing with a treasured doll belonging to Old Grandmother. Punishment follows. Perhaps Montgomery's memories of forbidden play had been kindled by the news recorded in her 1926 journal of the death of her earliest at-home playmate, Wellington Nelson. Marigold reflects Montgomery's remembered sense of insurgence and naughtiness. But the Marigold story also reflects rival theories about child play hotly debated in the public press in the mid-1920s, especially concerning Freud's theories of the sublimation of repressed emotions, through play. Montgomery's interest in play and theories of play was kindled by the activities of her two boys.

At six, Marigold leaves home for a series of visits to relatives and learns more about her mixed heritage of Lesleys and Blaisdells and Winthrops. Montgomery seems to be mocking the science of genetics, trumpeted by Dr. Helen MacMurchy. Marigold is analyzed by an extended family in terms of genealogy and family propensities. Marigold, like Emily and Montgomery herself, insists on her own independent personality. She also learns what it is to be homesick. Perhaps thoughts of Chester, away from home for the first time at St. Andrew's School revived memories of the devastating feelings she had experienced when she left Cavendish, even at a much older age than Marigold. Yet she accepted the need for a child to learn independence. Marigold's six-year-old growth is shown when she responds with dignity and sensitivity to the approaching death of "Old Grandmother." In a haunting scene, the little girl becomes friends with the old lady who has taunted and teased her. She listens to Old Grandmother's final memories, and finally is able to restore the old lady's private sense of identity, by agreeing to call the old lady by her first name, "Edith."

She is ready to leave home now. Her experiences in the real world of school are balanced by the private joy of her perfect imaginary friend Sylvia.

Marigold never talks about Sylvia in her encounters with two real little girls who now come into her life. Princess Varvara (Vere-de-Vere?), like Anne of Green Gables, lets her imagination run riot, but with harmful consequences. Gwennie is a role player, again like Anne, but again with negative results from her flights of imagination. They suggest a further re-thinking about imagination on Montgomery's part.

A crisis in Marigold's life comes when, at eight, she is forbidden by Young Grandmother to think about Sylvia. When Marigold goes into a kind of decline at this prohibition of her imaginary friend, Young Grandmother, as a modern woman, consults a child psychologist. Dr. Clow accepts the basic position of Sigmund Freud (whose work Montgomery had studied carefully). He explains Marigold's wasting away as the result of "neurosis caused by a suppressed desire for her playmate." Yet Dr. Clow adds to this Freudian diagnosis a phrase that could have been applied to Montgomery as a child: "She is not trying to deceive anybody. She has the wonderful gift of creation to an unusual degree." It takes a "Doctor of Psychology" to quell Young Grandmother and reaffirm the value of imagination. There had been no Dr. Clow in the 1890s, when Maud Montgomery offended her grandmother by talking about her imaginary friends, or in fictional Avonlea when Anne Shirley was chastised by Marilla for her flights of fancy. Wish fulfillment fuses with modernity in the triumph of Dr. Clow.

In the battle over Sylvia, Marigold's mother has been unable to stand up against the rational prohibition of the grandmother. After the long series of motherless heroines (Rilla and Valancy being the exceptions) Montgomery has at last created a child equipped with a mother. Herself virtually a single parent because of her husband's mental illness, she turned often to thoughts of her own mother, who had died before Maud could really remember her as a living presence. Montgomery's fictional magic gives Marigold all the mother figures she herself always wanted and never had: golden-haired Lorraine, stern but fair-minded grandmother Marian (Lorraine and Marian were names in the Webb family who now lived in Green Gables), and Edith, the old Grandmother who near her death had become a true intimate of Marigold. But Lorraine Lesley, though sweet, is an ineffectual person. In the mid-1920s Montgomery had become ruefully aware of the real helplessness of motherhood.[101]

Marigold has now reached the age of eight, an epoch of particular significance to Montgomery at this point. In 1923 Marjory MacMurchy, third of the MacMurchy sisters, had published a book with the odd title, *The Child's House: A Comedy of Vanessa from the age of eight or thereabouts until she had climbed the steps as far as thirteen*. Montgomery had first known Marjory MacMurchy years earlier when still in Prince Edward Island, as a novice writer being visited by an established member of the Toronto literary world.

When Maud came as a bride to Ontario, Marjory had drawn her into the literary circles in Toronto, acting as hostess at teas and luncheons honouring Montgomery's successive publications. On Montgomery's part, the friendship was an uneasy one. The journals include some snappish comments on Marjory's oddities, and in particular some mockery of her late marriage to Sir John Willison (rather like the marriage of Dr. Marigold to elderly Uncle Klon). Now Montgomery read MacMurchy's story of Vanessa in March of 1924. "It is not bad reporting, but Marjory cannot create," the journal says. "Still, of its kind, it is quite well done" (March 2, 1924).

Grudging praise; but in fact the book undoubtedly influenced the direction of *Magic for Marigold*. This is also a story of "steps," reflecting the stylish new theory of child psychology offered by Jean Piaget. Piaget was to the 1920s what Friedrich Froebel had been to the 1890s: the dominant educational theorist. Piaget postulated that all children move through certain clear stages, progressing from perception, to reasoning and judgment, and then to decision-making. Montgomery partly accepts the notion of "recognizable stages of development," but is too much a follower of Wordsworth not to see some of the development as a loss rather than an "upward" climb. She challenges the position of her friend and rival by beginning the story not at the age of eight but at infancy. This was the first time Montgomery had begun a story "at the beginning." Anne and Emily had come to her (and her readers) at about the age where MacMurchy's story of Vanessa begins and had gone on toward adolescence and maturity. But Marigold's story will end roughly at the point where the stories of Anne and Emily begin. Its concluding sections differ in irony and realism from the story of Vanessa.

Montgomery's vision of the years before puberty had come not just from Blatz and Freud and Piaget, but also from Wordsworth and Milne and a wide range of children's books, including Frances Hodgson Burnett's *The Secret Garden* (1911) and Kenneth Grahame's *The Golden Age* (1895), which suggested elements of meanness and slyness in older children as well as innocence and sweetness. Unlike MacMurchy, Montgomery also worked from direct experience of modern children. Chester's disruptive behaviour at school had become part of the reason for sending him away to boarding-school, and Stuart was showing the independence of any eleven-year-old. Montgomery was not so sure that the years between infancy and pre-puberty represented a climb.

The flurry of speculation and theorizing about the pre-school years had not yet expanded into equally innovative ideas about the problems and possibilities of early adolescence. The account of Marigold's progress between the ages of nine and twelve is less charming than the beginning movements. No more laughing and dancing. Dangerous emotions stir as Marigold matures. Jealousy and hatred flame against the thought of Clementine, the long-dead first wife of Marigold's father. In Marigold's mind, Clementine is like a hated stepmother. Perhaps a 1925 visit to Kirkfield, birthplace of Hugh Montgomery's hated second wife, had brought old tensions near the surface. A mocking campfire song, remembered by Montgomery from the Girl Scout Jamboree of 1926, serves to quell Clementine. Singing "Herring boxes without topses/Sandals were for Clementine," Marigold discovers feet of clay in the picture of the woman remembered as a bride more valuable than Marigold's mother Lorraine. In laughter, a bothersome "ghost was forever laid;" Marigold (and perhaps Montgomery too) can re-establish a belief in the parents' love for each other. That revelation cannot obliterate the subtext running through Marigold's story, in the evidence of half a-dozen families she visits, each a sardonic reversal of "ever after" happiness.

Another element that undercuts the sense of bliss in a little girl's life is the recurrence of tales of horror. Lazarre's folk tales and Old Grandmother's legacy of anecdotes are countered by the frightening impact when Marigold as an older child, entering the house of the "Weed Man," hears tales of a grave-robber, a wife-beater, a leprechaun, and a preacher who was stoned.

In following Marigold up the next steps toward adolescence, Montgomery swings attention to the presence of little boys. Montgomery's own earliest favourite among books had been *A Bad Boy's Diry* (1880). She had recently reread and enjoyed Booth Tarkington's *Penrod* (1914)—and had enjoyed the first *Delineator* editor's comment that her book was even better than Tarkington's. Marigold's all-female circle is enlarged to include some examples of post-war boyhood. Marigold's wit helps her survive the claims of a trio of unattractive boys: lawless, teasing Billy, hateful, flirty cousin Jack, and the more devious Hip Price, son of a minister, who wields a spurious and short enchantment. Hip Price may reflect some traits of Chester Macdonald, another minister's son, already manifesting troublesome qualities to his saddened mother.

Finally, in the last chapter, two boys named Budge and Tad become Marigold's friends. Their names echo the unusual names of the little boys in Habberton's ever-popular *Helen's Babies* (1876). In that old favourite, two little boys plague the life of their baby-sitting uncle with an unending store of mischief. Again, as with *Penrod*, a literary source ratified throwing a glow of humour over the boys' disloyal, obstreperous behaviour. Sadly, *Magic for Marigold* tells how faithless little boys can be, whatever their charms. Budge, thin and scrawny, with a dog named Dix and "fine, clear gray eyes" sounds like Stuart Macdonald, also twelve in 1927. Tad, again like imaginative Stuart Macdonald, is ready to "go Grailing" with Marigold. But these boys are not to be trusted. Very reluctantly, in order to hold Budge's friendship, Marigold tells him about her imaginary friend Sylvia—something she has never revealed to girl friends. But Budge tells Tad, ending her feelings of trust.

The more serious result is that Sylvia no longer comes in response to the magic rhyme. Marigold has climbed the years to disenchantment. Her mentor, Dr. Marigold, who is now married to Uncle Klon consoles her: "The dreamer's joy is worth the dreamer's pain." Marigold's more immediate consolation is the thought that Budge will return for her friendship whenever Tad is too busy to go fishing with him. Nature conspires toward the building of a new dream: "Presently a moon rose and there was a sparkling trail over the harbour like a lady's silken dress." There is no real remedy for the loss of imagined Sylvia, but there is amelioration in adult kindness and humour and in Marigold's new dream of growing up into womanhood.

Montgomery had presented a new view of the perils and pressures that wait for the laughing, dancing baby. But she had veiled the early troubles in laughter, and ended with a final smile at Marigold's acceptance of a new, ridiculously feminine dream.

Having dealt with a very young person in her last novel, it seemed natural for Montgomery to turn to a very old one in her next. She had already done a fine job with Marigold's feisty Old Grandmother. Furthermore, in 1927 a Canadian novel had become a world best seller, largely on the strength of the portrait of a conniving old woman. Did Montgomery read Mazo de la Roche's *Jalna* and react to Adelaide Whiteoak? At any rate, besides *Jalna*, other very popular novels focused on the inter-generational conflict: in 1929 John Galsworthy's *A Modern Comedy* had updated his *Forsyte Saga*.

In 1929, Montgomery's journal hummed with affirmations: pleasant memories of her grandmother, pride in her younger son Stuart, joy in the friendship of Ida and Ernest Barraclough in nearby Glen Williams. She was connecting with young people, directing drama groups in Norval and Union, addressing large groups of students at the Ontario Agricultural College at Guelph, and tangling herself in the romance between her protégé Marian Webb from Cavendish and Murray Laird of Norval. She enjoyed the beauties of Norval—the pretty bends in the Credit River, and the twilight and moonshine charms of the "Hill o' Pines." She was in a rare mood for seeing the funny side of life.

In a crucial journal entry she reported that in re-reading one of George Eliot's books she had noted reference to a woman's "best set of china," and had drifted into a reverie about her grandmother's "best set," voicing regret at not having inherited that treasure. Then, without transition she added, "I am now working on an adult story, centering around the old Woolner jug" (May 3, 1929). That "Woolner jug" inherited from her grandmother had come from England, with a romantic story attached to it. Montgomery had inherited it, and it remained a focus of her personal pride and her sense of difference from her current community.

She returned to her Island for a happy autumn visit—"warm, golden, dreamy" (September 28, 1929)—and the happy time of "brooding up" continued in Norval: "I look out of my window and, beholding the fine and beautiful austerity of my pine wood on this gray autumn twilight, feel comforted" (December 27, 1929). But by January of the New Year, her mood had descended. After an ice storm, the same pine trees look like "disgruntled old spinsters who had indignantly turned their backs on a derisive world" (January 8, 1930). In an increasingly dark mood, Montgomery admitted that she had been hovering on the brink of a nervous breakdown. Journal entries in early 1930 chronicle irritations, both physical (an ear and face ache) and professional (heavy bundles of fan mail "give me the willies"). Further unhappy pressure came from an eccentric young woman named Isobel Anderson who had begun to make disturbing and distracting demands for a close relationship. Early spring entries continued with thoughts of death.

Yet at that point, on March 17, 1930, she wrote in her journal, "Today I began the actual writing of the book I've been doing spade work on for a year. It has no name yet. It centres around the old Woolner jug. And it is to be a humorous novel for adults." If she could not exercise control over her life, she could do as she pleased in her fiction: draw a colourful group of people into her web, weave them together, and provide a laughable conclusion to all their troubles.

The first nineteen-part section of *A Tangled Web* presents a sharp-tongued old woman whose dearest possession is a family heirloom jug. She calls her clan together to hear what she plans to do with it at the time of her obviously impending death. With malice, mischief, and honesty old Aunt Becky Dark ("née Penhallow") unleashes sarcastic comments at all the family members who covet her treasure. The portrait of this imperious old woman has Shakespearean echoes, of King Lear, summoning his daughters to test their love for him, and of Prospero calling his old enemies to his island, to deal out rewards and punishments. If the opening movement reminds readers of Shakespeare, they may take it as a reminder of Montgomery's still-simmering ambition. After all, she renamed her home place "Avonlea"—suggesting a meadow near the shores of Shakespeare's river. (She will even call one of the characters in *A Tangled Web* "Tempest.") Aunt Becky's name also recalls another favourite adult book, *Vanity Fair*. Aunt Becky is a sharp old thing, as manipulative as Thackeray's hero.

Like Montgomery's Grandfather Macneill, she shoots "barbs" at everyone. As a young person, Montgomery had resented her grandfather's sharpness. Now she can use memories of his outrageous rudeness to make readers laugh. Aunt Becky in the book is in some ways an unbearable old woman, but like "Old Grandmother" in *Magic for Marigold*, she can respond to youth—and she is funny.

She controls her extended family by keeping her will a mystery, a theme that recalls Charles Dickens' *Bleak House* (1853). Montgomery dispenses Dickensian names to all the older male members of the Dark and Penhallow families, taunting us into guessing what the names suggest about the part each will play in her story. Old Uncle Pippin, for instance, bears the name of a Cox apple, grown from an unnamed pip; the only apple in which the pips rattle, since they are not connected with the flesh. Peter and the two Sams derive their names from the New and Old Testaments respectively. Other men who arrive at Aunt Becky's levee are suggestively named Dandy and Pennycuik, and Drowned John.

Almost every one of them wants the jug, out of possessiveness, rivalry, sentiment, or family pride. Although Montgomery treasured her own possessions, the china dogs Gog and Magog, the Woolner Jug, and the pictures of the cover art from her earliest books, she creates in *A Tangled Web* a picture of the way love of possessions can become grasping and cruel. "Possessions," a word dominant in woman's vocabulary, implying the pride of teacups, or quilts, old books, new clothes, also has another meaning. "That child is possessed!" suggests the old concept of demonic possession. As Aunt Becky welcomes each member of her clan with a barbed comment, she refers to what "possesses" them. One female kinswoman is twitted for being hopelessly in love, another for "chasing the boys," another for having just been kissed.

These are hints that even if the book begins in *Bleak House* it may well end in romance. When young Gay Penhallow walks into the levee in her daffodil dress, hope and affirmation touch every heart, withered or anaesthetized by Aunt Becky's malice and by individual covetousness. For all its satiric tone, something beside cynicism and possessiveness will slip into a Montgomery story, willy-nilly. As a young writer Emily Byrd Starr had been cautioned, "It is better to heal than to hurt." Montgomery packs both hurting and healing into this book, in a mischievous blend of cynicism and romance.

What follows the swift opening chapter in which Aunt Becky pounces upon the secret follies and yearnings of her relations is a slow exposition of their backgrounds. "Let us look at them a little more closely," the authorial voice says, and settles into an overlong exposition: thirty pages of explanation and analysis of the outer and inner lives of her cast of characters. Authors usually work out this kind of material in a notebook, filling out the characters back-stage, as it were, while preparing to shove them out in front of the footlights.

Why would a canny author like Montgomery ignore the timeless edict, "Show, don't tell?" After writing out the first bright interchanges Montgomery had dropped into a depressed mood. On April 9, 1930, she described her state of mind and body, "I am not well and I admit that today I have been blue-blue." At the end of the month she pasted into her journal a picture of Reverend John Mustard, with a wry comment "What funny kinks life does have!" Soon after these entries she became ready again to treat her readers to the "funny kinks" in the lives of the folk in her imagined world.

In this slow setting up of her *dramatis personae*, Montgomery lets slip secrets about her own nature. Old-maid Margaret with her lustrous eyes and her longing for a baby and a home of her own; young Gay, bedazzled by her first kiss—these seem like tiny bits of autobiography. So too, the story of the bride Joscelyn who experienced sudden wild rebellion against her husband Hugh's possessive kiss echoes the journal entry about Montgomery's own wedding day and her sudden fierce rejection of the idea of marriage to Ewan (whose name is the Scottish variant of "Hugh"). Charming Thora, married to despicable Chris, and patient Naomi, married to shell-shocked Lawson, are two variants of the story of young Leslie Moore in *Anne's House of Dreams*. Each is married to a husk of manhood, and here again, perhaps, is another veiled allusion to Montgomery's floundering marriage. Uncanny Oswald the Moon Man who once trained for the ministry hints at Montgomery's knowledge of the border state of mania in another theologian. The closeness of two women who vow to remain remote from romance, like Ellen and Rosemary West in *Rainbow Valley*, may be drawn from Isobel Anderson's devouring desire to monopolize Montgomery. Mrs. Fisher Dark leaves her door always open for her wandering son, and oh, how Montgomery's son Chester was wandering right now! *A Tangled Web* as a witty social study gains strength by transforming traits and actions in which Montgomery took personal pride into traits and actions clearly reprehensible.

The long section of exposition and analysis is redeemed by great flashes of characterization, of Drowned John, for instance, in a mood of fury, muttering,

It would be a damned outrage if Aunt Becky gave it to any one else and he'd tell her so, by asterisk and by asterisk. His very long face crimsoned with fury at the mere thought—a crimson that covered his ugly bald forehead, running back to his crown. His bushy white moustache bristled. His pop-eyes glared. By—more asterisks and very lurid ones—if anyone else got that jug they'd have to reckon with him.

All these vignettes are of interest to a student of Montgomery's, but they do not move the main story forward. Yet they are a reminder of the early Montgomery, story-teller supreme, who could create hundreds of believable people, involve each in a new short story, and create suspense as the reader waits to hear "what happens next." She is reminding her critics that she still has more in her quiver than chatty little girls. No child is to be seen in this novel.

After the long stasis, where Montgomery "tells," comments, and explains, Aunt Becky produces the old Dark jug, and the excitement resumes. This scene has mock-religious overtones. The jug is brought in like a chalice; an inept prayer is offered, "giving God information." Aunt Becky presides like a demonic priest, not listening to confessions but tearing the veil off the petty sins of everyone present, "airing the family skeletons." She distributes not alms but some of her less prized possessions. There is no justice in this ceremony. Everything is given to the wrong recipient. "The beautiful old Queen Anne bookcase went to Murray Dark, who never read books, and Hugh Dark got the old hour-glass—early eighteenth century—and wondered bitterly what use it would be to a man for whom time had stopped ten years ago." A shabby old book goes to Margaret Dark, an old spinster, who really needs a home and a room to herself, not a book. She is the only recipient that no one envies.

The mock-religious scene ends with sharper touches of heresy. Old maid Margaret admits to herself "the idea . . . that God was not fair." Hugh asserts, "Ah, verily, God had made a fool of him." If Montgomery's light mockery of the church in *Rainbow Valley* seemed daring, there is now a darker cynicism to wonder at. She was lashing back at new elements constricting her life. The Norval church had secret cliques and cabals, beginning to react meanly to the mistress of the manse whose métier was perhaps seen as interfering with her duties as wife of the minister. In Toronto there were more cliques and cabals: critics dismissing her work, if they mentioned it at all, as sentimental entertainment for children. While ardently proclaiming the strengths of Canadian literature, they assigned her no place in the Canadian canon in spite of her world-wide fame.[102]

Montgomery struck back. She gathered into Aunt Becky's levee a group of comic middle-aged men—Erasmus, Oswald the Moon Man, Homer, and a crowding of others—each harbouring petty pretensions and crooked intentions, all parodying the parishioners in Norval, or the self-important literary men in the Toronto Canadian Authors Association. Others with Prince Edward Island names like Palmer, Denzil, and Crosby pilloried Cavendish and Park Corner men, remembered sardonically from early years. Montgomery's sense of humour, so strong a part of the charm of all her books from *Anne of Green Gables* on, now directed itself at the people who had been important enough to annoy and frustrate her.

Yet in this section Montgomery also introduces notes of sympathy for young people, especially women in love. At Aunt Becky's levee, Donna the widow and Peter the wanderer look into each other's eyes, and fall in love. Joscelyn, who once fell passionately in love in a single instant, admits her folly to herself. These examples of sudden irrational love and its aftermath echo memories that resurfaced in the summer of 1929, when Montgomery visited Herman Leard's grave and remembered the power of her love for him and the desolation that followed his death.

Before the levee ends, Aunt Becky reveals that the fate of the old Dark jug will remain a mystery until next Hallowe'en, even if she dies before the time of revelation. Meantime, she lays out the conditions in which each member of her clan might hope to inherit the jug. Swearing, drinking, maintaining a bachelor's freedom—these and other behaviours that offend Aunt Becky will stand in the way of gaining the coveted jug. All of the potential legatees vow to forswear their sins. This comic emphasis on the power of an old woman's last will and testament was penned when Montgomery was concerned about her own literary legacy. From the late 1930s until her death Montgomery wrote and re-wrote her will, worried about her sons' relative ability to carry out her wishes. She had a special insight into Aunt Becky's desire to use her will to manipulate her relatives.

Aunt Becky dies tidily: with a "fresh sheet in unwrinkled purity. 'I've lived clean and I'll die clean,' said Aunt Becky, folding her hands on the sheet." But while waiting for Hallowe'en and the reading of her will, the men and women left alive re-knot themselves in a very untidy web of complications involving mating, and mismating. In her books for younger readers Montgomery had avoided the culmination of love. Even Rilla's "happy ending" had been reduced by the sadness of war's ending and by her childish lisp. But in the mid-section of *A Tangled Web*, Montgomery gave her fans as many love scenes as they could desire. They are sexless scenes, admittedly, except by allusions and metaphors, but definitely moving closer to passion than ever before. Yet, while Montgomery as author was prepared to dish out love scenes, Maud Macdonald was doing everything she could to prevent them in her sons' lives. She lashed out at Chester over his choice of a Norval girl, and prepared to mete out the same treatment to Stuart when his turn came: an amazing and amusing disconnect between the life and the art.

In art, if not in life, suspense must have a clear dénouement. All the threads in *A Tangled Web* must be tied up on Hallowe'en. Montgomery had been enjoying Agatha Christie's mystery stories and was ready to exploit suspense. Considerable underhand and wrongful manoeuvring erupts among the would-be inheritors of Aunt Becky's treasure. Pennycuik Penhallow, for instance, decides to marry, in order to conform to Aunt Becky's stricture against bachelor freedom, and makes a pompous offer to lonely Margaret. Similarly, coveting the jug impels all the older people into dubious behaviour.

Mischief also besets the young couples involved in rival courtships. In each case, it is the old dark jug that has brought unfortunate change into a happy life, since all the romantic troubles were set afoot at the levee. For each young couple the chief obstacle to reconciliation and happiness is a malicious, grasping woman. In particular, Nan, the glamorous flapper who comes from a more sophisticated world, wangles to separate Gay from her young fiancé. Nan is sharp, mean, malicious.

This tinge of darkness, appropriate in a novel for adults, perhaps reflects not only the concept of a new audience but also the depressing entry of criminality into Montgomery's consciousness. Sitting sadly in a Toronto courtroom with her old friend and cousin Mary Campbell Beaton, whose son was in trouble with the law, Montgomery caught a dark glimpse of young adulthood gone astray—a depressing experience for the mother of worrisome eighteen-year-old Chester. With this, among other reasons, her tone darkened. When, late in *A Tangled Web*, a famous preacher comes home to preach and pray, his religious certainty about the power of God is punctured by Stanton Grundy's comment, "There's still room for the devil at the edges."

Montgomery had reached this point in her novel around midsummer of 1930. Her work had stalled. "I cannot write and that unfinished book haunts me," she wrote in her journal on July 5, 1930. In August she was still admitting "Am trying desperately to catch up with my new book." Like Drowned John, she must have muttered rhythmically "By asterisk and by asterisk" and "by more asterisks and very lurid ones."

Inexplicably, late in the summer of 1930 Montgomery's narrative power revived. She worked out the plot and sub-plots of her novel briskly, confidently, ingeniously, with humour, realism, and vivid dialogue. First, she devised a car and bike accident that can bring Joscelyn and Hugh together, ending the separation caused by Joscelyn's romantic folly. The fortunate accident is caused by a pig. Like Anne when she hears of Gilbert's near-death in *Anne of the Island*, Joscelyn hears the false rumour of Hugh's death (by pig) and realizes how much she loves him. This reads like a grotesque mockery of the old convention of resolving a plot by a sudden stroke of fate. Or maybe the teasing resolution is Montgomery's response to critics who accused her of dainty sentimentalism. She had declared in both her novels and journals her preference for "violets" rather than "pig styes." Now she says, "I won't give you a pig stye, but here at least is a pig."

All the other young people who have been entangled in romantic illusions find ways out of the bad choices they have made. Old literary models suggested the devices that resolve the sub-plots in the novel. As in *Jane Eyre*, fire consumes the house of Dandy Dark, "Keeper of the Jug." The fire clears up two stories: Peter, rushing in to rescue the jug, rescues Donna, and ensures her commitment to a wandering life with him. A falling beam kills drunken Chris Dark, and Thora is free to be claimed by faithful Murray. Then, modelling on *Pride and Prejudice*, Montgomery lets scales fall from the heroine's eyes, when Gay sees Noel as he is, dapper, self-centred (like Wickham) and she finds true love with Roger, controlled and finer-souled (like Darcy). As in *The Taming of the Shrew*, when Joscelyn goes back to her husband Hugh, he coldly turns her away in an ugly power play, demanding that she come back to him dressed as a bride. Joscelyn humbly obeys.

Finally—and who but cat-crazy Montgomery would use this as a plot turner?—the death of a little boy's kitten sends him weeping to his mother's grave, where he finds Margaret, the lonely spinster who inherited Aunt Becky's unwelcome bequest of an old book. The old copy of *Pilgrim's Progress* has proved to be very valuable, and Margaret is now wealthy enough to buy a house that will shelter Brian.

"Finally, Brethren" is the sub-title that brings another levee. Here Dandy, holder of the precious letter that revealed the name of the jug's legatee has to make an inglorious confession. The letter has blown away—into the pig pen of course. "The pigs have et it." Another astonishing disaster follows. The jug is suddenly smashed to smithereens by the Moon Man, who has preached love, not possessions. The smash brings life and love back to a shell-shocked victim of war, in a variant of the improbable resolution in *Anne's House of Dreams*. For the other tales interwoven in the narrative web, however, Montgomery deftly produces realistic and appropriate and happy endings.

A final scene restores the cynical alternative. One aging cousin faces the long-lamented love of his life and sees her as she is: wrinkled, with yellowed skin and wattled neck, sleek black hair turned grey, the gracious curves gone. His anguished cry, "You've changed!" is countered by the lady's acid reminder, "You've changed a little yourself." The scene is cruel both ways. It is also a wry construct by a writer, now in her mid-50s, who had prided herself on her complexion.

But beauty, in a jug or a book or any other work of art, is in the eye of the beholder. The jug is gone, but another prized bit of crockery survives: the "statoo" of Aurora (the "Roarer"), goddess of dawn, beautiful to big Little Sam in her nudity, but offensive to prudish little Big Sam. At the end of the novel the two old boys move in together again, to enjoy the contentious "statoo," now bronzed, in consideration of Big Sam's prejudices. It may be de-bronzed soon, in deference to Little Sam's aesthetics.

So Montgomery concluded a novel that satisfied her intention of writing for adults, writing humorously, and celebrating her own dearest material possession while she mocked possessiveness. A century earlier, Sir Walter Scott had written, "Oh! what a tangled web we weave/When first we practice to deceive!"[103] Montgomery had "practiced to deceive" for over forty years before she created *A Tangled Web*. Like every novelist, she had made up characters and given them human foibles and mannerisms enough to fool readers into accepting them as real and wondering why they act as they do, or whether they could have been different—as if they were anything but pen-strokes on paper. Similarly, Montgomery had honed her skill at describing imaginary scenes until people came to believe in their actual existence. Now, on "Anne's Island" tourists wandered along the north shore, looking for "Green Gables," or "Lover's Lane," or the "Lake of Shining Waters" (September 22, 1929). As for Montgomery's plot lines, complete with hints and clues and foreshadowings, thousands of readers had willingly suspended disbelief and turned the pages to find out what would happen, without thinking about the author once upon a time chewing her pen to decide what the outcome should be.

Lots of practice; but when the creative writer actually spun out *A Tangled Web*, she wove in surprising new twists. In spite of all the light that the journals shine on her "real life" doings, the patterns in the web still appear mysterious.

~ Pat of Silver Bush ~

(Toronto: McClelland & Stewart, 1933)

Montgomery did not coin the phrases "kindred spirits" and "bosom friends," but her portrayal of intense friendships especially between young people was so memorable that the two phrases have come to be inextricably associated with her work. Most readers of *Anne of Green Gables* recall Anne's passionate eagerness to bond with Diana. Friendship bubbles over in *Anne of the Island*, where Anne and three other college students enjoy themselves at Patty's Place. In *Anne's House of Dreams*, the brilliant, unhappy Leslie Moore, at first resentful, becomes attached to Anne, the new bride and mother. Miss Cornelia offers inter-generational friendship. Anne's bond with Susan Baker, her housekeeper and confidante, is both inter-generational and inter-class. Youthful friendship glows between Emily and Ilse, the Story Girl and her cousins, the Blythe children and the Merediths. In *Magic for Marigold*, however, the idealization of youthful friendships diminished: the imaginary friend Sylvia was more beloved than any of the real little Varvaras and Gwennies. In *A Tangled Web*, there are no children, friendly or otherwise. Friendship as a fictional theme reappears in *Pat of Silver Bush*. Pat relates intensely to Bets, her bosom friend, and to Jingle, her kindred spirit.

From childhood, the friendships Montgomery documented in her journals had been strong, and funny to read about. Pensie, Amanda, Nate, and the Pritchard brother and sister, stand behind the happy young friendships in the early *Anne* books. Mary Campbell Beaton, Nora Lefurgey, the Campbell cousins, especially Frede, all helped fix images of older friends talking, teasing, exchanging secrets, enjoying common pleasures in the later *Anne* stories and the *Emily* series. As Montgomery grew older, she lost touch with some old friends, and new ones were hard to come by, given the tensions of her family life and the unspoken taboo against a minister's wife playing favourites among the parishioners, first in Leaskdale and later in Norval. By 1931, however, when Montgomery began to compose *Pat of Silver Bush*, two couples who had been friends of her youth emerged in freshly strong friendships. Alec MacNeill, a cousin, and older brother of Pensie, and his wife May, who had teased young Maud about Ed Simpson in old days, were now the Island friends who welcomed Montgomery to their home whenever she visited Prince Edward Island. (She would dedicate the new book to them.) Across the continent, Alexena McGregor, a school friend in Prince Albert, and her husband Fred Wright had offered a similar warmth when Montgomery made a western tour in fall of 1930. (She had dedicated *A Tangled Web* to them.)

The notion of friendliness had been soured lately by the intrusion of Isobel Anderson, an eccentric young woman who wrote adoring letters and proffered unwelcome invitations, and then announced that the cool reception she was receiving meant that Mrs. Macdonald was incapable of love. In answer, Montgomery wrote a paean to friendship, invoking the memory of Frede, calling on her to "answer from the grave" (February 8, 1932). In *Pat of Silver Bush*, the capacity for friendship is related to the possibility of tragedy.

In the spring of 1931, Montgomery was enduring what felt like family tragedy. Her son Chester, welcomed so touchingly at his birth, was now inflicting hurt. She faced Chester's failure at university, his troubling propensity to lie, cheat, and waste money, and his obsession with a young Norval woman at a time he should not be thinking about marriage. Her distress was compounded by household troubles. The maid she had relied on for several years had left, replaced by someone who made her uneasy. In this hurtful time, Montgomery turned to the memory of her great-aunt Mary Lawson. This woman had been acknowledged as the source of most of the tales in *The Story Girl* and *The Golden Road*. She had also been Maud Montgomery's consoler and confidante during the difficult time of her engagement to Edwin Simpson. She was the typical older visitor who moved from one family to another in those days, helping, cheering, passing along a hoard of family memories. On June 2, 1931, Montgomery took time to write out "Aunt Mary's account of the family." Copying out Aunt Mary's story was literary busy-work, a kind of doodling while the author's mind was turning over possibilities for her own composition. The literary result would be the creation of "Judy Plum," the mainstay of the Silver Bush household.

Memories of the Campbell home in Park Corner gave Montgomery an avenue into a new book. In July 1931, "rummaging through an old notebook to find an idea for a story," she was swept back to the winter of 1892 and a perfect moment of waiting for one of Aunt Annie's suppers while looking out the window to spruce-dotted hills. "I hate to think of all the lovely things I remember being forgotten when I'm dead!" she wrote (July 11, 1931). The journal entry included a reference to the "secret field" she and Alec and May MacNeill had discovered two years earlier. In midsummer 1931, while the idea of her new novel was still embryonic, Ewan went to the Island, leaving her, "a poor devil of an author," at home. Summer was the time when she was most filled with nostalgia, for the old summer kitchen, for the sand dunes and the trees around the farm. She began to brood up a story about a girl with equal or greater adherence to the world she grew up in. It was April 2, 1932, before she could say, "I began to write my new book today, *Pat of Silver Bush.*

As the book opens, Pat Gardiner is presented as a person who loves too keenly. "She loves things better than most, but they'll hurt her more," says Judy Plum, the Irish housekeeper at Silver Bush, Pat's home. She adds, "Ye have to take the bad wid the good." Judy Plum is an unending source of stories that delight, frighten, console, and amuse young Pat. Her incessant Irish dialect is a sign of Montgomery's literary times: Sean O'Casey and J.M. Synge and the Dublin Abbey Players were filling the theatres in Toronto as elsewhere, and W.B. Yeats was dominating the poetic world in the 1930s. Judy's Irish accent may also reflect the presence of many Canadians of Irish stock, including the McClures, in Norval, overlaid on memories of the many Irish people in Prince Edward Island. Aside from her stagey Irish brogue, however, Judy Plum has a lot in common with Great-Aunt Mary Lawson. From the outset of *Pat of Silver Bush*, Judy Plum helps little Pat Gardiner accept unwelcome changes by her tact and humour.

Pat has an almost pathological dread of change. That dread echoed Montgomery's own. She envied the women of previous generations: an "apparently changeless world. . . . And my generation! . . . Everything we once thought immoveable wrenched from its pedestal and hurled to ruins . . . before us nothing but a welter of doubt and confusion and uncertainty" (January 24, 1932). Her pain, and Pat's dread, reflect the troubles enveloping Park Corner, central in so many happy memories. Aunt Annie's grandsons, facing troubled times as farmers, bore the worst blows of the general Depression period. Montgomery "could not bear the thought of it and all its ghosts being sold to strangers" (February 26, 1932).

Little Pat is born into a family much like the Campbells. Not an only child like Anne or Emily or Marigold, Pat is deeply attached to brothers Joe and Sid, and sister Winnie. A new baby about to be added to the beloved sibling circle constitutes a frightening change—until Judy Plum offers funny consolation and advice on adjusting.

Equally, Pat loves her home. The fields of Silver Bush, the flowers in the garden (bluebells, lilacs, peonies), the food prepared in the old kitchen (eggs fried in butter, codfish cakes and bishop's bread and doughnuts), the furniture and the pictures on the walls, all are described with a passion that transmits Montgomery's own nostalgia. With Sid, Pat shares the discovery of a Secret Field, described in heightened style: "basking in a pool of sunshine, scented by the breath of the spice ferns that grew in golden clumps around it. Its feathery bent grasses were starred with the red of wild strawberry leaves." Pat loves Sid with particular intensity. As a very small child she plans to stay with him forever. "'And we'll always live at Silver Bush and I'll keep house for you,' said Pat eagerly./'Sure. Unless I go west; lots of boys do.'/'Oh!' A cold wind blew across Pat's happiness."

In the tenth chapter the new happiness of friendship is added when Pat makes her first friend outside the family. Hilary Gordon[104] (nicknamed "Jingle"), looks like a "hobbledehoy," to quote the term Montgomery's favourite author Trollope applied to a gangly insecure youth in *The Small House at Allington* (1864). With Jingle, Pat finds another secret place, the "Happiness Pool." They share a poetic response to beauty. Jingle, like Teddy Kent in the Emily books, is a creator. "Jingle took a bit of birch bark from a fallen tree near them and, with the aid of a few timothy stems, made under her very eyes the most wonderful little house . . . rooms, porch, windows, chimneys, all complete. It was like magic. . . . 'Some day when I'm grown up I'm going to build them really. I'll build one for *you*, Pat.'"

When she was planning her book, Montgomery, "rummaging" this time in the attic, had found letters from Nate Lockhart, her schooldays friend. "While I read them I was strangely happy, bewitched back into the past." As she drifted through these memories she asked herself, "Why am I scribbling on in this idle fashion? Just because I am lonely and homesick and like to write and think of events and people in those early happy days" (February 8, 1932). Doodling in the journal had again been a way of warming up for actual composition.

Five chapters later, she drew from more recent experiences. In 1930, she had been reunited with Laura Pritchard Agnew. Long ago, Montgomery had declared Laura and her brother, Will, "'my style' and I am right at home with them. We are kindred spirits" (December 10, 1890). Now, in May 1932, Laura's sixteen-year-old daughter Eleanor had come to Toronto to study violin. Welcomed to the Norval home in May, Laura's daughter brought a charming reinforcement of the warmth of early friendship.

Next, on July 2, 1932, Nora Lefurgey Campbell came for a visit and the two old friends "told stories and ragged each other and shrieked with laughter." When Maud first made friends with Nora in 1902, she had written, "We 'took' to each other from the start. . . . Nora suits me exactly" (September 21, 1902). Nora blessedly resurfaced in 1928, and "Ten minutes after we had met the twenty-four years were not. We 'clicked' as well as ever we did. . . . Apart from Laura Pritchard and Frede Campbell, Nora Lefurgey (who in some respects is much the same type of girl) is the only friend I have ever had before whom I could, in Emerson's fine phrase, 'think aloud'. . . . I feel as if I had been smothered and were now drinking in great gulps of clear gay mountain air" (September 23, 1928). From all these friends (and perhaps in defiance of debilitating Isobel) Montgomery drew the picture of Bets Wilcox, the friend who enters Pat's life in Chapter 15 of the new novel. The presence of Nora, added to the rediscovery of Laura, had allowed the author to return in some of the same happiness, to a secret field of love and companionship.

Bets moves into the "Long Lonely House" near Silver Bush farm. Gray-eyed, like Laura Pritchard, and pretty like her, Bets was born the same year as Pat (Laura and Maud had also shared a birth-year). Bets has "beautiful eyes, . . . large, dreamy gray eyes. . . . [Pat had] a queer feeling that she had known this girl always. Perhaps the stranger felt something of the same when she looked into Pat's eyes. . . . They were good friends before they spoke a word to each other." The friendship catches the charm and conviction of the earlier treatment of the love between Anne and Diana. But their repetition of the old vow made to Diana, "faithful till death do us part," comes shadowed by Judy Plum's sense of the transience of Bets's bloom.

At the mid-point of the book, Pat says, "I'm so happy I'm frightened . . . as if it couldn't be right to be so happy." While writing *Pat of Silver Bush*, Maud walked and talked with Nora, beside the Credit River, near its forks. "[We] went on up the river until we came to a place so breathtaking in beauty that we sat on a tree trunk for over two hours and just looked at it. . . . When we had to drag ourselves away we both felt that we had captured one of those things even time cannot destroy (September 11, 1932). The Ontario river was beautiful, when a friend was there to share the view. In the chapters Montgomery was writing at this time, young Pat is so happy she can't sleep. "'Drink all the happiness ye can, me darlint, when the cup is held to yer lips,'" says Judy Plum the story-teller.

Alas, soon Montgomery wrote in her journal, "The gods have presented their bill." The entry for September 14, 1932, reads,

> Last night a letter came from Eleanor Agnew, telling me that her mother had died a week ago. She was buried last Friday . . . when I was sitting with Nora by the moonlit river, feeling so happy! . . . If this had happened before my visit west two years ago I would not have felt it with this keenness of agony. But during that visit all my old deep love for Laura burst into a second blooming. (September 14, 1932)

She turned back to her writing. Into the last section of *Pat of Silver Bush* she added tragedy. Four-fifths of the way through, Pat's beloved "Bets" dies. She dies of flu-pneumonia, ever to be mourned, never forgotten. No sentimental wedding veil like Diana's for this friend, and no comic mockery of marriage either, just the sadness of loss, made so much sadder by the warmth of Montgomery's rediscovery of Laura on that October trip West two years earlier.

Montgomery had introduced the death of a young girl, Ruby Gillis, into *Anne of the Island*, and in *The Golden Road* she presaged the fate of Cecily. She could look for a literary model in the death of Beth in *Little Women*. But the handling of Bets's death is much more intense and personal, because of Montgomery's nearly neurotic clinging to the thought of her own dead friends. Never before had Montgomery allowed an event in her life to intrude so blatantly into her plot. There is no reason, logical or artistic, for Bets's death. The only logic for this sudden death must be that Pat is so melancholy a character that she invites tragedy. Alternatively, Montgomery must have justified this turn in the plot, both in the original composition and again in the time of revision, on the grounds of its relevance to the theme of change, as it linked in her mind now with the idea of friendship. In that sense she is offering an appropriate warning to readers who felt as deeply as she did not to trust fate to dole out anything but a tragic fate to one's friends.

A week before recording the death of Laura, Montgomery had experienced one of the strange dreams she took very seriously. It was a dream of Amanda ("Mollie") Macneill, her first "bosom friend," who seems to have suggested many of the happy-go-lucky qualities of Diana in *Anne of Green Gables*. In the dream, Amanda dissolved in tears, trying to tell of the death of a dear friend. Another part of the dream concerned Nate Lockhart, whose letters Montgomery had been re-reading at the time she was sketching the character of Jingle Gordon. Nate in the dream had aged. Like Amanda he was in tears (September 5, 1932). Montgomery interpreted this kind of dream as proving her psychic power, and as predictive of hearing of Laura's death. Psychology might instead read the dream as indicating the linkage in her subconscious between her real and imagined life. She was nearing the conclusion of the writing of *Pat of Silver Bush* and a general sense of tragedy was pressing on her. She had universalized her own sense that anything she loved was doomed.

Her mental health had been bad most of the summer. On July 10 she had written, "Today was dark and wet and on such days my nervous unrest is always intensified. I could hardly sit still in church. I don't understand these spells. I never had anything just like them before. They are very dreadful. Yet I seem to be quite well physically. . . . Yesterday my head was queer and I wrote at Pat with difficulty." Nora Lefurgey Campbell's visits ameliorated this mood, but the persistent intrusions of "that wretched Isobel" countered the happiness of Nora's friendship.

Montgomery's money troubles increased as she worked to finish *Pat of Silver Bush*. The effect of the general Depression had torn apart the financial security that she had built on her early royalties as a best-selling author. She had invested all her royalties plus the money awarded in her law suit against Page in the stock market in 1928. In 1929 the market crashed. Some of her investments were completely lost as companies declared bankruptcy; other diminished painfully. For example $14,000 invested in the Simpson Department Store Company diminished to $840 by 1932.[105] Another cry for help from the Park Corner family concerned her agreement to put George's daughter through Prince of Wales College; "It comes at a hard time for me" (September 12, 1932). She had made many loans to friends including those at Park Corner, but none were able to repay or to produce interest on these loans. Sales of her most recent book *A Tangled Web* were not going very well, perhaps because it was aimed at an adult audience new for her, but perhaps also because book sales like everything else were affected by the Depression. At this time, when the Depression was straining their finances, the Macdonald family needed the influx of new royalties to maintain their sons as students. Chester, who had failed his first year in Engineering at the University of Toronto, had wasted a year's worth of university fees and room and board. Stuart, who had been getting excellent marks and many prizes in school, had recently experienced a drop in his academic standing, lessening the probability of his getting a scholarship to attend the University in the fall. Small wonder that Montgomery experienced nights of nervous unrest as she wrote her way toward the end of her book.

She now created new loneliness for Pat, drawing on memories of her own youthful isolation. Jingle, whose story in many ways duplicates Montgomery's own, decides to leave the Island. A virtual orphan, Jingle had idealized his absent mother, as Montgomery idealized the mother she had never known. When, at the age of fifteen he realized that his mother had never loved him, he had sunk into a bitterness, clearly linked with what Montgomery felt when, at about the same age, she experienced her stepmother's cold rejection. When Jingle's love for Pat intensified, Pat tried to escape from the attraction that held her and Jingle together. Montgomery here draws on the puzzled summary of feelings she recorded in her current journal as she reminisced about Nate Lockhart: "Why, is it that all through my life the men I've *liked* best were the men I couldn't *love*?" (February 11, 1932). Excluded from Pat's life when she flirts with other "beaus," Jingle moves away from the Island to pursue studies in architecture. Pat lets him leave without allowing him to declare his love for her, dooming herself to a lonely future.

Pat has seen fundamental changes in her family, wrought by attrition rather than by tragedy. Joe has left, the wanderlust that is part of his heritage pulling him into escape to the sea. Sid has quit school, and spends too much time with the contemptible May Binnie. Pat's mother has gradually drifted into invalidism; her father has returned home discouraged by disappointment out west. For Winnie, the early rumours of her romance that distressed the child Pat with threats of change have shifted into the fact of marriage, a change which the older Pat must accept. Her only comfort is Silver Bush itself, the farm, the secret field where she can still find sunshine, and the kitchen where cooking offers some joy. Like Anne of Green Gables, and like Montgomery herself, Pat will stay home to keep the house going.

As she neared the end of her writing, Montgomery left Norval again for a brief autumn holiday in Prince Edward Island. She returned in November, "in body at least. Spiritually I am still on my Island—where I spent a happy month" (November 13, 1932). In spite of this buoyancy, certain changes such as the move of the old Cavendish schoolhouse left her desolate. Old Island friends now appeared literally old. The family at Park Corner seemed to be prospering at last, but a fatalistic feeling prevented Montgomery from feeling hopeful. She returned to her Secret Field with Alec and May Macneill, loving it "terribly—so terribly that I've been dying of homesickness for it ever since. I see it as I write, dark and still and full of secret wisdom." Then the journal continues, in the prevailing mood of depression: "It won't live long. Already its bents are feathered with tiny spruces and in a few years the woods will have taken it back."

All of these feelings drove the ending of *Pat of Silver Bush*. Bets is dead, Jingle has gone, but the beloved home place and its beautiful natural setting remain to be celebrated. On December 3, 1932, Montgomery wrote in her journal, "Today I finished *Pat of Silver Bush*." She added. "It has a setting after my own heart and 'Pat' is more myself than any of my heroines."[106] Sadly, this entry continues, "My nervous unrest and odd feelings in the head have returned. And so many things are worrisome and disheartening. . . . The 'Depression' shows no sign of lifting, . . . markets are dead—crude oil has crashed—my poor investments dwindle daily." In the new year, the Campbell family came to an agreement with "Aunt Maud" who loaned $700 to keep the farm in the family.

A sad aftermath to *Pat of Silver Bush* occurred in the sudden death of laughter-loving, affectionate Clara Campbell. Frede's older sister had been the prettiest of the happy Park Corner crew. Life seemed to have imitated art. Bets was dying again in Montgomery's "recurrent agonies of sorrow" (December 23, 1932). Eight months later when *Pat of Silver Bush* arrived in published form, she wrote, "I wish Frede had lived to read this book. It would appeal to her, for she loved her home with the passion I had for mine" (August 1, 1933).

For readers, that passion for home and the celebration of friendly love might counteract what is clearly a more depressive tone in *Pat of Silver Bush* than in any of the earlier works. For students of Montgomery there is certainly more here, sometimes—but not always—under artistic control, of her experiences of friendship and her nostalgia for the Island home.

Mistress Pat

(Toronto: McClelland & Stewart, 1935)

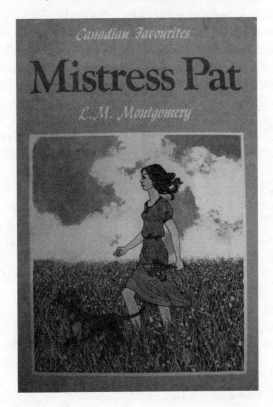

Pride had always been a component of Montgomery's personality. She laughingly quoted an Island saying, "From the pride of the Macneills, good lord deliver us." "To be born a Macneill was to be born to the purple in Cavendish," she once wrote, only half in fun (July 17, 1927). Far from Cavendish, Montgomery had been quite properly proud of her social position as a minister's wife, proud of her two sons, of her possessions and her accomplishments as a writer. The novel she began to write in January 1934 bears a proud title: *Mistress Pat*. Pat Gardiner, the little girl who had grown up in Silver Bush, was last seen when she became "chatelaine" of the family home. The sequel was to show her in control of her dear old house, and mistress, presumably, of her own destiny.

But Pat's creator suffered terrible setbacks since the time she worked on *Pat of Silver Bush*. Her older son Chester had been expelled in February 1933 from Engineering at the University of Toronto, a blow to pride so great that there is no journal entry specifying what had happened until three years later. He had made a fresh start studying Law, but at the end of his first term in that faculty, in December 1933, he was forced to reveal to his parents that he had secretly married a young Norval girl, and that they were expecting a baby. Montgomery was shattered. In the 1930s, when Victorian proprieties still prevailed in a small village, a proud minister's wife could hardly survive the gossip about a secret marriage followed swiftly by a baby's birth.

There was some consolation in the sympathy of Nora Campbell and of the Barracloughs, her friends in Glen Williams near Norval, and in the comfort of "Lucky," the beloved cat that "seems to *know* I am suffering" (December 8, 1933). On January 8, 1934, Montgomery visited John McClelland, her always supportive Toronto publisher. Maybe the combined encouragement by her friends and her publisher resulted in the entry for January 15: "I began work on a sequel to *Silver Bush*."

Mistress Pat begins with a replay of many earlier themes. Pat is still devoted to every flower, every tree, every animal on the Silver Bush Farm; every stick of furniture, every tradition, every accustomed meal in the old house. The food is still wonderful: "Grandmother Selby's jellied cabbage salad . . . Aunt Hazel's ginger cookies . . . Cousin Miranda's beefsteak pie . . . the Bay Shore pudding . . . Great-grandmother Gardiner's fruit cake . . . Old Joe Pringle's mince pie." Montgomery had always been able to recall sensual details in her use of nostalgic memories of Prince Edward Island: now it seems that the sense of sight and sound is being richly supplemented by memories of the taste of foods prepared by the Campbells, who were great cooks. The procession of the seasons on Prince Edward Island still brings Pat joy. Describing the beauty of Silver Bush in the autumn, she quotes Bliss Carman's "A Vagabond Song": "'The scarlet of the maples can shake me like a cry/Of bugles going by.'"

Pat is still "just a little different from other people, too. She had been different when she was a big-eyed child, . . . different when she was a brown, skinny little imp in her early teens . . . and still different, now that she was twenty and ought, so Judy Plum felt, to be having beaus." Judy Plum still cooks and gossips, now adding many proud stories of the fine castle in Ireland where she lived as a child.[107]

Two comic incidents will bring a little set-back to Pat's pride in her house and her family. An aristocratic lady comes to visit the Gardiners because of her friendship with their cousin in England. She comes, alas, ahead of time, leaving Judy to entertain her inadequately, in the kitchen. The incident ends happily: the Countess of Medchester thoroughly enjoys the Island homeliness and she allays Pat's embarrassment. A similar happy ending resolves the second humiliating occasion. At Christmas, Pat's scrupulous preparations are all undone when a strange black dog, coming with an uninvited guest, wreaks havoc. The food is ruined, the pretty arrangements come apart, Pat's best dress is spoiled. Again, however, in a happy aftermath, Pat's wandering brother Joe arrives in time for a post-Christmas feast, and sister Winnie gives birth, ahead of time, to a beautiful baby. On May 17, 1934, Montgomery had experienced a comparable "thrill of interest and excitement" at her first sight of her newborn granddaughter, Chester and Luella's child. Four days later she wrote in her Journal, "I wrote the Christmas chapter of *Pat II* today and lost myself for a few blessed hours in 'Silver Bush.'"

The happy, comic tone in this first section of *Mistress Pat* is reinforced by the arrival of Tillytuck the hired man. He rivals Judy Plum as a fantastic story-teller, and he is mercifully free of the stagey Irish dialect that makes Judy's sayings hard to read. In Silver Bush, as in real life, cats offer comfort.

Montgomery had had trouble "getting down to writing," but Nora Campbell continued to help her spirits in the spring. "When I am with Nora . . . I have not forgotten how to talk" (April 20, 1934). And she had not forgotten how to write, perched by the window in the Norval manse bedroom, glancing out at the beautiful pines on Russells' hill whenever her pen faltered. *Mistress Pat* began to take shape as spring passed.

Troubles erupted. In June Luella left Chester in Toronto and brought her baby, less than a month old, home to her father's house in Norval. Partly due to worrying over this situation, Ewan underwent a mental crisis, groaning and talking of suicide, sure that he was going to die and go to hell. Mrs. Thompson, the Macdonalds' maid, had turned hurtfully impertinent, and in July she announced she would be leaving in a month. Meantime, Montgomery compelled herself to write chapter after chapter, "in agony of mind" (May 29, 1934). Better return to the world of Judy Plum. There, reflecting dismay at the thought of Mrs. Thompson leaving, Montgomery put into Judy Plum's head the idea of going away from Silver Bush, for a visit back to Ireland.

Then, ignoring her fury over Chester's marriage, Montgomery set her fictional Pat into a laughing dance with a series of suitors. Old friend Hilary being far away in France, held there by Pat's refusal to consider him as other than old friend, Pat is free to encourage and then discourage a succession of fairly eligible young men. The air of romance is doubled, because little sister Cuddles, now to be known as Rae, is also enjoying some young romancing.

At the same point in the novel as the chapter where Bets first appeared in *Pat of Silver Bush*, newcomers move into the Long House where Bets once lived. Pat will once again enjoy friendship. Suzanne Kirk, a new kindred spirit, is garbed in a khaki shirt and knickerbocker outfit, very much like one Nora Campbell wears in a photograph pasted into Montgomery's journal. But Suzanne's slanted, grey-green eyes, sloe-black hair, and her "crooked clever mouth with a mutinous tilt" all sound like details in an older photo of Frede Campbell. Montgomery is giving Pat two gifts of friendship at once, for Suzanne's brother David also fits happily into Pat's circle. David is older, a war veteran and a widower, "with a mordant edge to his wit." A little troubling quality comes with his surname "Kirk," too reminiscent of Emily's "Priest."

In this second section of *Mistress Pat*, Montgomery adds family comedy. Uncle Tom Gardiner meets his long-ago love, now inordinately talkative and incredibly fat. "Can that be all one woman?" Tillituck asks. Uncle Horace Gardiner holds forth on fiction. He likes happy endings.

"These modern novels that leave everything unfinished annoy me."

"But things are often unfinished in real life," said Pat, who had picked up the idea from David.

"All the more reason why they should come right in books," said Uncle Horace testily. "'Real life!' We get enough real life living. I like a nice snug tidy ending in a book. I like fairy tales. Judy's yarns never left things in the air. That's why she's always been such a corking success as a story-teller."

This constituted a bit of self-congratulation for the real story-teller, who had been criticized for the too-sunny pictures of life in her fiction.

That summer brought Montgomery real-life troubles. Ewan's condition worsened so seriously that he had to be hospitalized in the Homewood Centre in Guelph, where psychiatrists and therapists could help him. He stayed at Homewood until August. From July to October there are no journal references to Nora Lefurgey Campbell. Presumably she was away with her own family on summer holidays. Mrs. Thompson departed, to be replaced by a new, young, less efficient maid. As prescribed by her doctor, Montgomery was dosing herself almost nightly with sleeping pills and tonics, some with strychnine, others with borine among their ingredients—and all in fact addictive and debilitating. She kept on writing *Mistress Pat*, although on August 15 her journal entry ran, "Managed to write a little but my head felt queer all day. I am afraid I am going to break down myself."

She opened the third section of *Mistress Pat* with a little happy ending of the sort Uncle Horace preferred: Judy Plum who has distressed the family by planning to travel to Ireland, changes her mind and stays on at Silver Bush in "The Third Year." The section titles are surprising. In earlier work, Montgomery had created intriguing chapter titles. Now she simply names the sections for the sequence of years, on and on until "The Eleventh Year." The heavy iteration of a non-changing, non-maturing adult life reflects a general diminishing of excitement in the story. In *Anne of Green Gables* Matthew once said to Marilla that Anne was "such an int'resting little thing." Pat Gardiner was an interesting little girl when she first appeared, but in her twenty-seventh, twenty-eighth, and twenty-ninth years, her interesting qualities wear thin. Young readers who had identified with the young Pat would be hard put to enjoy the elegiac tone of the older one. Even the beauties of nature seem diminished now. Winter whiteness, for instance, which once drew loving descriptions from Montgomery via John Foster in *The Blue Castle*, now appears menacing: "On a rare fine day the world seemed made of diamond dust, cold, dazzling, splendid, heartless. There was the beauty of winter moonlight on frosted panes and chill harpings of wind beneath cold, unfriendly stars."

Although Montgomery might well worry about losing her basic audience, she could still count on the older readers who still longed for "a new L.M. Montgomery novel." Whatever the losses in this sequel novel, many of the old strengths remained: sparkling bits of humour, sharp convincing dialogue, and a growing fascination with the theme of love of home, and the hope that nothing there will change.

Changes do come in "The Fourth Year" and "The Fifth Year." Pat's younger sister Rae storms off to take a college course at Guelph.[108] She leaves like a younger escaping Valancy, with "a little green hat tipped provocatively over one eye." Rae, dithering between two young suitors, sounds like Philippa Gordon in *Anne of the Island*.[109] Pat, however, is still so set on staying in Silver Bush that she refuses one charming suitor rather than move to another part of her home community with him.

More serious changes occur in "The Sixth Year." In *Pat of Silver Bush*, the vulgar Binnie family had threatened to take over the old home when the young Gardiners' father, Long Alec, was out West. That threat was avoided. Now it becomes an unavoidable reality. "Sid had brought May Binnie in and announced, curtly and defiantly, and yet with such a pitiful, beaten look on his face, that they had been married that day in Charlottetown." The scene is an ugly version of the moment when Chester announced his secret marriage to Luella Reid. One difference was that Luella was not arch, bold or brassy like May Binnie. She was a guileless young person who had always helped the Macdonalds with church events, especially musical programs. Her dying mother had trusted Montgomery to be kind to her. The picture of May Binnie reproduces Luella's situation rather than her character. May Binnie's name may have a literary source: Montgomery had read May Sinclair's novels in the 1920s and declared them "vulgar" which was the Silver Bush term for the Binnies.[110] The main difference from the situation Montgomery faced vis-à-vis Chester and Luella is that the focus in *Mistress Pat* is not on ensuing scandal but on intrusion into the home place. May Binnie is a completely wrong type of person to treasure and enhance Silver Bush. Even Judy Plum is crushed: "One does be thinking the world cud be run a bit better. I'm fearing this will break Patsy's heart." Indeed, Pat's fury suggests something neurotic in her possessiveness regarding Sid—not too different from Montgomery's feelings about her son Chester.[111] Pat's battle with the Binnies may also reflect the author's fury as she battled in the world of literature. She was horrified at the frankness of writers like Morley Callaghan who were turning a genre of writing that had always appealed to her sense of decency into something vulgar, where old taboos were disregarded.

Coached by Judy and Rae, Pat fights a quiet war at first, but in "The Seventh Year," the struggles become more desperate. This battling spirit reflects a new and frightening phase in Montgomery's life in Norval. Troubles were brewing in the church, directed against Ewan, who by now was virtually an absentee minister as a result of his mental illness; and there were also machinations against Montgomery as the minister's wife. These were bitter, bitter times for both husband and wife. In August, when Ewan came home from the sanatorium, not one member of the parish came to see him. While September wore away, there were behind the scenes efforts to unseat the minister. Montgomery swallowed her resentment and held her head high. She particularly resented the treachery of the McClure family. Garfield McClure had once declared "The Irish McClures would be loyal to the Scotch Macdonalds" (August 19, 1934). But now this member of Ewan's session was trying to oust the minister. Something of the same tension plays out in Silver Bush. In fiction Montgomery could muster her old sense of humour against vulgar Mrs. Binnie: "Gossip was her mother-tongue and grammar was her servant, not her master." She could vent her spleen against the Norval neighbour women when she wrote of the Binnies, "They had no comprehension whatever of people who did not think at the tops of their voices and empty out their feelings to the dregs." For Pat, not giving in to the Binnies, or responding in kind to their inroads into the gentle and genteel atmosphere of Silver Bush was a matter of pride. In both life and fiction, there seemed to be no escape from vulgarity. As for Montgomery, she had to say about her days in Norval, as she wrote in her fiction, "Life seemed sadly out of tune, struggle as bravely as one might."

Pat's unhappiness intensifies when Jingle writes of the glories of travel, seeing "Philae against a desert sunset . . . the storied Alhambra . . . the pearl-white wonder of the Taj Mahal by moonlight . . . Petra, that "rose-red city half as old as Time." Pat hears rumours that Hilary is engaged to a girl in Vancouver. Pat tells herself she is not hurt. David Kirk is still at the Long House with his sister Suzanne.

At this point in the composition of *Mistress Pat*, at exactly the same stage in the story as the moment marked by the death of Bets in *Pat of Silver Bush*, the new kindred spirit Suzanne Kirk is lost. She is torn away not by death, like Bets, but by her choice of marriage. Suzanne abruptly leaves her house and leaves the book. Again there is no build-up to this blow, and no logical reason why this new friend should go out of Pat's life. Montgomery seems intent on punishing Pat, here as in the first book.

At the news of Suzanne's going, Pat decides that she can marry David Kirk. Ominously, she tells her mother, "Our minds click. He loves the same things I do. . . . We'll always be good chums." To Rae she adds, more significantly, "I'll be *near* Silver Bush. . . . I can always look down on it and watch over it."

"The sad, hopeless rain of autumn that seemed like the tears of old sorrows on the window-panes of Silver Bush" opens "The Eighth Year." Montgomery had let her own dreariness trickle into her writing. On September 12 she told her journal, "If I am not getting any writing done. I don't see how I am going to get *Pat II* finished in time and if I don't things will be serious financially." As the Presbyterian plotters in Norval worked behind the scenes to oust Ewan, she realized that if he lost his church position his pension would be virtually valueless. Resisting her down-hearted mood, she sounded a wry comic note in her novel. Handyman Tillytuck is claimed by his abandoned wife. The reason for their separation turns out to have been that he refused to believe in predestination. Shades of poor Ewan Macdonald, whose mental instability had allowed the idea of predestination to obsess him! Perhaps the moment when L.M. Montgomery could find the heart to use this dreadful old theology for a bit of fun marked a changing point in her own spirits.

Hilary returns, only to hear May's gossip that Pat and David Kirk are engaged. He leaves again, wishing Pat happiness. Rare happiness does indeed come, from her garden, her kittens, and her home: "Silver Bush lying in its misty morning silence . . . *her* home . . . her dear, beloved, all-sufficing home." She has the mixed happiness also of playing with her elder sister's twin babies: "When Pat looked at the two absurd, darling, round-faced, blue-eyed mites on the same pillow she always swallowed a little choke of longing."

Working toward an ending, Montgomery worried in her journal. "October 8, 1934: I tried to work at *Pat II* and wrote half a chapter but find it very difficult to settle my mind to it." Small wonder: on October 13, the Norval Church management gave Ewan a leave of absence until December, with the edict that he would have to resign in the new year if unable to perform his duties then. Montgomery's dejection at this time was offset by the happy ending to the on-and-off romance of Marion Webb, who had grown up in the house that had been the inspiration for "Green Gables," and Murray Laird. Ewan was able to officiate at their wedding in the Norval manse. Montgomery promptly wrote the same kind of happiness into her novel, but she assigned it not to Pat but to her younger sister Rae.[112] The Silver Bush family puts together a short-notice, beautiful wedding (like

Marion Laird's). The section ends with Pat alone, quietly happy in her home. In the journal, Montgomery entered a sadder cry about the love of home: "The thought of leaving Norval hurts me horribly. I love it so—my hills, my trees, my river, my garden, the beautiful church I've loved and worked for, the pretty roads all around" (November 5, 1934).

Five days after writing this, she discovered how hurtful Norval could be. Her old foe Garfield McClure led the Norval Dramatic Society in excluding her from their meetings and plans, in spite of the fact that she had created and led the play-giving in the community ever since arriving there. She bitterly swallowed the insult to her pride rather than add to Ewan's difficulties with his parishioners. When Ewan, now on leave, departed for Prince Edward Island, she returned to her book with relief. "November 26: My first *livable* day for months. . . . I wrote a whole chapter of Pat II this morning and found it quite easy though I cannot take pleasure in it. But it was wonderful to be able to write without Ewan coming in every few moments with some bogey to be laid. And such a relief to my mind to find I can really write again when the strain is lifted."

She writes relief into her book. On "a dear, gentle evening with the 'ancient lyric madness' Carman speaks of loose in the air," David Kirk generously offers to free Pat from the engagement which he realizes she now regrets. She can remain at Silver Bush, and will not be quite alone with May and the other Binnies, since Judy is still there.

But the inexorable author told her journal on November 28, 1934, "I had a fairly good night and felt better all day. Wrote a *Pat* chapter—'Judy's' death." In the grimmest days of her life in Norval, Montgomery killed off her alter ego, the story-teller. Judy Plum had kept the novel lively with her apparently inexhaustible fund of stories to entertain, teach, amuse, and scare her audience. Near the end of the book she is still strong enough to retell some of the old stories, and to confess that some of them had been far-fetched: a fine ending for a fine story-teller. Judy's death climaxes the dark foreboding strains in the novel.

What follows is a tragic ending to a long sad story. Inexplicably, Silver Bush, the beloved house at last about to be Pat's own again, since Sid and May are now to move into their own place, burns to the ground. (Not completely inexplicable, for there are hints that May Binnie's mismanagement of the old kitchen stove was the cause.) In describing this conflagration Montgomery was invoking thoughts of several fires: the historic fire at the landmark Norval mill, gone up in flames four years earlier; the archetypal fire that burns at the end of *Jane Eyre*, destroying Rochester's house; the comic fire near the end of *A Tangled Web* that threatened to destroy the jug once the favourite possession of a proud old lady; and perhaps the fires of hell that burn away all pride.

Pat's response to the fire that burns down her home is "'If I could ever be glad of anything again . . . I'd be glad that Judy died before this happened.' Her heart was like an unlighted room and nothing, she thought she knew, could ever illumine it again." "Life has beaten me," Pat tells herself.

There is personal pain in Montgomery's decision that Silver Bush should be destroyed. She too was about to lose a dear home. Not her own, of course, and subject to the congregation's decisions as to roofing, painting, plumbing; yet dear to her for its garden, its view of the river, and its memories of happier days when her sons were young. When Pat's house goes up in smoke the tragedy suggests the hopelessness of the author, as a writer and as a homeless woman. Her author was inclined to agree. Two days after writing of Judy's death, on her sixtieth birthday, she wrote, "I got the last chapter of *Pat II* done. . . . I never wrote a book in such agony of mind before" (November 30, 1934).

In fact, however, she had gone beyond the fire to write a final chapter in which a happy ending is ground out—for the Uncle Horaces of the world who "like a nice snug tidy ending in a book." In another "gentle and almost windless evening" like the one when David Kirk freed Pat from her engagement to him, Jingle returns. He has been called back by a letter written by Judy Plum on her deathbed. He comes to claim Pat and to tell her that he has built a new home for her, out in Vancouver. The story ends with a sound that suggests the closest thing to a love scene that Montgomery could write, "the low yielding laugh of a girl held prisoner by her lover."

A snug tidy happy ending. Or perhaps not entirely so happy. In *Pat of Silver Bush*, young Pat had recoiled at the idea of her father's going West, and taking the Gardiner family with him. "Going out west would be the death of her." Jingle has always talked about the house he would build for Pat some day, but never did he hint that the site might be a continent's remove from Silver Bush. He admits the problem: "I know what this tragedy of Silver Bush must have meant to you . . . but I've a home for you by another sea, Pat." So of course she agrees to go West with Jingle, leaving the farm, and the burnt-out remnants of her home.

A world of readers had been grateful to Montgomery for her earlier happy stories. Nevertheless, in even the most bubbly of those early books, the endings had been at best ambivalent, and in tone subdued. Anne walked quietly with Gilbert as she approached the bend in the road, in contrast with the ebullience of her earlier *joie de vivre* when she stamped her furious foot at Mrs. Lynde, or leapt onto old Aunt Josephine. Emily's ending was ambiguous also when she switched her ambitions into submission to Teddy's career. Valancy settled in ominously with old Doc Redfern as a father-in-law. The ending of *Mistress Pat* is considerably more troubling than any of these earlier conclusions. Most of the book had reflected the sombre mood in which Montgomery recorded her own disappointments, losses, resentments. Too swiftly it returned to the expected affirmative tone of an L.M. Montgomery book.

Many years earlier, Robert Louis Stevenson wrote to J.M. Barrie regarding the happy ending of *The Little Minister*: "It ought to have ended badly; we all know it did." Stevenson added, in an Uncle Horace mood, "We are infinitely grateful to you for all the grace and good feeling with which you lied about it." Montgomery's "grace and good feeling" toward her readers gave them the satisfactions that life was snatching away from the humbled author.

~ Anne of Windy Poplars ~

(Toronto: McClelland & Stewart, 1936)

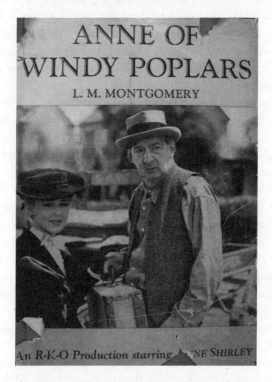

An eager audience greeted the news that L.M. Montgomery had started on a new "Anne" book. The success of a 1934 moving picture of *Anne of Green Gables* would guarantee a substantial market for a new sequel. Such a move had long been urged by her publishers and fans, but the real impetus came from the need for house-buying funds. Since L.C. Page had bought the copyright to *Anne of Green Gables*, the successful moving picture was bringing no royalties to Montgomery. She began *Anne of Windy Poplars* hopefully: "I mean to try to fill in the gap between *Anne of the Island* and *Anne's House of Dreams* when she was teaching school in Summerside. If it proves possible to 'get back into the past' far enough to do a good book it ought to do well commercially after the film" (March 9, 1935). The awkward expression of this hope seems very different from the deft way she had formerly composed entries for her journal.

Present reality was not readily furnishing raw material for an "Anne" book. The see-saw of hope and dread caused by her sons' academic and

romantic affairs, by financial problems and world news, and by continuing worry over her husband's mental ill-health left Montgomery in a
perilously fragile state of mind. Yet she knew that writing always revived
her spirits, and that once she found her way into a new book her mood
would be elevated. She could pull up her own miseries (including sad
memories of herself as a child) and assign them to characters in a story.
She could use the emotions that were paralyzing her, make them either
comical or heart-rendingly melodramatic, and in the process improve
her own state of mind.

So she began doing "spade work," re-reading the earlier "Anne" books to
get back into the youthful mood. She also began perusing her early journals,
particularly the pages referring to her days as a very young teacher, in
Bideford, Belmont, and Bedeque. In these quarries, she found an infusion
of romance and high spirits.

In the new book, Anne will be putting in the three years that intervene
between her time in college and the time she married and moved into her
first home. Sandwiched this way between two already published books, the
new novel can show no change in the relationship between Anne and
Gilbert, no change in Marilla's life, and no rebirth of Anne's writing career.
Instead Montgomery does what is really her best trick. She creates a series
of chapters, each a story in itself, funny or sentimental or pathetic, all linked
very loosely by the presence of warm-hearted Anne.

This episodic form is reminiscent of *Chronicles of Avonlea*. There, in
1912, Montgomery had assembled a group of short stories, many of them
published earlier, and had created connective links by introducing "Anne
Shirley" into each of them. With the successes of her full-length novels
from that point on, Montgomery had hardly had time to write short stories, publishing only one or two a year between 1910 and 1924. Then in
1924–26, the *Delineator* had bought eight short stories, all of them to be
woven later into the *Emily* books and *Magic for Marigold*. This double use
of material was obviously profitable, so when financial problems brought
on by the Depression became urgent in the 1930s, Montgomery went back
to writing short stories to sell to magazines. The *Family Herald*, a long-
established farm paper published in Montreal, bought sixteen unconnected
short stories between 1933 and 1936, many of them destined to be re-used
in *Anne of Windy Poplars*.[113]

When Montgomery began to write up her "new" book in 1935, she was
in part stitching together materials she had already sold once. She was doing
more than that, however. These stories, unlike the *Chronicles of Avonlea*, had
been written with a new *Anne* book in mind. The adaptations from *Family
Herald* stories begin in chapter nine of *Anne of Windy Poplars*. Before re-
using them, Montgomery had to create a new beginning for Anne.

In her journal entry for March 9, 1935, she mentions beginning "spade work on a new Anne book," and adds, "I had a strange feeling when I sat down to my work. Some interest seemed to return to life."

In an episodic novel like *Anne of Windy Poplars*, Montgomery could expand her cast of characters almost indefinitely. The swarm of themes, characters, and sub-plots of *Anne of Windy Poplars* places it in an important Canadian genre, the "Sketch-Book" type of fictional local history popularized by Stephen Leacock and Duncan Campbell Scott. Like these popular contemporary writers, Montgomery builds a recognizable sense of eccentric people in a complex web of relationships.

From the beginning, *Anne of Windy Poplars* builds on Anne's interaction with eccentrics in the school and town. She boards with the widows Aunt Kate and Aunt Chatty, and their "far-off cousin" Rebecca Dew, plus a huge cat called Dusty Miller. Her neighbours are old Mrs. Campbell, her Woman (that is, her housekeeper), and her granddaughter, Little Elizabeth. Soon she will meet her pupils, some responsive, some not; and the Summerside adults, Dovie Westcott and her father, Pauline Gibson and her mother, Miss Minerva Tomgallon; and a town-full of others, each with a story in which Anne can become involved.

Montgomery's magic touch in describing houses, gardens, and rooms is revived. "Windy Poplars" presents a typical Prince Edward Island picture: "a white frame house . . . very white . . . with green shutters . . . very green . . . with a 'tower' in the corner and a dormer-window on either side, a low stone wall dividing it from the street, with aspen poplars growing at intervals along it, and a big garden at the back where flowers and vegetables are delightfully jumbled up together." Anne moves into a room that suits her exactly, "engoldened by the light that came through the corn-colored curtains" with "the rarest tapestry on the whitewashed walls where the shadow patterns of the aspens outside fell, . . . always changing and quivering."

All these people and places will be described to Anne's fiancé Gilbert in an avalanche of letters. Through this correspondence, the novel tells the story of Anne's three years of waiting, while Gilbert Blythe, her fiancé, finishes medical school. Montgomery could remember a comparable period in her own life. After becoming engaged to Ewan Macdonald in the fall of 1906, she had been separated from him until 1911. During this period when he was overseas in Glasgow doing advanced studies in theology, and later when he served in parishes in the far western end of Prince Edward Island, there had been a constant flow of letters between them. None of these letters survive, although there is frequent reference to them in Montgomery's journal. On the other hand, a wonderful body of her letters to two earlier friends, George Macmillan in Alloa, Scotland, and Ephraim Weber in Alberta, has survived and been published. Montgomery's letters are perhaps more thoughtful and philosophical than those of the fictional Anne, but they have the same engaging quality of random comment on the passing events of the day.

The epistolary form is a very old-fashioned one, popularized in the eighteenth century by Richardson's *Pamela* (1740). The first known Canadian novel, Frances Brooke's *The History of Emily Montague* (1769), used this form, a very appropriate one in a colony where correspondence formed the precious link with the old country. In Prince Edward Island, as in other older settled parts of Canada, many families treasured collections of such letters. They proved how much life could be condensed into epistolary form. The genre had been revived early in the twentieth century and used effectively for example by Jean Webster, one of Montgomery's rivals in the field of young adult fiction. *Daddy-Long-Legs*, a best seller in 1912, consisted of a sequence of letters from a young girl to her patron and friend. The form allows the story to unfold from the concentrated point of view of the protagonist.

The form might be old-fashioned, but Anne Shirley, as letter writer, is a modern young woman. She has progressed in her profession to the point of becoming Principal of the High School in Summerside, the second largest city in Prince Edward Island. She writes to Gilbert as an equal, just as Montgomery did in her letters to Macmillan and Weber, where she speaks as a successful professional writer to others in the same trade. Montgomery could also model young professional Anne on the memory of her loved cousin Frede Campbell, who took a teaching position out in Red Deer, Alberta, after graduating from Macdonald College, returning later to her alma mater to join a lively staff of women teachers and extension workers. Letters from Frede and other friends scattered widely had been a constant joy to Montgomery, whether she was in Leaskdale, Norval, or Toronto.

Anne of Windy Poplars was originally titled *Anne of Windy Willows*, an echo of the name of one of her favourite books. *The Wind in the Willows* (1908) by Kenneth Grahame is the story of a small animal leaving home, venturing out into the wide world. It was an appropriate model for this story of Anne in her away-from-home years. The tone of Montgomery's most recent book, *Mistress Pat*, had been very different. There the old home still absorbed young Pat as an obsession. But in the new book, Montgomery would show Anne, her most famous heroine, striking out cheerfully, leaving Avonlea to make a life of her own. Montgomery was buoyed up by having found a new home and looking forward to a new life. Going from Montgomery's troubled 1935 journal to a reading of *Anne of Windy Poplars* is like suddenly getting a whiff of fresh air, suddenly sharing a fit of the giggles, suddenly noticing how pretty young women are, suddenly believing in love. The creative power to invent romances counterbalances the journal's dreary record of actual family life and shows the persistence of sympathy for the girls (like the younger self Montgomery remembered) who have not found "happy endings."

At the time she began writing this novel, Montgomery too was striking out. She was leaving Norval, leaving the last of the church-owned manses, which had never been her own. She was moving to Toronto, to the house she called "Journey's End." In spite of the change in residence, however, Montgomery's journal began to show the recurrence of depression. A sign of her negativity is the introduction into her novel of a new kind of twins. Not a balanced pair like Davy and Dora, one well-behaved and the other mischievous, these twins are both unmitigated imps, a pair of "holy terrors."

As she continued work on *Anne of Windy Poplars*, however, Montgomery tried to use the experience of shaping and composition as a means of elevating her spirits. In earlier days, she had relished the experience of "rinsing out her soul" by talking over her woes with Frede and making them laughable. Now, in the later years, without Frede, with a husband sinking into deep depression, and two sons wrapped up in their own studies and love affairs and resisting their mother's intrusions in both, she no longer had anyone to laugh with. She began complaining in her journal about experiencing "waves of hopeless unreasoning despair" (November 24, 1935).

For consolation and escape she turned to "Windy Poplars." She found it possible to neutralize her miserable thoughts about herself by giving some of her worst traits to characters in her books and making light of them. Young Jen Pringle sets out to make Anne's life miserable, as Maud had undoubtedly done with Miss Robinson, the teacher she despised. Lugubrious cousin Emmeline shares Montgomery's medical problems, lying awake with pains shooting down her lower limbs. Ridiculous, manipulative Mrs. Gibson exerts neurotic control over her daughter, as Montgomery was trying to do in her dealings with Chester and Stuart.

Other characters in the book give her a chance to work off old suppressed resentments. Little Elizabeth Grayson lives with her undemonstrative grandmother because her mother is dead and her father has gone elsewhere on business, as Hugh John Montgomery had done. Cyrus Taylor's daughters live in fear of the terrible sulky spells with which, like Montgomery's irascible Grandfather Macneill, he keeps the girls' would-be suitors at bay. Aunt Mouser, pouncing, like a cat on a mouse, always finds something disagreeable to say, just like Montgomery's Aunt Emily in Malpeque.

Even more suggestive of subliminal self-awareness is the character of Miss Minerva Tomgallon. She lives in a decaying gothic house, romanticizing her dead relatives, and believing that there is a "curse" on her family. Montgomery makes particular fun of Miss Tomgallon's Dickensian surname, and Anne wryly observes that she is a melodramatic old woman who seems to positively enjoy the idea of the family curse. Yet Montgomery herself had become morbidly convinced during the 1930s that there was a curse on her own house, afflicting everyone she loved. Miss Minerva, named for the goddess of wisdom, is perhaps wise enough to recognize the reality of the "curse." The novel thus treats the possibility of a curse ambivalently; but in the journals Montgomery is deadly serious when she writes about her own sense of doom.

The acid picture of a strange, rude young woman named Katherine Brooke seems at first sight to be drawn from a young woman who was now intruding persistently into Montgomery's life. Katherine in *Anne of Windy Poplars* is uncannily like Isobel Anderson, a teacher in Acton, Ontario, who had first introduced herself to Montgomery as a fan but soon began bombarding her with passionate letters pleading for love. Katherine Brooke shares Isobel Anderson's bitterness, loneliness, lack of concern about her own appearance, and also her unpleasantness as a teacher. Her pupils live in fear of her sarcasm. She has no friends and wants none. Katherine, however, is not driven like Isobel Anderson by a powerful attraction to Anne but instead dislikes and resents her. Sharp-tongued Katherine repulses Anne's sympathy. "'I can't pretend things,'" she tells Anne; "'I haven't your notable gift for doing the queen act . . . saying exactly the right thing to everyone.'" The Acton school-teacher similarly attacked Maud for her universal friendliness.[114] Over a long period, Montgomery tried to help the unhappy Isobel, with no effect. In the novel, Anne, detecting something pitiful in Miss Brooke, works to help her become happier, and finally convinces her to leave the teaching profession and find work she could enjoy.

Katherine is not just a disguised picture of a real-life neighbour and nuisance. She is partly, again, self-portrait. She embodies Montgomery's resentment of forces working against her, in Norval and in the literary circles of Toronto. Montgomery was baffled by and coldly furious at the treatment critics were now giving her books. Katherine releases that fury. Like Katherine, also, she was less and less able to relate to young people, though she still managed to send off hundreds of cheery, friendly letters in response to fans still writing to her from Sweden, Palestine, Australia, and of course from the United Kingdom, the United States, and Canada.

Montgomery had assigned to Anne her own genuine desire to help others. What she does not give her is anything of the unpredictable charm of the earlier *Anne of Green Gables*. No more funny "scrapes," no comical results of good intentions: the grownup Anne infallibly helps dysfunctional families and solves the problems of difficult characters. She wins the whole community over not by startling rhetorical pronouncements like young Anne's, laughable in their inappropriateness to everyday life, but by "saying the right thing to everyone." All difficulties dissolve before the charm of "Queen Anne."

It is a dream of control. For female readers, *Anne of Windy Poplars* could ratify the tenets of feminine persistence and patient tolerance. Like Anne, it seems, a young well-trained and well-intentioned teacher could wield a gentle and finally triumphant battle against a Katherine Brooke or a troublesome student named Pringle who is the Summerside equivalent of the insufferable Pyes.

Montgomery's study of the politics within a secondary school is a *tour de force*. She knew very little about teaching as a modern profession. Her own experience had been in very small one-room schoolhouses, at the end of the nineteenth century. By the time her sons were old enough to go to High School in the 1920s, she had sent them away to a boys' boarding school, so was never involved in Parent-Teacher Associations, or in teacher-parent manoeuvring. She did know some post-secondary school educators: Frede Campbell, Ephraim Weber, and Dr. MacMurchy, father of the three redoubtable MacMurchy sisters and Principal of Jarvis Collegiate in Toronto. She had also absorbed the high school atmosphere in a long series of visits to schools as a welcome and admired visiting speaker.

Although her direct connection with classroom work and teacher-student interaction was very limited, she realized how much teaching and schools had changed during her lifetime, and how much of that change involved a changed status for women in the profession. She herself remembered when the first "lady teacher" came to Cavendish. Now she was living in a period when ambitious women were beginning to dominate the teaching field. Several major Toronto schools appointed women Principals in the 1930s; well-trained women were emerging from Schools of Education in ever greater numbers and finding satisfaction in their work. The story of Anne's achievement as a High School Principal, though set at the beginning of the twentieth century, reflected a reality of the 1930s.

For Montgomery herself, working out this triumphant story served another purpose. Creating the story of Anne's success in taming her school colleagues and winning over her hostile pupils served as a sublimation of her personal miseries. It served as a rinsing out of her troubled soul. Recent medical research on depression suggests that in people like Montgomery with a tendency to depression the rational mind can start swarming with negative thoughts. In such a state, cognitive faculties of the brain tend to suppress the emotional ones. Modern cognitive therapy treats such people by helping them face and oppose negativity.

Without psychiatric help, Montgomery found a similar way to control some of her misery and anxiety. She recognized some of her darkest feelings, and turned them into powerful characters. She added dramatic conflict to her plots by letting her personified worries swarm against each other, in conflicts between rationality and excessive emotion. She looked for the funny side of such conflicts.

An excellent example of this sublimation is in the scene where Esme Taylor brings her young man home for dinner, only to find her father in one of his horrible sulky moods. Montgomery must have sat through many a meal with a glowering silent Ewan sulking at the head of the table, locked into his own misery. Now she dramatizes the situation. Anne pretends to recognize Cyrus Taylor's silent sulks as the impervious aloofness of a deaf man. The daughters jump at the opportunity to recall all their father's irritating activities, knowing that he will not break his sullen silence to respond. Eventually, the fun goes too far and the father explodes against their revelations of his supposed cruelties. There are two effective and unexpected bits of drama. Tension is heightened by the fact that the young suitor is "the new Head of the Modern Languages Department at Redmond and dreadfully clever." Dr. Carter comes to dinner, "undeniably handsome and distinguished-looking, with crisp dark hair, brilliant dark eyes and silver-rimmed glasses." It is a recognizable picture of Montgomery's former professor at Dalhousie University, Dr. Archibald MacMechan. In his *Headwaters of Canadian Literature* (1924) MacMechan had paid small attention to the former student whose writings were very much better known than his own. Now Montgomery lets Anne dismiss him, recalling memories of her days at Redmond, where he seemed "a rather pompous young bore." Yet in the end, Montgomery through Anne takes a second look at the academic she remembered. "Perhaps after all he was not pompous, thought Anne . . . only young and shy and over-serious." The same switch from malice to kindliness appears when Esme is impelled by justice to add a reference to her father's kindness. It is this which finally brings him to break his silence and relax into geniality.

Montgomery's essential kindliness shines again in the final chapters of the novel. She is kind to the characters, doling out appropriate rewards to all of them. Rebecca Dew's cat is restored to her, guaranteeing that she will go on looking after Aunt Chatty and Aunt Kate. Pauline Gibson meets an old beau, in spite of her mother's tyranny, and is eventually truly freed by her mother's death. Dovie marries, her grumpy old father turning out to have wanted this happy ending all along. Happiness comes to "poor Nora" Nelson when Anne interferes and brings Nora's young man back to her. Katherine Brooke, advised by Anne to leave the teaching job she hates, emerges well-satisfied as private secretary to a "globe-trotting M.P." In arranging affairs so optimistically, Montgomery is indeed kind to those of her readers who like a "snug tidy ending." Such cheerfulness fits better into this picture of young and hopeful Anne than it did into the story of lachrymose Pat Gardiner.

For Montgomery as novelist, the balance of moods always tipped toward hope rather than despair. A description of the house of Miss Minerva Tomgallon symbolizes this recurring movement toward affirmation. Anne says of the house, first, as she might say of herself in darker moments,

> This was really rather a terrible old house, full of the ghosts of dead hatreds and heart-breaks, crowded with dark deeds that had never been dragged into light and were still festering in its corners and hidey-holes. Too many women must have wept here. The wind wailed very eerily in the spruces by the window. For a moment Anne felt like running out, storm or no storm.

But she continues at once,

> Then she took herself resolutely in hand and commanded common sense. If tragic and dreadful things had happened here, many shadowy years agone, amusing and lovely things must have happened, too. Gay and pretty girls had danced here and talked over their charming secrets; dimpled babies had been born here; there had been weddings and balls and music and laughter.

In the later Toronto period Montgomery suspected that she might have been the author of her own misfortune. Such an insight came when she enumerated in her journal the ways in which her family and everyone she loved seemed indeed to be under a curse. She could not, of course, know that in 1936 many beside her own sons were moving into the shadow of a world-wide curse, the return of war.

Yet she could have said, with more accuracy, that in spite of personal distress she was the author of a long shelf-full of books. And there was more to come before the war broke out. She edged into this "more" with yet another of the happy endings lavished on *Anne of Windy Poplars*. Little Elizabeth, who had always longed for Tomorrow-land, finds it at the end, and in a way of deepest significance for Montgomery. Anne writes to Elizabeth's father, and he comes to claim his child at the end of the novel. Anne takes Elizabeth to join him on Flying Cloud, a perfect islet off the coast near Summerside. Old Mrs. Campbell, the harsh grandmother with her menacing shadowy Woman beside her, is defeated. Unlike feckless Hugh John, Elizabeth's father promises that they will never be separated again.

If such a dream could bring so much happiness, why not dream it again? In the Tomorrow-land of Montgomery's fiction, there will be a successor to Little Elizabeth. This strong new character, without sentimentality or pathos, will be named Jane Victoria.

Jane of Lantern Hill

(Toronto: McClelland & Stewart, 1937)

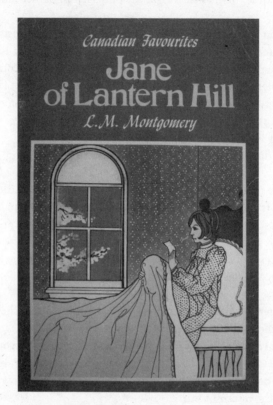

On January 27, 1936, Montgomery pasted into her journal a photograph of her new Toronto house, which she called "Journey's End,"and wrote a note about the final typing of *Anne of Windy Poplars*. In April she inserted an old photograph of "Cavendish Shore" and in May she mentioned "my new book whose heroine I have named Jane." Jane, an eleven-year-old girl, will swing from the Toronto of her wintry life to the summery Prince Edward Island of her dreams. There she will find a father.

For Montgomery, it was a recurring motif. Two years earlier, *The Canadian Home Journal* had published her short story called "Tomorrow Comes," about a little girl who finds a picture in a magazine, cuts it out, and hides it, without realizing that it represents her unknown father. That story hinged on a grandmother's jealous effort to keep her away from the charming man she resembles. As in the similar tale of "Little Elizabeth" in *Anne of Windy Poplars*, the 1934 story takes place on the Island. By 1936

Montgomery had found a new setting for the darker side of the story, the home place of the jealous grandmother.

The Macdonalds had moved to Toronto, into a newly-built house in a stylish west-end suburb. It seemed like an idyllic setting: a friendly life with interesting neighbours, a nearby library, bird-watchers and poetry-reading clubs. But when Montgomery walked a couple of blocks to the streetcar stop and went downtown to enjoy literary associations, and to renew old friendships with fellow Torontonians like Mary Beal and Nora Lefurgey Campbell, she saw a different life. From the streetcar she could see heavy old mansions on dark streets, and shabby alleys where the Depression was leaving its dirty mark. She had found a correlative for the unhappy side of Jane's bi-polar story.

Jane Stuart is about the age of Anne Shirley when she first came to Green Gables from an orphanage, and of Emily Byrd Starr when she is brought to New Moon from her father's impoverished little house. But *Jane of Lantern Hill* will present a much sharper photograph of the life that is left behind when a child comes to a new home on the Island. Only in *The Blue Castle* is there a comparable sense of the difference between a world of stagnation and a world of charm, and Jane Stuart's Toronto is a more deadly place than the village from which Valancy Stirling must escape. In a pretentious mansion at 60 Gay Street, survivor from a former era, locked in by iron gates, Jane has lived since she was three years old. In this stagnant, repressive world, Jane is ironically called "Victoria."[115] She is unhappy in her grandmother's stately establishment, unhappy when her Aunt Gertrude leads her through joyless religious exercises.

Jane's life in Toronto is a version of the myth Montgomery had spun about her own early years. She remembered a restricted life, bound to an unbeautiful religion, and made to feel inferior in her tastes by unsympathetic aunts, harassing cousins, and a stern grandmother. She remembered feeling excluded, wanting to belong somewhere, and knowing she was physically like the absent father scorned by her maternal clan. In all these ways Jane Stuart is a portrait of Maud Montgomery as she remembered herself and recorded her memories in her journal.

For readers, Jane's life is also a recognizable example of the life many modern children were enduring in the Depression, with distracted parents; a situation soon to be intensified when World War II swept so many fathers to greater distances. *Jane of Lantern Hill* would come to its full popularity after 1939.[116]

In Jane's Grandmother Kennedy, Montgomery created, perhaps unconsciously, another self-portrait. Like the older woman fiercely intent on keeping her daughter away from the man she loves, Montgomery was trying to control her sons, to break up Stuart's relationship with a girl she found inferior, and to keep her older son Chester from wandering away from home.[117] In *Jane of Lantern Hill*, Mrs. Kennedy keeps her daughter Robin with her, having convinced her to leave her husband. She is a social snob, feeling superior to her neighbours, as Montgomery the minister's wife had formerly felt about many of her small town parishioners.[118] Like old Aunt Becky controlling the young ones through her material possessions in *A Tangled Web*, both the fictional Mrs. Kennedy, and the real Mrs. Macdonald, could use money to exercise authority, being lavish to their children, while keeping them away from "undesirable" people of their own generation—always without success.

Unlike Anne and Emily, Jane has a mother, beloved and lovable but more than a little childish. She is a social butterfly, rather like Rilla Blythe, or Marigold's pretty young mother, or the giddy flappers in *A Tangled Web*, or Valancy's socialite cousin in *The Blue Castle*. Montgomery's memories of the frivolous fun of her own young days makes the portrait of Robin Stuart sympathetic. The author also assigns to her something of her own present situation. Like Montgomery, Jane's mother disguises her loneliness from the world. She presents a facade of social adaptation, hiding her grief at a lost loving partnership.

Jane, like Anne, Emily, Pat, and young Maud Montgomery, has a beloved girl friend (pathetic orphaned Jody, in Jane's case) with whom she can escape briefly from the heaviness of daily life. Jody lives in poverty, in a city squalor and exploitation beyond what Anne Shirley or Mary Vance knew in the Maritimes, where the division of rich and poor was less absolute. Powerful Mrs. Kennedy of Gay Street lives next to the shabby boarding-house, detritus of the Depression, where the waif Jody cowers. Montgomery had recognized the economic and regional dissonance that existed between metropolitan power struggles and rural neighbourliness. She had found in Toronto "the City of Destruction," to quote Gabriella Ahmansson.[119] Although she had apparently settled into suburban complacency, she had maintained the sensitivity that once imagined the cruelty that a child like Anne could experience on the mainland of social and economic reality.

Jane's rebellion against the restriction and sterility of her life consists of pretending to shine up the moon, and wangling opportunities to play a part in the servants' preparation of food. These secret domesticities cannot counter the general dreariness of her Toronto existence. The first eleven chapters end with Jane saying, with vigorous rebellion, "God is no good."

In the month when she first names "Jane," Montgomery was locked into despair. She had discovered that Luella and Chester were expecting a second child—a discouraging complication for a young man still studying to be a lawyer and an infuriating development for his mother, who had received a promise of "no more babies" in return for continuing to support his studies. By August, when she had finished the spade work on her new book and was beginning the actual writing, she was staggered again, when the distressing news of the death of their admired friend Mr. Barraclough sent Ewan into deep depression. "I am broken and defeated," she wrote (September 29, 1936).[120]

In October her spirits recuperated through a trip to Prince Edward Island, the first in four years. "It seems always as if deep dear old gladnesses are kept here for me and take possession of me again" (October 3, 1936). At the end of her stay she wrote, "I must leave my dear Island again. And I don't want to—I don't want to. I *belong* here" (October 27, 1936). Back in Toronto, she returned to her writing, and to her double life. The manuscript of *Jane of Lantern Hill* shows, as Jennifer Litster says, "the split between the author living imaginatively with her heroine on an island haven and the woman functioning in Toronto as bread-winner, business head, and practical mainstay of her household."[121] Montgomery rarely wrote on fresh sheets, using instead scraps of bills, old letters, old sermons of Ewan's, and business correspondence with her agent and publisher.[122] The reverse side of the first pages of the manuscript of *Jane* shows Montgomery buying and selling stock in oil companies, and happily attending authors' meetings and Press Club lunches. Leading this double life, Montgomery created a bi-polar pattern in her new narrative.

Jane too now finds an alternate life. Her absentee and unknown father Andrew Stuart writes to demand her presence in Prince Edward Island. Jane's friend Jody says dubiously, "I hunted up P.E. Island on the map. . . . There's such an awful lot of water round it. Ain't you afraid of falling over the edge?" Jane travels alone to the Island, with trepidation.

There she sees "the loveliest thing on earth . . . a June morning in Prince Edward Island."

> A wave of fragrance broke in her face from the lilac hedge. . . . The poplars in a corner of the lawn were shaking in green laughter. An apple-tree stretched out friendly arms. There was a far-away view of daisy-sprinkled fields across the harbour where white gulls were soaring and swooping. . . . "Why . . . why, P.E. Island is a pretty place," thought Jane half grudgingly.

Montgomery's poetic prose goes beyond mere prettiness here. It charms with its rhythms, its sentence structures, its sequencing. It exploits the kinetic force of present participles: "shaking," "soaring," "swooping." It mixes appeals to different senses, of sight and smell ("wave" of "fragrance"), of colour and sound ("green" "laughter"). It creates an island, not just as a place in a book, but a place to see, smell, hear, and to taste "the sea tang in the air. Jane sniffed it for the first time . . . sniffed again . . . drank it in."

As Montgomery wrote she recaptured the sensual appeals of the Island, but she does not endow Jane with a "flash," or let her erupt into ecstatic cries like "Oh, Mr. Cuthbert! Oh!" Nor does she let Jane look for metaphors for her experiences. No vision of a cathedral's rose window when Jane sees a sunset. Yet Jane, like the girl Anne who once seemed to stand at the writer's elbow, "with her eager, starry eyes" (January 22, 1911) reacts in her own memorable, and idiosyncratic way. After one night on the Island, and one day with her long-lost father, Jane says, "I owe God an apology."

A country house halfway to Lantern Hill brings Jane to earth, with ginger cookies, wild strawberry jam, golden-brown beans, Johnny-cake, and a big fat doughnut. The central theme of cookery expands. In Lantern Hill, not a rainbow-glorified valley but the happy homely house where her father lives, Jane's inner toughness and executive ability surface. She cleans house, scrubs floors and finds curtains; fishes, rides the hay wagons; visits and is visited; explores the sea shore with her father. She is a friend of all the world, loved by the tumble of Island children, Min and Ding-Dong and especially Shingle (echo of Jingle?). She is petted and given gifts by the older Island eccentrics like Little Aunt Em and Step-a-Yard and the Jimmy Johns.

This is a new, dramatically energetic version of the dream world. Unlike lonely misty Mistawis in *The Blue Castle*, it is realized in concrete terms of work and daily life and a multiplicity of friends. Valancy in *The Blue Castle* donned a moonlight gown of blue and silver and drifted in a solitary dream, paddling her bare feet, sitting and doing nothing in the beautiful silence, dining on berries and trout. Young Jane puts on Prince Edward Island overalls, weeds her garden, and bakes a perfect pie for her father. Feminists might deplore the implication of domestic subservience as happiness. But Jane—and many of her readers—accepts the idea of nurturing as a new part of her destiny. Jane is a sturdy girl, and her author treats her with none of the sentimental whimsy that marred many of her short stories (including "Tomorrow Comes"). No cute talk like sweet Little Elizabeth maundering about "Tomorrow-Land;" Jane lives by the calendar, ticking off days as she latches into housework and community life. Her father has faith in Jane's ability to cook because of her genes. Jane prefers to put her trust in her good cook book, *Cookery for Beginners*,[123] and in the advice of neighbours.[124] As Montgomery grew older (and fatter), she perhaps dreamed more about food. But the chief focus here is not on eating but on preparing and sharing food. Jane treats the children from poorer families to cakes and cookies. In turn she receives friendships and the knowledge of generations.

Near this mid-point of the novel, Jane's father offers other nourishment: a pleasurable reading of the Bible. The fearful theology imposed by Aunt Gertrude in Toronto is replaced by a new aesthetic: joy in the Bible as poetry and myth. Of course there is trouble in paradise. Aunt Irene, the saccharine yin to Aunt Gertrude's sour yang, mentions the threat of Miss Morrow, "an old sweetheart of your father's, lovey," and hints at the possibility of a United States divorce. Her spiteful, harmful gossip, like the rumours that endangered Joscelyn's happiness in *A Tangled Web*, marks Montgomery's insistence on the darkness of gossip as a shadow menacing serenity. The horror of divorce was particularly poignant for the mother of a young man whose marriage seemed very shaky.

Jane's worry about her father's possible divorce and re-marriage remain unresolved when she returns from her summer in the Island, to spend nine colder months in Toronto. Jane is now taller, better looking, and more self-assured. After spending three months becoming "superior Jane," standing up to Grandmother in defence of the Bible as literature is easy. "While she was reading the Bible chapter to grandmother and Aunt Gertrude in that terrible unchanged drawing-room, she was reading to dad on the old Watch Tower . . . with a triumphant clang of victory in her voice." ("I should prefer a little more reverence," says Grandmother.) Buoyed by the memory of a crowd of friends on the Island, Jane emerges at her Toronto school as effective and popular. New-found confidence enables her to bake a Christmas cake and send it to her father.

Jane can survive Toronto, because she has her creator's power to live an inner life on her island. Because she has internalized the Island, Jane can now find, at the western edge of Toronto, a perfect house overlooking the Humber River ravine. Just as Montgomery had described it (March 12, 1935), Jane's find has "casement windows . . . some of them beautifully unexpected. . . . It was built right on the edge of the ravine over-looking the tree-tops, with five great pines just behind it." Looking at this new-found beauty, Jane sees "the banners of a city at night . . . being flaunted in the sunset sky behind the pines. . . . She could be happy here. . . . She could love the lake even if it did not have the sparkle and boom of the gulf seas."

Jane is back on the ferry from Cape Tormentine very soon, ready for a second Island summer. When Montgomery writes about Jane's second summer on the Island, she slips into a radical change of tone. Thinking back to her memory of that last visit to Prince Edward Island, and re-reading her journal account of it, she admitted a sense of decay and change. In retrospect although it had been in some ways a triumphant visit—being feted, entertained at Government House, praised by her friends, and welcomed to all her old haunts—she had brought back sad memories. The central "haunt," her old home, had been destroyed by her uncle John, and now he himself was dead, as was his wife, their deaths incised into a tiny corner of a family gravestone. Amanda's house, "sad and ramshackle," waited to be torn down when the National Park took over the property. "Green Gables" itself, the home of her dear friends the Webbs, was due to be remodelled.

Changes everywhere; Montgomery had maintained a "surface gaiety" but "I was immeasurably sad" (October 2–28, 1936).

Back now in a Toronto November, back into the writing routine and ready to take Jane back to the Island, Montgomery could only write in a different mode. Like a person waking from a dream and trying desperately to savour it for a few more minutes, she over-writes the second of Jane's Island summers. In place of the realism of Jane's practical accomplishments in her first summer, Montgomery gives her fabulous—and unlikely—successes. There are comic victories: Jane diminishes a snobbish Toronto cousin by saving her from the menace of cows. She can cure a self-pitying old woman of her death wish by doling out some unwelcome truths. ("Hand me my teeth," says Aunt Elmira as she gets off her death bed in response.) She can convince two old maids to adopt little orphan Jody from Toronto. She can defeat Aunt Irene ("the Wicked Witch of the East," to quote Jennifer Litster[125]) by outdoing her as a pastry cook. She can, finally, astonish the whole Island by coping with a lion.[126] A lion? Tame, elderly—but still straining conviction. The slackening of realism reflects another period of depression in Montgomery's life, when she seems to mock her own achievement and ridicule her own narrative. The story of Jane's double life is becoming more mythic, closer to a Proserpina story designed to feed a desire to believe in the return of springtime hope. It is a narrative becoming more clearly a correlative of Montgomery's periods, increasingly drastic, of depression and relief.

November ended in gloom, fatigue, and illness. December added the troubling universal worry about King Edward VIII, the man who had charmed the British Empire in the past, only to distress it now with the revelation of his "nauseating" love for a "middle-aged divorcée with two living husbands" (December 7, 1936). This general distress at the idea of divorce was probably felt with extra poignancy by Montgomery because of her worry that Chester might be contemplating a break-up of his marriage to Luella. Christmas 1936 followed, bringing to Montgomery a feeling of being "imprisoned and smothered."

In her writing she brought Jane back to Toronto, a place whose menace is moderated now by the knowledge that is contains its own kind of beauty in the secret house by the ravine. Further, she now enjoys two ironic signs of victory over her grandmother. In a conciliatory gesture, Grandmother Kennedy has had Jane's room done over in pink silk and shimmering curtains (a "wonderful splendour" though not to Jane's taste). This gesture leads to a further (and equally irrelevant and inappropriate) gift: the presentation of a glamorous Persian cat called "Snowball," a cat that even Montgomery seems unable to love.

A melodramatic letter breaks Jane's false sense of comfort. Aunt Irene, sweet, smooth, and deadly, reports as a certainty that Jane's beloved

father is indeed proposing to divorce Robin and marry again. The sudden
terror that Jane feels carries with it some of the terrible fears Montgomery
was experiencing as her sons seemed to be moving toward harmful stages
of life. More deeply it recalls the slower growth of agony when as a girl she
was faced with her beloved father's remarriage. In real life, she fled from
Prince Albert, back to the Island. In the novel, Jane flees from Toronto to
her own dreamed-of Island.

But "her Island was not beautiful now." Montgomery counters the early
idyllic descriptions with a tone poem of hostility in nature. Jane struggles
five miles on foot through a Prince Edward Island March rain, thin and
chilling. She comes at last "past the forlorn and muddy garden where the
poppies once trembled in silken splendour." Beyond the soggy garden, however, stand a lamp-lit house and a man who shouts a denial of the rumour
about his divorce—before Jane justifiably collapses, her arduous trip having
brought on pneumonia. This sudden onslaught, used here for an abrupt
shift in the narrative, is better motivated than Gilbert's plot-shifting illness
in *Anne of the Island*. Jane having walked five miles through cold rain
deserves (unlike Gilbert) to have a life-threatening illness.

As she devised that threatening development, Montgomery faced new
blows in her own life—and reacted to them in an astonishing manner.
Stuart was showing too much interest in a girl who was completely unacceptable to his mother: "I *cannot* think Stuart will ever ask me to accept that
bootlegger's spawn as a daughter," she fumed in her journal, when Island
friends reported hearing gossip about this romance (October 23, 1936).[127]
January 1937 brought what was to her another devastation, the death of her
cat Lucky. She could not finish the book. "Only passionate cat lovers will
understand this" (January 25, 1937). Not so. Anyone can see that her
response to the death of a cat (twenty-two pages of grief in the published
version of the journal) is a displacement of other sorrows. All the repressed
moans and howls of many years are released over the death of the gray cat
Good Luck. Then she regained control. Within a few weeks, when she discovered that Chester, though still married to Luella, was carrying on a serious affair with another young woman named Ida Birrell, she grimly
restricted comments on this infidelity to a cryptic, laconic statement: "All
happiness departed from my life forever."

On February 1, 1937, she tried to write, "but couldn't do it."
Nevertheless, on February 3 she "managed to write the last chapter of *Jane
of Lantern Hill*, my heart bleeding at every word."

Bleeding or not, Montgomery created a miraculous "have-your-cake-
and-eat-it" ending. Though her sons were assaulting her by their indulgence
in romantic follies, and though literary critics were no longer extolling her
work, and though Good Luck had died in Toronto, on the island of fiction

she could create glorious good fortune. Jane's near-death situation will draw butterfly Robin back to her marriage to Andrew Stuart and back to the magic of life in Lantern Hill, and Jane's restored family can be accepted by old Grandmother Kennedy. Further fortunately, Jane's father, in fiction, can be offered a half-time job in Toronto. Montgomery could counter her professional colleagues' sneers by creating an author (albeit a male) who not only reunites his family but also snatches victory as a professional writer.

Dad, Mummy, and Jane can divide their time between the summer Island and the one fine part of the winter world, the grey stone house on the edge of the Humber ravine. The Island ideal and the Toronto reality can be melded, reconciled, in this fabulous happy ending. Jane can live in Prince Edward Island and also in Toronto, in the house that is an idealized version of "Journey's End."

~ Anne of Ingleside ~

(Toronto: McClelland & Stewart, 1939)

Montgomery was living in "Journey's End" when she composed the last part of her "Anne" saga. In the book, Anne lives not in her house of dreams, but in a home called "Ingleside." There is irony in both names. Montgomery's Toronto home was named in memory of a happy song in Shakespeare's *Twelfth Night*, "Journeys end in lovers' meeting," but there would be no meetings of lovers there, no "pretty sweetings" lurking in pursuit of Chester or Stuart, let alone any dalliance between the sixty-four-year-old author and her apathetic, delusional husband. Nor would "Ingleside" produce cosy scenes in a nook by a happy hearth in Montgomery's novel, which is focused mostly on Anne's little children as they foray into a cold world. In this last of the Montgomery books published in her lifetime, the warmth of the family falters against the fires of hostility, resentment, and jealousy. Yet this late book has a new bite of realism and the extra appeal of ingenious structuring. It is built like a series of boxes within boxes, with a treasure at the centre—a vignette about author-ship. It has a stability and symmetry sadly lacking in the author's life.

Montgomery's journal in this late period of her life is sparse and hectic. After the histrionic entry on January 29, 1937, "All happiness departed from my life forever,"[128] she withheld from her journal the richness of com-ment of earlier years. She entered a case history of Ewan's nervous break-down, and brief notations of how badly she had slept and how ill she felt, and what medicines she had taken in order to sleep better and suffer less. In the face of such paucity, an unusually detailed account of her progress in the writing of *Anne of Ingleside* shines. Considering that the earliest journal never recorded her work on *Anne of Green Gables* until the glorious moment of the manuscript's acceptance by L.C. Page and Company, it is astonishing to see this detailed account of her movement into the world of her imagin-ing. The novel, packed as it is with people and incidents, obliquely eluci-dates the life that the journal doesn't care to, or dare to report.

In a retrospective passage written in January 1938, she pronounced her life since August 22, 1937, as "plain *hell.*" Yet an entry on April 26, 1937, three months after finishing *Jane of Lantern Hill,* reports "three hours of spade work on *Anne of Ingleside*," and references to spade work continue throughout spring and summer 1937, until October 28, 1937, when she wrote, "finished the spade work. But will I ever be able to write it!" Indeed, the year 1937 ended without any further references to actual writing.[129]

Depression deepened. From March 8, 1938, on, most journal entries began with sad reiterations: "A very bad day;" "I had a sleepless night;" "A very miserable day." She refrained from describing her terrible distress over Chester's infatuation with a young woman other than his wife. Finally, on April 3, she wrote Chester a "bitter letter," threatening to cut off all finan-cial support from him while he finished his law studies, unless he promised to re-establish his marriage. Then on April 5 she had a business meeting with her publisher John McClelland. Her writing life began again. On April 27, 1938, a year and a day after first beginning *Anne of Ingleside,* she could write, "I was a little better today and did a little spade work at intervals."

Spasms of depression recurred. She called for help from the doctor who lived across the street. He gave her a hypodermic injection in the hip, "'to tone up the nervous system'" (May 3, 1938). More hypodermics, May 8 and May 16, did little to allay her trouble: "I am possessed with a desire to *die,*" she wrote part way through the treatments (May 5, 1938). May ended: "A terrible, terrible May." Then the terrible tension ebbed, partly because she learned in mid-June that Chester had passed a crucial set of examination. At the height of this worry, she had reiterated the cry she remembered voicing soon after Chester was born, "Oh, motherhood is *awful*—motherhood is awful!" (June 15, 1938).

On July 19, in a significant upswing, "My old 'flash' came again, at sight of some pine trees." The pines edging down to the Humber River had triggered the same response as the old-time leafy walk through Lover's Lane used to do. By early September 1938, Montgomery could brag again (as she had done in October 1937), "This cold rainy day I finished the last bit of spade work on *Anne of Ingleside*."[130] She was now "absolutely ready to start writing it," but she admitted, "I *dread* trying to begin it. What if I find I cannot write?" She experienced five days of blockage. September 12 brought relief: "On this hot dark muggy day I sat me down and *began to write Anne of Ingleside*." After "a year and nine months . . . [a] burden rolled from my spirit. And I was suddenly *back in my own world* with all my dear Avonlea and Glen folks again."

The new novel would be another bridging book (like *Anne of Windy Poplars*), covering the years between *Anne's House of Dreams* and *Rainbow Valley*. It would present the Blythe family, in the days of childhood of Walter and Jem, Nan and Di, and Shirley (the little boy born after the era of *Rainbow Valley*). Within the time-frame of the new story, the birth of Rilla will complete the Ingleside family, and she will grow old enough to venture away from home and enjoy or endure relations with the world outside.

That much was planned in the brooding-up phase. In the actual working out of the story, Montgomery did more than unfold the family narrative. She also created a unified structure, suggesting by the very shape of the narrative a number of sub-texts: about gender differences, levels of personality, family dynamics, and the faltering of artistic certainties. The story would open and end on a happy note, but troubling elements would be built in, focused in the centre of the story on an insight into Anne as disappointed author.

Two gloriously happy opening chapters of *Anne of Ingleside* find Anne, back at Green Gables, interacting with Diana, Mrs. Lynde, Marilla and Dora and Davy, the twins who were Anne's surrogate children in the days before her marriage and motherhood. Another picnic in Hester Gray's dreamlike abandoned garden concludes the happy time, before Anne returns to the realities of being Mrs. Blythe, mother of Jem, Walter, the twins Nan and Diana, and little Shirley.

Montgomery had begun her new book with a kind of flashback to the old happiness at Green Gables. Presumably she had intended to move from these glimpses of Avonlea into a story of the different kind of happiness Anne finds in the life of her new family at Glen St. Mary's. (The place name suggests the holiness of the mother.) But somehow the planned family idyll gets off the track. When Anne returns to Gilbert and her children she finds her home dominated by a new and sinister character. Aunt Mary Maria comes to visit and stays to torment. She is a second cousin of Gilbert's, imposed on the family by his clannish sense of obligation.

Aunt Mary Maria is no kindly Marilla, but an annoying character, malicious, petty, and spiteful. She hides her negative feelings under a pretence of amiability and compliance. She almost destroys Anne's happiness. This cynical observer, ready to blame Anne for worrying too much, seems like an incubus that can never be banished from the Blythe home. The darkness she brings reflects the frightening world events that were erupting. On September 13, 1938, Montgomery marked two facts in her journal: "Wrote another chapter. . . . It is heavenly to be able to *lose myself* again in my work. But . . . Hitler is still shrieking defiances." Another interleaving of world politics and desk work on the novel appeared on the next day, September 14: "The 'war news' is worse. . . . Finished another *Anne* chapter and came back reluctantly to the fears and dreads of this present world."

Aunt Mary Maria continues to tilt Anne's story off-balance. Her unwelcome presence adds depth and bite to the picture of the mature Anne, surrounded by apparent success. Aunt Mary Maria watches superciliously when disobedient little Jem is lost for four chapters, and when over-sensitive Walter is sent away from home for three chapters. She tries to spoil the boys' Christmas happiness: "'You surely don't believe in Santa Claus *still?*' said Aunt Mary Maria. . . . Luckily Jem had paid no attention to Aunt Mary Maria." Perhaps the troubles that beset the boys reflect Montgomery's fears for her sons, with a new war impending. Remembering the years before World War I in which she is setting her story, she embedded awareness of the horrors awaiting happy boys. Both her sons were now of military age. In the novel, the mother's fears are made even more unbearable by the presence of a mocking, judgmental old lady who derides them.

Montgomery was herself becoming a bitter, judgmental woman, harsh in her criticisms of her sons, her husband, and her neighbours.[131] Behind a bland social facade like Aunt Mary Maria's she too was seething with resentments and frustrations. Her creative imagination sublimated these tensions and she drew from the hidden side of her personality this vivid portrait of an older woman who hides self-absorption and self-pity behind a mask of helpfulness. She was writing her way out of the tensions of an unhappy family, and the terror of war.

When Rilla, last of Anne's babies, is born in the spring, Anne stumbles on a way of ridding the house of Aunt Mary Maria. She ousts the evil spirit by kindness and humour. Anne plans a special fifty-fifth birthday party for her, a celebration of her presence. The old woman departs, nonplussed by having to confront a welcome when she expects to arouse hostility, and furious because the truth about her age has been revealed. Light and laughter rid the house of the presence of malice. For Montgomery, too, the lift of composition had perhaps brought temporary relief from her neuroses.

The tone shifts after Aunt Maria leaves. Two chapters amusingly concerned with adult life in Glen St. Mary's follow. In the first, Miss Cornelia and Susan Baker gossip about local families. In the second, Anne decides to act as matchmaker for young people she barely knows and is amusingly reduced by the outcome of her match-making. Montgomery was perhaps remembering with a chuckle her own attempts at match-making in Norval, and the successful outcome when Murray Laird and Marion Webb married. She was also restoring notes of kindness and fun to the picture of Anne. Although this chapter introduces a touch of cruelty—Walter being teased creeps to Anne for comfort—it ends with the apotheosis of Anne as mother: "What else are mothers for, darling?"

The next chapters are sentimentally focused on little Jem (the idealized version of a treasured eldest son). Jem takes his troubles to his mother—whom he calls "Mother dearwums,"[132] and he explains, complacently, "Mother knew everything." Montgomery was now weaving in threads that obliquely show the continuing strain of her obsession with Chester's affairs. Her journal entry for September 20 runs, "I wrote a good deal today and it has left me feeling tired. I am enduring a certain gnawing suspense these days which is hard to endure." She was so distressed and angered by Chester's continued involvement with Ida Birrell that she could not write about it directly in her journal. She could however interject the complexity of her mood into the ongoing novel. Her anxiety was intensified by the news of the week: "War seems certain!" (September 27, 1938).

She had reached the mid-point of her book, Chapters 21–22 of a 40-chapter novel. In this central incident, attention swings away from the children to Anne herself, the Anne who once dreamed of becoming a writer. Montgomery had sent her Story Girl into a wider world to thrill audiences with her eloquence. She had imagined her Emily, creating a little fantasy that would begin her publishing life, and later creating a book that would win great acclaim. Now she was bitter enough about the writing life to debunk the whole business of writing. Anne is talked into doing a bit of writing, a poetic obituary for a neighbour, and manages to create something fine. Then her "obitchery" is mocked by gross, ignorant editorial work. The mordant twist in the story is that the reader who requested the composition loves the mangled work. Bitter, but funny, the tiny incident mocks the aspiration of authorship in Anne, and the small-mindedness and impercipience of her audience. This sardonic interlude correlates with Montgomery's disappointment when her erstwhile admirers in the Canadian Authors Association manoeuvred her out of a leadership position in the society. It is also a bit of mockery of second-rate writing and of an audience whose respect for Montgomery's own delicate expertise was diminishing.

By October 17 she could write in the journal, "I have about half of *Anne of Ingleside* written." After this central point, the story returns to the troubles of Anne's children, presented now in encounters with a very ugly world. Again the chronology of the story meshed with the on-going life of the story-teller. Montgomery had begun to be more concerned about her grandchildren, Chester's young daughter and baby son. The second half of her novel begins with Jem and Walter facing sorrows over the loss of pet dogs; then turns to Anne's little daughters when they start off to school.

In twinned chapters, each child faces a problem, and is granted a solution. The structural device is reminiscent of the paired chapters early in *Anne of Green Gables*, where each of Anne's "scrapes" was followed by a triumphant resolution. Now, however, the scrapes are not comic but seriously distressing. In Chapters 25–26, Nan strikes an unhappy bargain with God; the stimulus for her unhappiness turns out to be her desperate love of mother Anne and desire to protect her. After Nan's happy ending, and a chapter when "Ingleside rang with laughter," Diana moves into the spotlight. In Chapters 28–29, Di is fooled by a mean little girl named Jenny Penny. This treachery leads into a sequence of stories about bad friends, in contrast to the olden-days love between Diana and Anne. In Chapters 30–31, another cruel little girl named Dovie fools Nan into believing she is not Anne's child.[133] The world of Glen St. Mary presents a scary array of little girl meanness, deceptions, teasing, lying.

Each of the stories about mean little children shines with extraordinary power, embedded as they all are in a generally upbeat novel. Although Montgomery ends each misadventure with a picture of Anne gently offering solace to her children, the portraits of spite are surprising, Here was a novelist who had made a specialty of portraying the attractiveness of children like Anne, Emily, and Pat. The new stories of Glen St. Mary demonstrate unexpected growth of darkness in the aging writer's view of childhood.

As she neared the end of her book, Montgomery dropped the stories of children and introduced two chapters which counterbalance two of the earliest chapters. In the first of these Miss Cornelia and Susan shared friendly gossip; in the second, Anne indulged in match-making. Now Montgomery presents, first, a quilting party where the gossipy members of the Ladies' Aid laughingly recount all the funny things that happened over the years, at local funerals. One well-remembered funeral was that of Peter Kirk. In the second of this pair of central chapters, Montgomery focuses more darkly on that memorable event. She presents Anne's recollection of the way one woman released a stream of vitriolic hatred as she stood by the dead body of Peter Kirk. This man, with the name that links with Dean Priest and David Kirk, had blighted his first wife's life. "He tortured and humiliated her . . . he *liked* to do it. Oh, he went to church regularly . . . and made long prayers

. . . and paid his debts. But he was a tyrant and a bully . . . his very dog ran when he heard him coming." At the climax of this vignette, Kirk's second wife rises in silent corroboration of marriage as victimization. At about the time she was composing this chapter, Montgomery, on her sixty-fourth birthday, November 30, 1938, noted in her journal that Ewan "has been very grim and melancholy of late and his thoughts are again centred only on his own sensations and phobias. He cannot help it." Anne herself comments that the story of Peter Kirk is "no story for children."

Then she returned to writing stories of childhood. In Chapters 35–36, Nan's romantic dream leads to cruel disillusionment; in the next two chapters, Di finds and unmasks another bad friend named Delilah, who is as devious as her Biblical model. Misadventure follows for Rilla, now old enough to venture into Glen St. Mary's on her own. Her small-girl pride leads to humiliation. Not one of these late chapters reads like a "story for children."

In her earlier books, Montgomery had introduced some less than lovable little girls such as Josie Pye in *Anne of Green Gables*; vain, self-centred Felicity in *The Story Girl*; Rhoda in *Emily of New Moon*; the Pringles in *Anne of Windy Poplars*; and the teasing visitors in *Magic for Marigold*. The tonal weight in those books had always been on the lovable amusing qualities in little girlhood. Now Montgomery has dropped her trademark.

Working from her unerring sense of symmetrical structure, Montgomery now chose to complete her novel by reverting to her opening theme—the workings of subtle adult malice. Aunt Mary Maria was the invader of Anne's peace at the outset; Christine Stuart plays that role at the end. Again it is Gilbert who brings the invader into Ingleside. Anne has been troubled by Gilbert's absorption in his own profession of medicine. When Christine Stuart, once seen as a rival for his affection in college days, appears as guest of honour at a medical dinner in Charlottetown, Anne becomes consumed by jealousy. Anne's insecurity and unhappiness disrupt the sunny security of her role as consoling mother. Montgomery makes Anne's jealousy funny for the reader, if not for poor Anne. It evaporates when Gilbert reveals the true professional cause of his absorption. Anne has the further comfort of recognizing that beautiful Christine, "sleek, well-preserved" has "substantial" feet (like the hated Clementine who roused little Marigold's jealous torments) and "a terrible mouthful of teeth." Perhaps the mocking treatment of jealousy is at some level directed against Ewan's displeasure at her fame as "L.M. Montgomery." The satire is also aimed at her own possessiveness and pride.

To complete the symmetry of the novel, she needed to conclude with a parallel not to Aunt Mary Maria's invasion, but to the golden peace of the opening visit to Green Gables. On December 7, 1938, having announced, "I wrote a chapter of *Anne of Ingleside*. Have only one more to do," Montgomery could add on the domestic scene, "Ewan seems pretty cheerful but his bronchitis is bad," and end her entry with a happy note, in which life seemed to be imitating art: "Today Chester called me 'nice little mother' for the first time in over a year." Then she could indeed write a final chapter that includes a closing moment of peace and pride in her family and herself.

The structure of symmetry is complete. The book began and ended with happiness. If the final happy resolution of all problems seems escapist, Montgomery had a lot to escape from, what with two military-aged sons, a mentally unstable husband, worries about her own health, diminishing dividends and royalties, and perceptible changes in readers' taste. The facile resolution of problems rises from desire, not clarity of vision. The bulk of the book remains shadowed by its recognition of cruelty. At its core, Montgomery had set an ironic comment on art, in the "obitchery" farce, a mockery of Anne as a would-be writer, scribe for her society.

Was the whole structural plan complete when Montgomery finished the "spade work" or did it emerge as pressures of her life suggested parallels and opposites? The answer is probably a composite. Montgomery planned very carefully, working out bits of dialogue and characterization as she "brooded up" her story. She was also sensitive to the kinds of changes and enrichments that life could bring to her consciousness. In either case, the clarity and control of the structure stands in stark conflict with the increasing misery and confusion of her life.

The last stage of the process of producing the book was tainted by real unhappiness. On January 24, 1939, as she typed and revised her manuscript, Montgomery wrote, "Ewan . . . came up to our room this evening when I was trying to work and made a terrible scene. I am so sick of these scenes—twenty years of them. I cried a little but soon returned to my work. It is surprising how one can grow used to intolerable things—and tolerate them." She survived, and when the end of the task of typing came, wrote on March 21, 1939: "I went down town after lunch yesterday to take the completed MS of *Anne of Ingleside* to Mr. McClelland" (her publisher). Immediately she added in an ominous return from fiction to fact, "Hitler has seized Czechoslovakia and a new war scare is in the offing."

Montgomery had gone back to her magic island one more time, and found it, like Shakespeare's isle in *The Tempest*, invaded by self-centred and threatening newcomers. It seemed no longer "a brave new world." But there are still "such people in it!": survivors like Susan Baker and real rebels like the women who tell the truth about Peter Kirk. It was still an island worth visiting as Montgomery wrote her way through her last sorrows, both the real ones and the ones that were exaggerated by her recurrent depressions.

Her earlier themes, nature, rural life, nostalgia, social customs, and feminism, had all shifted in meaning during the Depression period and the years leading to World War II. This last novel shows a surprising ability to introduce, in however veiled a manner, several modern fields of interest: aging, family studies, child psychology, childhood bullying, dysfunctional marriage. The emergence of such modernism perhaps accounts for the way Montgomery's popularity continued to hold up in an era so different from the one in which she embarked on her career.

On the day she completed *Anne of Ingleside*, Montgomery sadly expressed her suspicion that her writing days might be coming to a close. "I always wonder now if I will ever write another one. There are lots I want to write—but I *am* getting a little tired. I love to write still—I will always love it. But—."

Indeed, no more Montgomery novels were published after 1939. *Anne of Ingleside* remains as the last work that the author finalized and saw through the press before her death in 1942. Yet in the years after she finished *Anne of Ingleside*, Montgomery continued to live in imagined time as well as in reality. She continued to write, composing a series of stories that she planned to weave together in a book to be titled "The Blythes are Quoted." Anne appears in these stories as the subject of local gossip, among other roles. One story is set in the 1920s, following close behind the era of *Rilla of Ingleside*. Others include later anecdotes about Anne's grandchildren, including Rilla's son, Gilbert Ford, and Walter Blythe, the child of Faith and Jem. In one late story, Dr. Blythe is an elderly man, whose son has followed him into the medical profession. The last of the stories is set around 1940; it mentions the fact that another war is going on.

Not ready for publication in Montgomery's lifetime, these fragments remained in manuscript until her son Stuart Macdonald published them, as *The Road to Yesterday*, in 1974—one hundred years after her birth in 1874, and thirty-two years after her death in 1942. The stories appeared in truncated form, because the publisher, McGraw-Hill Ryerson, had removed the linking intervals in which Anne and Gilbert mull over the stories they have been telling each other. The publisher also rearranged the order of the stories.[134] Knowing her addiction to infinite revision, we can only wonder what the final form of *The Blythes are Quoted* would have been if she had overseen it. As any good story-teller would do, Montgomery had left her readers with a suspense at the end.

— Conclusion —

L.M. Montgomery may have longed, like Virginia Woolf, for "a room of one's own." She never had one from the time she married, but all through her troubled life she always had "an island of her own." Two islands, in fact: the one she had grown up on, and the one she created, the fictional island the rest of us can access. The Island on which she had matured was a plastic to be moulded into the permanence of art. It remained in her memory as a beautiful place, yet she recognized the imperfections it presented to her as an adult. She could not and would not move back in fact, but in fiction it served well throughout her life. Even when she was away from the real Island it provided her basic plot, her stock of natural charm, and her range of convincing colourful people.

Her fictional island is a world of mysterious sights and sounds, signals and mists, babble and echoes. Shakespeare in *The Tempest* depicted an isle "full of voices." When powerful Prospero in the Shakespeare play calls people from the real world to his magic isle, they find there two opposed figures: Ariel, the imaginative free spirit, and Caliban, the near-inarticulate intractable half-beast. Readers coming to the totality of L.M. Montgomery's work find there the same opposed forces: the magic isle of her fiction hums with Ariel's whimsy and charm, but it is roiled by the darker Caliban force of resentment and meanness, creating a chiaroscuro of ambiguity and complexity. Montgomery had thrown into her romances the spice of a darker irony. Her fiction presents dichotomies of irony and naïveté, simple fun and farce, sweetness and cruelty.

The idea of an island always stirs ambivalent feelings. Deep water surrounds every isle. For the islanders this gives a sense of centred unity, of security. Shakespeare called his own island, "This precious stone set in a silver sea,/Which serves it in the office of a wall."[135] Yet Matthew Arnold described those silver separating waters as "the unplumbed, salt, estranging sea."[136] From the point of view of the mainland, the island is marginal, a place of isolation and exile. Shauna McCabe, a modern art curator, summarizes the dichotomy: "Romanticized and promoted as places of ideal perfection, of intimacy, retreat, and renewal, islands also offer stark realities of exile, isolation, seclusion."[137]

Montgomery's stories expand the duality of island/mainland into a triad: the island, the mainland, and the creative artist. The artistic creation of an imagined world, an island set off from the mainland of reality, seemed sinister and suspect in the past, when Puritans denounced fiction as lies, a usurping of the one Creator's prerogative. Something of that attitude survived in the community of Montgomery's youth, an attitude personified in Emily's Aunt Elizabeth (though Montgomery showed Aunt Elizabeth as capable of being converted to a surprised joy in Emily's fiction). For the older Montgomery as a wife and mother, and as responsible adult in a community depending on her services, the escape to an imagined world still trailed some sense of guilt. Perhaps it was that sense that led her increasingly to assign the role of creator not to her central figure but to another character, often one who came from or planned to return to the mainland. Consciously or unconsciously she drew into her stories the figure that obliquely represented her own ambivalence toward herself as a woman artist.

The voyage through her fictions reveals many other haunting ambiguities. Adults may play supportive, fostering roles in relation to young artists—or hindering ones. Idealized landscapes may appear in a rainbowed Valley, of a lantern-lit Hill. Houses may be beloved and welcoming, or disappointed and menacing; at worst, they burn to the ground. Doubles recur, but even in twins, male and female principles are opposed.

Voyaging through these islands of fiction leads to recognition of some recurring features in the whole archipelago. First, there is the sensual detail of the island: colours, sounds, movement, pulsation, energy, skies, paths, woods; and each novel creates also a sense of the island as social space. Second, there is a dweller in the island, usually female, who is ecstatic in response to the sensual and social stimuli. Sometimes this person is also a story-teller, writer, or performer; sometimes she is friend or companion to such a person, a portrait painter, an architect, a would-be novelist, a successful essayist. Third, there is another place, a mainland not of ecstasy but of meanness, malice, incomprehension. Sometimes this is the adult world closed to a child's energy; sometimes it is the home of an uncomprehending friend or suitor.

In *Anne of Green Gables*, Anne is the imaginative, story-telling child who comes to the Island from away, to live with rather stiff older people until she finds her way into maturity. Anne comes to Green Gables from a mainland of cruelty (and twins). On tiny Victoria Island, the isle within the Island, she writes little stories. Later, however, though she has won a scholarship for Literature and has dreamt of going to college on the mainland, she stays on the Island. Because of Green Gables, Marilla, and Gilbert—rootedness, duty, and romance—this first novel concludes, "not yet."

"Not yet" again in the sequel. Anne becomes a power and a beautifier of Avonlea and she copes with the twins, dynamic Davy and dull domestic Dora. She has little time for writing, but there are two creative writers at the margins of this book. Middle-aged Mrs. Morgan is a homely, successful novelist, who comes from the mainland for a brief visit. Young, oversensitive poetic Paul Irving also comes "from away." He is whisked back to

Boston, when his father marries Miss Lavendar, Anne's white-haired surrogate. Paul will come back for summer visits to the Island and to lonely "Echo Lodge"; Anne prepares to leave for Kingsport.

In *The Story Girl* and *The Golden Road*, the Island is the place where two boys come from mainland Toronto, to find family warmth and memories and a circle of cousins in the old orchard, a fruitful island within the Island. Here they find a flaming creative girl, who is yearning for her absent father. At the end of *The Golden Road*, the boys' father calls them back to Toronto and the Story Girl's artist father will take her farther from the Island, to Paris, so that her talent can develop fully.

Kilmeny repeats and intensifies these motifs. For the voiceless girl, the island-in-island orchard is doubly walled by her disability and her history—mother's "sin" and grandfather's cold, numbing fury. She drifts with her violin, waiting for a lover to come from away. A single man comes as schoolmaster to the Island, in spite of mainland mockery of his decision. For love of him, Kilmeny frees herself from silence. The Master, abetted by his father, prepares to take her from the Island to Queenslea, the college town on the mainland.

Back to Anne, now of/off the Island—as Montgomery now found herself. Married to a minister, taken by him to a village near Toronto, the author now imbued her remembered and imagined isle with greater complexity. Anne goes off the Island not to "Queenslea" but to "Kingsport" where a threatening little fortress island oversees her abortive romance with Royal Gardiner. She finds a new off-Island "bosom friend" named Philippa, who marries a gawky but attractive minister. Back on the Island Diana is engaged to dumpy Fred, while Ruby Gillis dies, bitterly denied love and life. "Not yet" changes to "at last" when Anne accepts Gilbert after he too hovers at the point of death.

In *Anne's House of Dreams* Anne's married story unfolds, but the book's centre of gravity lies in another young woman's destiny. Leslie Moore, married to a mindless husk, is eventually carried away from her loneliness by Owen Ford, a man who has had success as a writer of short stories, and who dreams of writing a novel. The other creative person in this novel is old Captain Jim. He dies as the book ends, and Anne moves away from dreams to Glen St. Mary—the valley of sanctified motherhood.

So Montgomery's fictional island loses its creative artists in these early books, and in the two sequels about Anne's children. In *Rainbow Valley*, they play with their counterparts, the minister's children, but also with Mary Vance, an Anne without her vivid colouring, a girl with washed-out eyes and a mean tongue. In *Rilla of Ingleside*, Mary Vance mocks Anne's youngest daughter, Rilla, for her efforts at mothering. This sequel ends when Anne's poet son Walter leaves for the mainland of war and is killed, and Rilla lisps her way into romance.

Then a new moon rises in the Island. Young Emily Byrd Starr grows through writing to her father and for Mr. Carpenter. But adult Emily, in the sequels, though she has quested and climbed and published books, finally waits unhappily for the call from another (male) artist. When, as a successful portrait painter, Teddy finally takes Emily away to his mainland world, she can still anticipate summers on the Island, not in Echo Lodge but in "the Disappointed House." The *Emily* series is pulled from a late stage of the author's life, and from a deeper probing of her sense of the writer's psyche: it maps a different nook in her experience.

Midway through writing about Emily, Montgomery broke away to *The Blue Castle*. Valancy's island is not Prince Edward Island, but an imaginary isle in Ontario's Muskoka district—mysterious Mistawis, a dream world where a lover from away is waiting, once the young woman can escape from a fatherless family to find him. Valancy's triumph is the finding of Mistawis isle, *and* a rich and successful writer-husband. Barney Snaith has returned from wandering as far as the Yukon, to go on with his writing in a special Bluebeard's chamber (where perhaps a Sister Anne is hanging, as in the old Arabian Nights tale). After the book ends, Snaith/Foster/Redfern will take Valancy to the Alhambra and to Samarcand, and then to a home near Montreal with Mistawis as a summer retreat. Divided years, divided residence, like Emily's and Miss Lavendar's, in each case dominated by a male artist's successful career.

Montgomery's next two books take Prince Edward Island for granted as a complex society where very young Marigold Leslie and very old Becky Dark stand at the poles of life. *Magic for Marigold* concentrates on the wonders of open-hearted childhood, even a fatherless childhood. Uncle Klondike, who has wandered as far as the Yukon, the farthest away of any Islander, comes home to marry the other Marigold. Dr. Marigold is a successful professional woman. *A Tangled Web* sardonically dramatizes the social effects of wilfulness on the Island's un-magic adult world.

Then comes Pat Gardiner, moving sadly from one pole of life toward the other. The first half of *Pat of Silver Bush* is dominated by the birth of Rae, the second half by the death of Bets. Pat is the most deeply islanded of all the Montgomery characters: obsessed with Silver Bush, the house, the property, the landscape; with the family (a circle rather like the Kings' in *The Story Girl*), and with the resident story-teller, Judy Plum. Withered, comic, earthy, Judy Plum is the Story Girl, debased in many ways but still vigorous and varied in her Island. In *Mistress Pat*, after Judy dies, the family dissolves, and the house burns down; but Jingle, the successful architect returns from the far west, to take Mistress Pat off the Island "for good."

Finally, two more Annes appear, wrapped around a Jane. In the retrospective *Anne of Windy Poplars*, young Anne appears as troubled school principal, lonely letter-writing fiancée, and worried colleague of a young woman suffering from depression.

Jane of Lantern Hill signals the eruption of optimism. The Island is at last again a beacon, a high place drawing a girl up and away from the dark sardonic lowland of Toronto. Jane's writer-father calls her to the Island, not away from it. The reunited family will live in two perfect houses, on and off the Island. With Jane, the dream of a perfect Prince Edward Island revives. Here a girl can find a father, a métier, friends, and ultimately the chance for a second start.

"Ingleside" in the other final Anne title means hearthside and enclosed safety, but the story turns on the meanness, envy, and bullying tendencies of children and the boring intrusiveness of an old woman. The last portrait of the artist, Anne herself as a writer of obituary, appears in the final Anne novel.

The total sequence of books constitutes a fluctuating, complex commentary on life and art. Behind the complexity stands a mysterious creator, a mature craftsman, absorbedly at work. Montgomery had recognized and relished her gift of transcendence, her ability to lift the curtain of reality and rapturously re-enter a more perfect land. She created characters with a comparable capacity of escape into a world of beauty and accomplishment, comedy and pathos. Unlike most of her characters, she concentrated on brooding up her dreams, doing spade work, separating herself from daily concerns while she wrote a first draft, returning to that draft to revise improve, delete, add. She worked at each manuscript until it came close to satisfying her desire for wholeness, progression, surprise, and reassurance.

Knowledge of Montgomery's life suggests a deep source of the ambiguous creations that emerged from this assiduity. From her youth, she had suffered wild mood swings. In her husband's case, such affective disorders became a clinical form of depression, a malady that certainly stained her later years as well as his. But given her inexplicable literary gift, Maud Montgomery was able to divert her manic tendency, to exploit the mood swings by converting them into opposed characters and opposed symbolic landscapes. Her novels can be read as a gifted writer's conversion of the pressures, evasions, and releases of her own life into complex fictions. In fact, her fiction reveals depths of personality of which she herself was probably unaware.

Beyond this psychological hypothesis, however, thanks to research and readings of the journals, we can also set the novels a little more accurately within vectors of time and place. In her lifetime Montgomery had moved from a late-Victorian, early-Edwardian set of values and literary conventions, through the disruptions of style and vision enforced by the war and its aftermath, on into the Depression and toward the coming of another war. Against this drama, her own life seemed relatively quiet. Yet by dogged persistence, she had produced eight sequels in the *Anne* series, fourteen other books of fiction, an autobiography, a book of poetry, roughly four hundred and fifty uncollected poems, five hundred short stories, and over five thousand pages of diaries. In the same life span, she had also married, given birth to three sons, and run Presbyterian manses in small villages in Ontario.

Biography does not explain the alchemy of art. Readers recognize much more than confession or auto-therapy in the Montgomery novels. They find, for one thing, deep symbolic meditations on art and life, male and female, home and away. Such wisdom is surely not attributable simply to an individual's mood shifts.

What she did with her island reveals the mystery of talent, or genius. She gathered bits of memory and observation, fitted these into a construct of chapters, and launched new creations, books much more than the sum of their explicable parts. The rhythm of each novel seems foreordained yet each is full of surprises and thrills of unexpected recognition.

Such creative art is a mystery indeed, and one that can be illuminated by comparison with the achievements of genius in other media. Art is common, genius is rare. Most of us can sing a little tune, but it takes a freak of vocal chords and a richness of feeling to sing as Pavarotti did. Most of us can hold a paint brush and make strokes on canvas, but it takes an odd combination of physical eye and hand and spiritual vision to produce a work like a Tom Thomson picture of a northern isle, or a binocular vision of enraptured voyage like Alex Colville's "To Prince Edward Island." As for storytelling, we can all pass along an anecdote, but the instinct for pace, proportion, and progression is rare. An inborn instinct, maybe, or a matter of genetics. Some day neurologists may trace the flukey heritage path to a Pavarotti or a Thomson, or the genetic thread that gives narrative genius to an Austen, an Aesop, a Montgomery. Meantime, let's call it magic.

— Notes —

Introduction

1. *Selected Journals of L.M. Montgomery*, Vol. V, eds. Mary Rubio and Elizabeth Waterston, 264. The quotation comes from Montgomery's entry of June 25, 1938. Further quotations drawn from the *Selected Journals* will be identified by the date of the entry.

2. The scrapbooks are held at the Confederation Centre in Charlottetown and at the University of Guelph; the photographs are at the University of Guelph and are discussed very effectively in Elizabeth Epperly's *Through Lover's Lane*; the letters appear in *The Green Gables Letters*, ed. Wilfrid Eggleston, in *After Green Gables*, eds. Hildi and Paul Thiessen, and in *My Dear Mr. M.*, eds. F.W.P. Bolger and Elizabeth Epperly. The manuscripts are held at the Confederation Centre and the University of Guelph. See the bibliography for details.

3. Mollie Gillen's *The Wheel of Things* is an older but still very useful biography; Mary Rubio's *The Gift of Wings* presents and interprets more recent research.

4. Details of the translated editions of all Montgomery's novels, and lists of the short stories published before 1895 appear in *Lucy Maud Montgomery: A Preliminary Bibliography*, eds. Ruth Weber Russell, D.W. Russell, and Rea Wilmshurst.

5. Clarence Karr surveys Montgomery's reading in "Addicted to Books: L.M. Montgomery and the Value of Reading."

6. Two seminal studies suggest the intention and methodology followed in this study of factors leading to creative achievement: Jerome Beaty's *Middlemarch: From Notebook to Novel: A Study of George Eliot's Creative Method*; and John Livingstone Lowes's *The Road to Xanadu*, on S.T. Coleridge's "Kubla Khan."

7. An intriguing set of comments on the effects of reading and re-reading Montgomery's work appears in the tributes to her in *Everybody's Favourites: Canadians Talk about Books That Changed Their Lives*, edited by Arlene Perly Rae.

Anne of Green Gables

8. The revisions to *Anne of Green Gables* are preserved in manuscripts held at the Confederation Centre, Charlottetown, Prince Edward Island. A copy of all the changes is presented on the web site www.lmmrc.ca.

9. Because there are so many editions of each of the Montgomery books, no page references are given here. One quick way to find the quoted passages in their context is to "Google" the title of the book and add "Gutenberg" to see a text online.

10. Publishing data on all these best-selling novels appears in Frank Mott, *Golden Multitudes*. Montgomery knew all these books, and Mark Twain and Kipling remained among her lifelong favourite authors.

11. See F.W.P. Bolger, *The Years before Anne*, 86–131.

12. See Russell, Russell, and Wilmshurst, *L.M. Montgomery: A Preliminary Bibliography*, 65–84.

13. Ewan Macdonald had been inducted in Cavendish as the Presbyterian minister in 1903.

14. See Epperly, *The Fragrance of Sweet-Grass*, 32–33.

15. Critical comments on the ending of *Anne of Green Gables* appear in Epperly, *The Fragrance of Sweet-Grass*, Chapter 1, and in Gabriella Ahmansson, *A Life and Its Mirrors*, as well as in many articles.

16. Montgomery's notes of revisions to selected chapters, including the final one, are reproduced in the Norton Critical Edition of *Anne of Green Gables*, ed. Mary Rubio and Elizabeth Waterston.

17. See Yuko Katsura, "Red-haired Anne in Japan."

Anne of Avonlea

18. See Carole Gerson, "'Dragged at Anne's Chariot Wheels': The Triangle of Author, Publisher, and Fictional Character," in *L.M. Montgomery and Canadian Culture*, eds. Irene Gammel and Elizabeth R. Epperly.

19. For comments on the twin theme as used by another major Canadian writer, see Robert Rogers, *A Psychoanalytic Study of the Double in Literature*, and Elizabeth Waterston, "Double is Trouble: Twins in *A Jest of God*."

20. For example, *Scribner's* in 1907 published "The Garden as a Picture" by Edith Wharton's niece Beatrix Jones; nine years earlier the *Atlantic Monthly* had published N.S. Shaler's "The Landscape as a Means of Culture."

21. The spelling of "Lavendar" is unusual. Montgomery used the more conventional form in her short story "Lavender's Room," *East and West* (1905).

Kilmeny of the Orchard

22. A direct hint of the extent of "Kailyard" influence among American writers appears in Alice Hegan Rice's title, *Mrs. Wiggs of the Cabbage Patch*.

23. Montgomery used this identical Browning quotation in the description of Anne as she prepared for her public performance.

24. See also *My Dear Mr. M.*, eds. F.W.P. Bolger and Elizabeth Epperly.

The Story Girl

25. A boy from Quebec comes for a summer visit to an uncle's farm in Prince Edward Island in "Our Charivari," published in the Philadelphia magazine *Golden Days* in 1896.

26. For example, two stories with suggestive titles had appeared in 1903: "The Running away of Chester" in *Boys' World*, and "Ted's Double" in *Men of Tomorrow*.

27. Because of the popularity of *Anne of Green Gables*, Montgomery had recently welcomed many visitors "from away" to her home province. These visitors included Ontario writers such as Florence Livesay and Marjory MacMurchy. Perhaps these experiences also suggested the choice of an Ontario narrator. The male narrator's name is "Bev"—first of a series of androgynous names assigned to male characters by Montgomery. Others will include "Hilary" and "Shirley."

28. There was a fourth member of the Campbell clan, Frederica, too young to play much part in the early days at Park Corner; but later to become a very dear friend. It was Frederica who launched the phrase "the race that knows Joseph"—a phrase quoted in Maud's journal just before she began to write *The Story Girl*. In Cavendish another large family of cousins, children of Uncle John Macneill next door, were also early playmates.

29. Both "A Pioneer Wooing" and Sara's story retell the story of the Macneills' great-grandmother who asked her sister's suitor, "Why not marry me?"

30. In 1909, when Montgomery was writing *The Story Girl*, Ewan Macdonald was working in the parishes of Bloomfield and O'Leary, in the western end of the Island. He moved to Ontario at the end of 1909 and was inducted into St. Paul's Presbyterian Church in Leaskdale in January 1910.

31. In an "Afterword" to *The Story Girl* (1991), Mary Rubio and Elizabeth Waterston suggested that the brothers Bev and Felix might be seen as two versions of Ewan Macdonald—the young enthusiast who stirred Cavendish into beautification, and the "grave and stodgy" person he became. See the "Afterword" for further notes on the dominant themes of the novel.

32. See Irene Gammel, "'I loved Herman Leard madly,'" in *Intimate Life of L.M. Montgomery*, ed. Irene Gammel.

33. The Montgomery scrapbooks are preserved in Charlottetown and Guelph. Reproductions of them are available on-line in "Picturing a Canadian Life: L.M. Montgomery's Personal Scrapbooks and Book Covers: The Virtual Museum of Canada. 2002," http://lmm.confederationcentre.com.

34. By 1910 there were 342 titles from named magazines, as listed in the Wilmshurst bibliography, plus 40 more titles from clippings in the scrapbooks (which do not give the names of the publications), plus roughly another 60 named only in her business ledger list.

35. See Rachel Blau DuPlessis, *Writing Beyond the Ending.*

Chronicles of Avonlea

36. *The Green Gables Letters*, ed. Wilfrid Eggleston, 49.

37. *My Dear Mr. M.*, ed. Bolger and Epperly, 32.

38. Mary Rubio suggests that the repeated choice of an Ontario narrator may reflect the author's thoughts of Ewan Macdonald, now in Leaskdale, Ontario, looking to the Island where his story-telling bride is.

39. Mary Rubio interprets this comment as indicative of Ewan's self-contained, undemonstrative nature, rather than as dismissive of his bride's importance.

Anne of the Island

40. For comments on the *bildungsroman* as it relates to male characters, see Jerome Buckley, *Season of Youth: The Bildungsroman from Dickens to Golding*. A shift of focus to the development of women was notable around 1913, when Montgomery wrote *Anne of the Island*. Major demonstrations in the UK and US urged suffrage for women; changes occurred that year in the status of women in Australia, most Scandinavian countries, and many American States. The *Montreal Witness*, Montgomery's first publisher, was a leader in the women's movement in Canada. Carrie Derick became Canada's first woman Professor in 1913.

41. On these theories, see Ahmansson, *A Life and its Mirrors*, 114 ff.

42. Montgomery's friend Marjory MacMurchy in a book titled *The Woman— Bless Her* (1916) urged that a scholarly woman should hold a position of authority and management in university affairs affecting young women. "What a barren place a university would be for young men if there were no older men in the university for them to learn from, to respect and copy, more than all, admire!" In this sense, college life for Montgomery (and also for Anne) was a barren place.

43. Years later in a handbook on Canadian literature Archibald MacMechan would mention Montgomery kindly, without mentioning that she had been his student for an important year of her life.

44. Reproduced in The Norton Critical Edition of *Anne of Green Gables* (2006), ed. Rubio and Waterston.

45. Tennyson, "The Daydream," *English Idylls and Other Poems* (1842).

46. Montgomery might remember receiving a proposal in 1894 from Lem Mcleod, who had "no brains, culture, or breeding" (October 2, 1894).

47. As a student in the Canadian Maritimes, Montgomery followed American conventions of spelling. Quotations from her work follow this convention (e.g., "harbor,") although set here into a text that follows British-Canadian conventions (e.g., "harbour").

48. Yet, ambiguously, Montgomery also touches onto the description of Hester Gray's garden specific echoes of the charms of Patty's Place with words like "golden," "kindled," and "purr."

49. This is the view of Owen Dudley Edwards of University of Edinburgh, as recounted by Dr. Jennifer Litster in a lecture at University of Prince Edward Island, June 2006.

50. It could be argued that the sketch about wild flowers and domestic garden blooms confronts the question of freedom and containment, the main themes in the containing novel.

51. Significantly, she changed the name of the mainland city, which had appeared as "Queenslea" when she wrote *Kilmeny of the Orchard*, to "Kingsport" in her present state of irritation at the strictures of male critics in the world outside her Island.

52. A similar worry perhaps underlies the attribution of literary power not to Anne but to Stephen Irving in Montgomery's previous novel, and to Owen Ford in her next one.

Anne's House of Dreams

53. The allusion is to Washington Irving's travel book, *Tales of the Alhambra* (1832). Montgomery had indirectly indicated her debt to Irving by giving his name to the famous writer who comes to rescue Miss Lavendar from her life alone in Echo Lodge.

54. See Epperly, *Lover's Lane*, for comments on the metaphoric significance of the details in Montgomery's photographs of the Leaskdale manse. Particularly interesting is the visual link between the arch over the front porch of the manse and the arched Wine Gate at the Alhambra, as shown in Epperly, figures 34, 35.

55. Captain Jim had appeared in a story published in the *Housekeeper* (August 1909) as "The Life-Book of Uncle Jesse."

56. The "house-wife's" care in keeping her house shiny and tidy links with her supervision of village mores and kindness to the needy. In *The Poetics of Space*, Bachelard writes of "woman's construction of the house through daily polishing" (690).

57. See Rosemary Ross Johnston, "Landscape as Palimpsest, Pentimento, Epiphany: Lucy Maud Montgomery's Interiorisation of the Exterior, Exteriorisation of the Interior."

58. This part of the dream is used in the powerful scene when Anne dances on the sea shore on a calm evening after a storm, "whirling round and round, laughing like a child."

59. The story was published in *Everywoman's World* in July 1917. This Canadian magazine was concurrently publishing Montgomery's autobiography, *The Alpine Path*, in serial form (June–November 1917).

60. Saunders's last publication with Page appeared in 1913. After switching to McClelland & Stewart she began to use Canadian settings for her stories for the first time since the 1880s. Most of her Page-published books were set in Maine or Vermont, although she lived mostly in Nova Scotia. See Elizabeth Waterston, "Marshall Saunders," in *Silenced Sextet*, eds. Carrie Macmillan, et al. (Montreal: McGill-Queen's University Press, 1992), ch. 5.

61. One of Miss Cornelia's more unsettling comments concerns a man who "worried so much over believing that he had committed the unpardonable

sin that he died in an asylum" (200)—a creepy foreshadowing of Ewan's eventual breakdown.

Rainbow Valley

62. See Rubio, "L.M. Montgomery: Scottish-Presbyterian Agency in Canadian Culture," *L.M. Montgomery and Canadian Culture.*
63. Montgomery relished Charlotte Brontë's portrait of St. John Rivers, the obsessive minister in *Jane Eyre*; but she also enjoyed the lighter touch of Anthony Trollope in portraying the Dean in *Barchester Towers.*
64. A harsher view of the minister may be implied in his name, perhaps an allusion to the novelist George Meredith, whose best known work is titled *The Egoist* (1879).
65. An article on Mary Vance refers to her as a "hoyden." Rosamond Bailey, "Little Orphan Mary: Anne's Hoydenish Double."

Further Chronicles of Avonlea

66. See Gammel, ed., *The Intimate Life of L.M. Montgomery.*
67. The arrival of a Cavendish kitten named Daffy reconciled her to her exile in Leaskdale when she was a bride, and Daffy became a constant treasure, eventually mourned and then replaced by Good Luck—on whose death Montgomery indulged in a forty-page elegy.
68. John Simpson and John Ayto, eds., *The Oxford Dictionary of Modern Slang.*
69. Cutler, Charles L. *O Brave New Words! Native American Loanwords in Current English.* Norman: University of Oklahoma Press, 1994.
70. Montgomery presented a paper on his *The Sky Pilot* to the Hypatia Club of Uxbridge in 1912.
71. Unsigned comment found online, on "Tannis" December 20, 2006.
72. The editor of these volumes, Rea Wilmshurst, had for years been tracing the early Montgomery stories to their originals; her selections were insightful and sensitive.

Rilla of Ingleside

73. Named for angular old Marilla, her name has been softened to fit the play of a little brook. Perhaps this softening also reflects the change in Maud Montgomery's memories of her Grandmother Macneill, the woman who was in part Marilla's original, and who—like Marilla and Rilla—was thrust unwillingly into a nurturing role.
74. The manuscript of *Rilla of Ingleside*, with corrections appended, is in the archives at the University of Guelph.
75. Another character who seems drawn from family memories is "Cousin Sophia"—a sad, sighing woman, critical of everything and everyone— much like Frederica's sister Stella Campbell, who had come to Leaskdale to

help when the new baby Stuart was expected, and stayed on and on, complaining, unhelpful, and bossy.

Emily of New Moon

76. Mary Rubio, in private correspondence to me, suggests that the picture of Aunt Elizabeth is also in part a "hate-portrait" of Montgomery's own darker side, rising from subconscious recognition of the harshness of her treatment of her sons (2007).

77. Montgomery perhaps considered the Ontario system, curriculum, and standards, as manifested in a small town, and as compared to the Prince Edward Island system, not good enough for her sons. Mary Rubio suggests in private correspondence that this was also an elitist choice on her part. Chester's early troubles in the local school reinforced the decision to opt for a distant school (2007).

78. A footnote attached to Wordsworth's poem attributes these two essential lines to his wife: "Line 21 and 22 were composed by Mrs. Wordsworth."

79. Ernest Raymond, *Through Literature to Life* (London: Cassell, 1928), 248–49.

80. Alice Munro says this was a watershed book for her. So does Jane Urquhart. Margaret Laurence said it recreated exactly how she felt as a budding artist.

Emily Climbs

81. Mary Rubio expands on this situation in *The Gift of Wings* (2008).

82. Perhaps an oblique reference to Ewan Macdonald, whose awkward table manners were commented on as reflecting his farm origins.

83. Marie Campbell, "Wordbound." Unpublished Master's Thesis, University of Guelph, 1985.

The Blue Castle

84. According to Isabella Valancy Crawford's great-niece, the family pronounced her name Valáncy, from Valencia, a family name since the Peninsular war. Valancy Stirling's middle name is plain "Jane." She takes after her great-grandfather Wansbarra (an odd name—somewhat reminiscent of the name "Barraclough," the name of new friends in Norval; or of "Gainsborough," the epitome of romantic painters).

85. For analysis of the way Victorian women exploited illness as a way of evading the reality of powerlessness, see Elaine Showalter, *The Female Malady*, and Athena Vrettos, *Somatic Fictions*.

86. Montgomery saw *Saint Joan* on stage October 10, 1924. It was produced in 1923 in New York, 1924 in London.

87. See Hutton and Jackson-Hutton, *Lucy Maud Montgomery and Bala*, 75.

88. See Hutton and Jackson-Hutton, *Lucy Maud Montgomery and Bala*, 46–53.

89. In private correspondence, Barbara Garner has argued for the identification of Bliss Carman as the original of "John Foster"; Elizabeth Epperly finds

echoes in his portrait of another Maritime writer, Charles G.D. Roberts, and Mary Rubio identifies John Burroughs (1837–1921) as notably close to "John Foster" in style.

90. When Carman died, Montgomery offered a powerful tribute (June 18, 1929).

Emily's Quest

91. In fiction, Teddy seems destined to marry another woman; in real life, Nathan Lockhart's marriage was not just a "seeming" but an actuality. He married a Nova Scotian woman in 1906.

92. Russell, Russell, and Wilmshurst, *L.M. Montgomery: A Preliminary Bibliography*, 96–109.

93. See Rachel Blau DuPlessis, *Writing Beyond the Ending*.

94. Barbara Godard, "Structuralism/post-structuralism," in *Future Indicative*, ed. John Moss, 46.

Magic for Marigold

95. These would reappear in modified form in *Magic for Marigold*, chs. 1, 5, 10, 12.

96. See Sandra Sabatini, *Making Babies: Infants in Canadian Fiction*. The emergence of professionals devoted to various aspects of child-rearing was part of a general modern trend.

97. The Lesley family lives in a town called "Rexton" in the *Delineator* short story. In the novel, Montgomery drops this name, so redolent of male monarchy. The town is now called "Harmony," suggesting a more feminine ideal.

98. See Laurie Ricou, *Everyday Magic*, on the phenomenon of child language. Experiments like Joyce's appeared in many books of the period, including *Mary Olivier* (1919) by May Sinclair, which Montgomery had read and discussed a few years earlier.

99. Marigold's home had been called "Cloud o' Pines" in the *Delineator* short story.

100. In the *Delineator* stories the imaginary friend is called "Gertrude," an old-fashioned name up-dated in the novel (to quote Donna Campbell) to the more stylish "Sylvia."

101. See Margaret Steffler, "Performing Motherhood: L.M. Montgomery's Display of Maternal Dissonance," *Storm and Dissonance*.

A Tangled Web

102. This dismissal was slow to dissipate. As late as 1964, the first edition of the *Literary History of Canada* (Toronto: University of Toronto Press, 1964) assigned treatment of Montgomery's work to a children's librarian. In a later edition (1976), Sheila Egoff, the respected expert on children's literature, wrote dismissively of the Montgomery books.

103. Walter Scott, *Marmion* (1808), Canto VI, Stanza 17.

Pat of Silver Bush

104. "Hilary" is one of several androgynous names used by Montgomery. During the time Montgomery was working on *Pat of Silver Bush*, she also did some writing for periodicals for the sake of quick cash. In February, the *Canadian Home Journal* bought a story called "The Mirror." The mirror in the title is a family heirloom, like the mirror mentioned at least twelve times in descriptions of "Silver Bush." Intriguingly, the heroine is a shy girl named "Hilary." This strange use of the name she had already assigned to the boy who is Pat's hobbledehoy friend indicates her identification with his story.

105. See Rubio's study of Montgomery's finances in *The Gift of Wings*, which is based on Montgomery's account books, as interpreted by financial experts.

106. In a letter to Roberta Sparks, Saskatchewan, July 4, 1933, now held in the University of Guelph archives, Montgomery wrote, "I gave *Anne* my imagination and Emily Starr my knack of scribbling; but the girl who is more myself than any other is 'Pat of Silver Bush'—my new story which is to be out this fall. Not *externally* but spiritually, she is 'I.'"

Mistress Pat

107. Perhaps this comes from a memory of her grandfather Montgomery playing up his supposed resemblance to the Earl of Eglinton: a proud story Montgomery passed along at this time to her future daughter-in-law Luella.

108. The reference to Guelph is a gracious tribute to the Ontario Agricultural College, where Montgomery had addressed a very large crowd of students in 1929. Rae will presumably register in Macdonald Institute of Household Science, getting the kind of training that Frede had at Macdonald College of McGill. In 1907 Frede had also taken a summer course at Guelph.

109. Presumably there is no link between Philippa and Hilary "Jingle" Gordon, let alone with Neil Gordon long ago in *Kilmeny*. Montgomery still had no trouble thinking up funny names for older people like Mr. Butterbloom or Mrs. Pennyduck, but the old power of deeply suggestive naming for central characters seemed to be in remission.

110. Perhaps the Binnies' last name is a blurred echo of Mr. Bennie, a minister at Uxbridge whom Montgomery disliked.

111. Margaret Doody detects an incestuous quality in Pat's feelings for Sid (*Storm and Dissonance*). The suggestion is evocative, in the light of Montgomery's horrified over-reaction a few years earlier to Valentine Dobrée's 1927 novel, *Your Cuckoo Sings by Kind*. Dobrée's introduction of a scene of incest into this story of an eleven-year old girl appeared "worse than dirt—it was verminous. I poked it into the fire and held it down with the tongs and watched it burn" (November 17, 1929).

112. Rae marries Brook Hamilton, whose name recalls John Brook, the kindly man that Meg married in *Little Women*, but in *Anne of Windy Poplars* Montgomery will assign the surname again to difficult Katherine Brooke.

Anne of Windy Poplars

113. Beth Cavert notes that this title echoes a phrase from a poem by Bernard Trotter: "a row of wind-blown poplars." Montgomery and her friend Nora Campbell quoted the poem to each other in August 1932; it is quoted again in *Jane of Lantern Hill* by Jane's father. See Cavert, "Summoning voices in Diaries and Memoirs," in *The Intimate Life of L.M. Montgomery*, 116.

114. Rubio reports from interviews she conducted in Acton that people there still remember that they lived in dread of the year their children would be in Isobel Anderson's class, given her angry and caustic sarcasm.

Jane of Lantern Hill

115. Donna Campbell notes the double-naming in "Tomorrow Comes," which concerns a child "whose mother called her Judy and whose grandmother called her Hester." Other oddities appear in the 1934 story: the name "Tillytuck" is recycled from *Pat of Silver Bush*, and "Flying Cloud" and "Grandmother and her Woman" will reappear in *Anne of Windy Poplars*. In *The Blue Castle* "Victoria" reappeared as Valancy's middle name, perhaps presaging her victory over a life as restrictive as Jane's. An earlier example of double naming appears in *Mary Marie* (1920) by Eleanor Porter, author of *Pollyanna* and one of the L.C. Page authors. In the Porter story the father calls a little girl Mary, while her mother calls her Marie. "A divorce, you know."

116. I remember reading to my two little cousins who came to live with us when their father went overseas and their mother went to work in a factory. I couldn't understand why they preferred to hear about Jane rather than Anne. I understand now. Gabriella Ahmansson spoke movingly about the effect of this book on a bereaved child in "Jane Victorious: the Magical Journey to Lantern Hill," a paper presented at the L.M. Montgomery Institute, June 25, 1994.

117. A short story, "The Man Who Forgot," *Family Herald* (January 1932), dealing with a parent's interference with a young person's choice of mates, foreshadowed her own interference in the early choices of Stuart and Chester.

118. Montgomery would soon evince the same feeling of superiority with regard to Mrs. Cowan, her next door neighbour in Toronto.

119. See "Jane Victorious: the Magical Journey to Lantern Hill."

120. Litster adds a comment that a terrible heat wave in Toronto in the summer of 1936, causing distress and deaths, may have contributed to the Montgomery's depression and her use of prison metaphors in the description of Jane's Toronto life. Lecture at the University of Prince Edward Island, June 2006.

121. Litster has made a detailed study of the manuscript, which is held in the Archives of Confederation Centre, Charlottetown, Prince Edward Island. Lecture at the University of Prince Edward Island, June 2006.

122. Montgomery could not bear to waste paper: "I for example, *cannot* discard any piece of blank paper. I *must* save it to write on."

123. Donna Campbell notes that Montgomery wrote a blurb to appear on the back cover of the first Canadian edition of *Jane of Lantern Hill* promoting one such cookbook, *The Country Kitchen*, by Della Lutes (1936).

124. Jennifer Litster also connects the cooking prowess with Jane's conquest of her "Wicked Witch of the East," Aunt Irene. Lecture at the University of Prince Edward Island, June 2006.

125. Lecture at the University of Prince Edward Island, June 2006.

126. Maybe that lion taming is a deliberate allusion to Una in Spenser's *Faerie Queene* whose control of her lion symbolizes the power of purity. Maybe this comic lion-taming is connected with the other Una, in *Rainbow Valley*, who braved something worse than a lion—a potential stepmother.

127. A short story, "The Man Who Forgot," *Family Herald* (January 1932), dealing with a parent's interference with a young person's choice of mates, foreshadowed her own interference in the early choices of Stuart and Chester.

Anne of Ingleside

128. She had probably stumbled on the annual January exchange of letters between Chester and Ida Birrell, and discovered the state of their affair.

129. It is possible that she had in fact been "brooding up" a different story, and in transcribing the journal later misnamed it: one guess is that she envisaged a sequel to *Jane of Lantern Hill*, as was her normal procedure in the wake of a successful book. In 1939 she did in fact refer to "my new Jane book," perhaps titled "Jane and Jody."

130. There is a curious discrepancy in the journal references to work on this novel. On August 3, 1938, she mentioned in her journal doing "spade work" on "the new Anne book"—ten months after announcing that she had "finished the spade work."

131. At this point Montgomery harboured a particular grudge against her Aunt Emily, who had remained uninterested in the display of the insignia awarded to Montgomery on her induction into the Order of the British Empire (October 25, 1936). Aunt Emily is one of the models for Aunt Mary Maria.

132. When Chester first went away to boarding school, Montgomery's journal entry recalled sadly the way he had once spoken of her as "his 'mother dearwums'" (September 11, 1925).

133. This story of Nan, deceived by a malicious girl, had been published earlier as a short story titled "I Know a Secret." In 1984 "I Know a Secret" would be converted into an effective film by Atlantis Films.

134. When Benjamin Lefebvre publishes this important manuscript in its original form it will be of great interest to Montgomery's admirers.

Conclusion

135. *Richard II*, 5, lines 46–47.

136. Arnold's poem, "To Marguerite—Continued" (1849), begins, "Yes! in the sea of life enisled/with echoing straits between us thrown,/Dotting the shoreless watery wild,/We mortal millions live *alone*."

137. Shauna McCabe, Introduction to the catalogue of an "Islands" Exhibition, Confederation Centre, Charlottetown, Prince Edward Island, July 2004.

Appendix

Additions to manuscript of Chapter 15, *Anne of Green Gables*. Additions to original text are set in **bold** within the relevant passage.

The way Anne and Diana went to school *was* a pretty one. **Anne thought those walks to and from school with Diana couldn't be improved upon even by imagination. Going around by the main road would have been so unromantic; but to go by Lover's Lane and Willowmere and Violet Vale and the Birch Path was romantic, if ever anything was.**

Lover's Lane opened out below the orchard at Green Gables

And it's a very pretty name, don't you think? **So romantic! We can imagine the lovers into it, you know. I like that lane because you can think out loud there without people calling you crazy."**

Anne, starting out alone in the morning

under the leafy arch of maples—**"maples are such sociable trees," said Anne; "they're always rustling and whispering to you,"**—until they came to a rustic bridge.

a long hill straight through Mr. Bell's woods, **where the light came down sifted through so many emerald screens that it was as flawless as the heart of a diamond.** It was fringed in all its length with slim young birches

a rabbit skipping across the road if you were quiet—**which, with Anne and Diana, happened about once in a blue moon.** Down in the valley the path came out

old-fashioned desks that opened and shut, **and were carved all over their lids with the initials and hieroglyphics of three generations of school-children.** The schoolhouse was set back

down to the Lake of Shining Waters. **There are a lot of nice girls in school and we had scrumptious fun playing at dinner time. It's so nice to have a lot of little girls to play with. But of course I like Diana best and always will. I *adore* Diana.** I'm dreadfully far behind the others.

wear her bead ring all the afternoon. **Can I have some of those pearl beads off the old pincushion in the garret to make myself a ring?** And oh Marilla she hastened to add, "that anybody would."

Anne sighed. She didn't want her name written up. But it was a little humiliating to know that there was no danger of it.

"Nonsense," said Diana

"Nonsense," said Diana, **whose black eyes and glossy tresses had played such havoc with the hearts of Avonlea schoolboys that her name figured on the porch walls in half a dozen take-notices.** "It's only meant as a joke."

Mr. Phillips didn't see her—**he was looking at Prissy Andrews**—but I did.

climbed the fence of the main road. **"Gertie Pye actually went and put her milk bottle in my place in the brook yesterday. Did you ever? I don't speak to her now."**

When Mr. Phillips was in the back of the room

drawing pictures on their slates, **and driving crickets, harnessed to strings, up and down the aisle.** Gilbert Blythe was trying

With her chin propped on her hands **and her eyes fixed on the blue glimpse of the Lake of Shining Waters that the west window afforded,** she was far away in a gorgeous dreamland

slate, not head—clear across.

Avonlea school always enjoyed a scene. This was an especially enjoyable one. **Everybody said, "Oh" in horrified delight. Diana gasped. Ruby Gillis, who was inclined to be hysterical, began to cry. Tommy Sloane let his team of crickets escape him altogether while he stared open-mouthed at the tableau.**

Mr. Phillips stalked down the aisle

Anne returned no answer. **It was asking too much of flesh and blood to expect her to tell before the whole school that she had been called "carrots."** Gilbert it was who spoke up stoutly.

he said in a solemn tone, **as if the mere fact of being a pupil of his ought to root out all evil passions from the hearts of small imperfect mortals.** "Anne, go and stand on the platform into my soul, Diana."

Diana hadn't the least idea what Anne meant but she understood it was something terrible.

"You mustn't mind Gilbert

said Anne with dignity. **"Gilbert Blythe has hurt my feelings *excruciatingly*, Diana."**

It is possible the matter might have blown over without more excruciation if nothing else had happened. But when things begin to happen they are apt to keep on.

Avonlea scholars often spent noon

singing softly to herself, **with a wreath of rice lilies on her hair as if she were some wild divinity of the shadowy places,** was latest of all.

buried her face in her arms on the desk. **Ruby Gillis, who got a glimpse of it as it went down, told the others going home from school that she'd "acksually never seen anything like it—it was so white, with awful little red spots in it."**

To Anne, this was as the end of all things.

it would be of no use to try. **Her whole being seethed with shame and anger and humiliation.**

At first the other scholars looked

said Anne sadly. **"I'd let myself be torn limb from limb if it would do you any good.** But I can't do this

It's tremendously exciting. **And we're going to learn a new song—Jane Andrews is practising it up now; and Alice Andrews is going to bring a new Pansy book next week and we're all going to read it out loud, chapter about, down by the brook. And you know you are so fond of reading out loud, Anne."**

Nothing moved Anne in the least.

awful stubborn if she takes the notion. Far as I can make out from her **story, Mr. Phillips has been carrying matters with a rather high hand. But it would never do to say so to her.** I'll just talk it over with Rachel.

"About Anne's fuss in school, I reckon," she said. **"Tillie Boulter was in on her way home from school and told me about it."**

"I don't know what to do with her,"

I never saw a child so worked up. **I've been expecting trouble ever since she started to school. I knew things were going too smooth to last. She's so high-strung.** What would you advise, Rachel?

punished as well as Anne, that's what. **And I don't believe in making the girls sit with the boys for punishment. It isn't modest. Tillie Boulter was real indignant. She took Anne's part right through and said all the scholars did, too. Anne seems real popular among them, somehow. I never thought she'd take with them so well."**

"Then you really think I'd better let her stay home,"

if his uncle hadn't been a trustee—*the* trustee, **for he just leads the other two around by the nose, that's what.** I declare, I don't know

this Island is coming to."

Mrs. Rachel shook her head, as much as to say if she were only at the head of the education system of the Province things would be much better managed.

Marilla took Mrs. Rachel's advice

did she love Diana, **with all the love of her passionate little heart, equally intense in its likes and dislikes.** One evening Marilla

And oh, what shall I do? **I hate her husband—I just hate him furiously.** I've been imagining it all out

the wedding and everything—**Diana dressed in snowy garments, with a veil, and looking as beautiful and regal as a queen; and me the brides-maid, with a lovely dress, too, and puffed sleeves, but with a breaking heart hid beneath my smiling face.** And then bidding Diana

⟶ Works Cited ⟶

Books Read by L.M. Montgomery

Alcott, Louisa May. *Little Women*. Boston: Roberts, 1868, 1869.

Aldrich, T.B. *Story of a Bad Boy*. Boston: Fields, Osgood, 1870.

Arabian Nights Entertainment. Ed. Andrew Lang. London: Nimmo's, 1866.

Barrie, J.M. *Auld Licht Idylls*. London: Hodder & Stoughton, 1888.

———. *The Little Minister*. London: Cassell, 1891.

Brontë, Charlotte. *Jane Eyre*. London: Smith, Elder, 1847.

Brontë, Emily. *Wuthering Heights*. London: Thomas Cautley Newby, 1847.

Bulwer-Lytton, Alfred. *Zanoni*. London: Saunders and Orley, 1842.

Burnett, Frances Hodgson. *Little Lord Fauntleroy*. New York: Scribner, 1886.

———. *The Secret Garden*. New York: Stokes, 1911.

Carman, Bliss. *The Kinship of Nature*. Boston: L.C. Page, 1904.

Connor, Ralph. *Glengarry Schooldays*. Toronto: Westminster, 1902.

Crockett, Samuel. *The Stickit Minister*. London: Fisher, Unwin & W. Pollock Wylie, 1893.

Deacon, W.A. *Poteen*. Ottawa: Graphic, 1926.

Dickens, Charles. *David Copperfield*. London: Bradbury and Evans, 1849–50.

Dobrée, Valentine. *Your Cuckoo Sings by Kind*. London: Knopf, 1927.

DuMaurier, Gerald. *Trilby*. London: Osgood, McIlvane, 1894.

Eggleston, Edward. *A Hoosier Schoolmaster*. New York: Grosset & Dunlap, 1871.

Gray, H.T. *A Bad Boy's Diry* [sic]. New York: J.S. Ogilvie, 1880.

Hogg, James. *The Queen's Wake*. Edinburgh: Blackwood, 1819.

Hope, Anthony. *The Prisoner of Zenda*. Bristol: Arrowsmith, 1894.

Hudson, T.J. *The Law of Psychic Phenomena*. Chicago: A.C. McClurg, 1893.

Irving, Washington. *Tales of Alhambra*. New York: Putnam, 1832.

Johnston, Annie Fellows. *The Little Colonel*. Boston: L.C. Page, 1895.

Kipling, Rudyard. *Kim*. London: Macmillan, 1901.

———. *Stalky & Co*. London: Macmillan, 1899.

Longfellow, Henry Wadsworth. "Hymn to Night." *Voices of the Night*. Cambridge, 1839.

MacLaren, Ian. *Beside the Bonnie Brier Bush*. London: Hodder & Stoughton, 1894.

MacMechan, Alexander. *Head-Waters of Canadian Literature*. Toronto: McClelland & Stewart, 1924.

MacMurchy, Marjory. *The Child's House: A Comedy of Vanessa from the Age of Eight or Thereabouts until She Had Climbed the Steps as Far as Thirteen*. London: Macmillan, 1923.

———. *The Woman—Bless Her*. Toronto: Gundy, 1916.

Milne, A.A. *When We Were Very Young*. London: Methuen, 1925.

Porter, Eleanor H. *Mary Marie*. New York: Houghton Mifflin, 1920.

————. *Pollyanna*. Boston: L.C. Page, 1913.

Rice, Alice Hegan. *Mrs. Wiggs of the Cabbage Patch*. New York: Century, 1903.

Roberts, Charles G.D. *The Heart that Knows*. Boston: L.C. Page, 1906.

Roberts, Theodore Goodridge. *Brothers of Peril*. Boston: L.C. Page, 1905.

Roberts MacDonald, Elizabeth. *Our Little Canadian Cousins*. Boston: L.C. Page, 1904.

Saunders, Marshall. *Beautiful Joe*. Philadelphia: Bowker, 1893.

Schreiner, Olive. *The Story of an African Farm*. London: Chapman and Hall, 1883.

Scott, Walter. *The Lady of the Lake*. Edinburgh: Black, 1810.

Sinclair, May. *Mary Olivier: A Life*. London: Macmillan, 1919.

————. *The Romantic*. London: Macmillan, 1920.

Spenser, Edmund. *The Faerie Queene*. London: Ponsonby, 1590.

Stevenson, Robert Louis. *The Strange Case of Dr. Jekyll and Mr. Hyde*. London: Longmans, Green, 1886.

Stratton Porter, Gene. *Freckles*. New York: Doubleday, 1904.

————. *A Girl of the Limberlost*. New York: Grosset & Dunlap, 1909.

Tennyson, Alfred. "Lancelot and Elaine." *Idylls of the King*. London: Moxon, 1859.

Trollope, Anthony. *Barchester Towers*. London: Longman, 1857.

Twain, Mark. *Huckleberry Finn*. New York: Webster, 1884.

————. *The Prince and the Pauper*. New York: Webster, 1891.

Von Arnim, Elizabeth. *Elizabeth and her German Garden*. London: Macmillan, 1898.

Webster, Jean. *Daddy-Long-Legs*. New York: Scribner's, 1912.

Wiggin, Kate Douglas. *Rebecca of Sunnybrook Farm*. Boston: Houghton Mifflin, 1903.

Interpretations and Backgrounds

Ahmansson, Gabriella. *A Life and Its Mirrors*. Uppsala: Almqvist and Wiksell, 1991.

Atwood, Margaret. Afterword. *Anne of Green Gables*. By L.M. Montgomery. Toronto: McClelland & Stewart, 1992.

Bachelard, Gaston. *The Poetics of Space*. New York: Orion, 1964.

Bailey, Rosamond. "Little Orphan Annie: Anne's Hoydenish Double." *Canadian Children's Literature* (1989) 8–17.

Beaty, Jerome. *Middlemarch from Notebook to Novel: A Study of George Eliot's Creative Method*. Urbana: University of Illinois Press, 1960.

Bettelheim, Bruno. *The Uses of Enchantment*. New York: Knopf, 1975.

Bolger, F.W.P. *The Years before Anne*. Charlottetown: Prince Edward Island Heritage Foundation, 1974.

———— and Elizabeth R. Epperly, eds. *My Dear Mr. M: Letters to G.B. Macmillan*. Toronto: McGraw-Hill Ryerson, 1980.

Buckley, Jerome. *Season of Youth: The Bildungsroman from Dickens to Golding*. Cambridge: Harvard University Press, 1974.

Cavert, Mary Beth. "Summoning Voices in Diaries and Memoirs." *The Intimate Life of L.M. Montgomery*. Ed. Irene Gammel. Toronto: University of Toronto Press, 2005.

Doody, Margaret. "L.M. Montgomery: The Darker Side." *Storm and Dissonance: L.M. Montgomery and Conflict*. Ed. Jean Mitchell. Newcastle, UK: Cambridge Scholars Publishing, forthcoming in 2008.

Droz, R., and M. Rahmy. *Understanding Piaget*. Trans. Joyce Diamenti. New York: International Universities Press, 1976.

DuPlessis, Rachel Blau. *Writing Beyond the Ending*. Bloomington: Indiana University Press, 1985.

Eggleston, Wilfrid, ed. *The Green Gables Letters*. Toronto: Ryerson, 1960.

Epperly, Elizabeth R. *The Fragrance of Sweet-Grass*. Toronto: University of Toronto Press, 1992.

———. *Through Lover's Lane*. Toronto: University of Toronto Press, 2007.

Gammel, Irene, ed. *The Intimate Life of L.M. Montgomery*. Toronto: University of Toronto Press, 2005.

——— and Elizabeth Epperly, eds. *L.M. Montgomery and Canadian Culture*. Toronto: University of Toronto Press, 1999.

Gillen, Mollie. *The Wheel of Things*. Toronto: Fitzhenry and Whiteside, 1975.

Godard, Barbara. "Structuralism/Post-Structuralism: Language, Reality and Canadian Culture." *Future Indicative*. Ed. John Moss. Ottawa: University of Ottawa Press, 1987.

Goddard, Ives. *The Origin of the English Word "Squaw."* Report to the Arizona Board on Geographic and Historic Names, 1996.

Heilbrun, Carolyn. *Writing a Woman's Life*. New York: Ballantine, 1988.

Hutton, Jack, and Linda Jackson-Hutton. *Lucy Maud Montgomery and Bala: A Love Story of the North Woods*. Gravenhurst: Watts, 1998.

Johnston, Rosemary Ross. "Landscape as Palimpsest, Pentimento, Epiphany: Lucy Maud Montgomery's Interiorisation of the Exterior, Exteriorisation of the Interior." *CREArTA* 5 (2005): 13–31.

Karr, Clarence. "Addicted to Books: L.M. Montgomery and the Value of Reading." *CCL: Canadian Children's Literature* 113–14 (2004): 17–33.

Katsura, Yuko. "Red-haired Anne in Japan." *Canadian Children's Literature* 34 (1984): 57–60.

Lecker, Robert. *Making It Real: The Canonization of English-Canadian Literature*. Concord, ON: Anansi, 1995.

Lowes, John Livingston. *The Road to Xanadu*. New York: Houghton Mifflin, 1930.

Macmillan, Carrie, Lorraine McMullen, and Elizabeth Waterston. *Silenced Sextet*. Montreal: McGill-Queen's Press, 1992.

McCabe, Shauna. Introduction to the catalogue of an "Islands" Exhibition, Confederation Centre, Charlottetown, PEI, July 2004.

Montgomery, L.M. *The Selected Journals of L.M. Montgomery*. eds., with introductions by Mary Rubio and Elizabeth Waterston. Toronto: Oxford University Press. Vol. I, 1985; Vol. II, 1987; Vol. III, 1992; Vol. IV, 1998; Vol. V, 2004.

Mott, Frank. *Golden Multitudes*. New York: Bowker, 1947.

Radway, Janice. *Reading the Romance: Reading, Patriarchy and Popular Literature*. Chapel Hill: University of North Carolina Press, 1984.

Rae, Arlene Perly, ed. *Everybody's Favourites: Canadians Talk about Books that Changed their Lives*. Toronto: Viking, 1997.

Raymond, Ernest. *Through Literature to Life*. London: Cassell's, 1928.

Ricou, Laurie. *Everyday Magic: Child Languages in Canadian Literature*. Vancouver: University of British Columbia Press, 1987.

Rogers, Robert. *A Psychoanalytic Study of the Double in Literature*. Detroit: Wayne State University Press, 1970.

Rubio, Mary. *The Gift of Wings*. Toronto: Doubleday, 2008.

———. "L.M. Montgomery: Scottish-Presbyterian Agency in Canadian Culture." *L.M. Montgomery and Canadian Culture*. Eds. Irene Gammel and Elizabeth Epperly. Toronto: University of Toronto Press, 1999. 89–105.

Russell, Ruth Weber, D.W. Russell, and Rea Wilmshurst. *L.M. Montgomery: A Preliminary Bibliography*. Waterloo: University of Waterloo Library, 1986.

Sabatini, Sandra. *Making Babies: Infants in Canadian Fiction*. Waterloo: Wilfrid Laurier University Press, 2004.

Showalter, Elaine. *The Female Malady: Women, Madness and English Culture, 1830–1980*. New York: Pantheon, 1985.

Simpson, John, and John Ayto, eds. *Oxford Dictionary of Modern Slang*. Oxford: Oxford University Press, 1993.

Spacks, Patricia. *The Female Imagination*. New York: Knopf, 1972.

Steffler, Margaret. "Performing Motherhood: L.M. Montgomery's Display of Maternal Dissonance." *Storm and Dissonance: L.M. Montgomery and Conflict*. Ed. Jean Mitchell. Newcastle, UK: Cambridge Scholars Publishing, forthcoming in 2008.

Thiessen, Hildi, and Paul Thiessen, eds. *After Green Gables*. Waterloo: Waterloo University Press, 2006.

Vrettos, Athena. *Somatic Fictions: Imagining Illness in Victorian Culture*. Palo Alto: Stanford UP, 1995.

⟿ Acknowledgements ⟿

My primary debt is to Mary Rubio, friend and colleague, who provided invaluable comments and criticisms for the present book; over many years we have collaborated in writing and speaking about L.M. Montgomery's fiction. Dr. Stuart Macdonald, Montgomery's younger son, who permitted Dr. Rubio and me to edit *The Selected Journals of L.M. Montgomery*, had helped me in the 1960s while I was preparing a chapter for *The Clear Spirit*, a Canadian Centennial project at the University of Toronto Press, supervised by Francess Halpenny. In the wake of that publication I met Father Francis Bolger in Charlottetown and Wilfrid Eggleston in Ottawa, and welcomed their encouragement, as well as that of Carl Klinck and James Reaney at the University of Western Ontario. In 1975, Mary Rubio, Glenys Stow, Bob Sorfleet, and I founded *Canadian Children's Literature/La littérature canadienne pour la jeunesse,* which became a focus for people interested in Montgomery, including Rea Wilmshurst, Barbara Garner, and many others. William Toye at Oxford University Press contributed greatly to the elegance of the *Selected Journals* from 1982 on. While preparing their own key studies in the 1980s, Betsy Epperly and Gabriella Ahmansson shared their insights; they have continued to influence my own readings of Montgomery. Most recently I have benefited from the enthusiasm and advice of Beth Cavert in Minnesota; Jennifer Litster of Edinburgh; and Donna Campbell of "Walden Farm" near Lindsay, Ontario; Carole Gerson in Vancouver; and Benjamin Lefebvre in Winnipeg. I owe thanks to the enthusiasts at Leaskdale and Norval, to Linda and Jack Hutton of Bala, Jean Hendry of Guelph, Barbara Garner of Ottawa, Clara Thomas of Strathroy, Kevin McCabe in St. Catharines, Irene Gammel in Toronto, and Catherine Ross and Nancy Schiefer in London. Many librarians and archivists have helped me: Michael Ridley, Bernard Katz, and Lorne Bruce at the University of Guelph; the late J.J. Talman at the University of Western Ontario; Kevin Rice at the Confederation Centre in Charlottetown; and Simon Lloyd at the University of Prince Edward Island. Over the years, Jennie and John Macneill, George and Maureen Campbell, and Elizabeth DeBlois have made me feel welcome in Prince Edward Island. I am now particularly grateful to Jennie Rubio, for excellent editorial work on this book. Finally, I thank my son and daughters for constant support and enthusiasm, my granddaughters (Katie in particular) for their research help, and my friend and husband Douglas, who has survived sixty years of L.M. Montgomery with me.